IMITATION & DESIGN

IMITATION & DESIGN

AND OTHER ESSAYS BY

REID MacCALLUM

EDITED BY

WILLIAM BLISSETT

UNIVERSITY OF TORONTO PRESS: 1953

Printed in Canada
London: Geoffrey Cumberlege
Oxford University Press

Reprinted in 2018

ISBN 978-1-4875-7691-2 (paper)

PREFACE

IT is a pleasant duty to express gratitude for kindnesses to me during my work as editor. These range from simple courtesies to great personal benefaction. For permission to quote copyright material, acknowledgment must be made to the following: Messrs. George Allen & Unwin (Fung Yu-lan, *History of Chinese Philosophy*, 1947), the American Psychological Association and the *Psychological Review* (Clark L. Hull, "Mind, Mechanism, and Adaptive Behavior," 1937), Messrs. Constable and Company (*Letters of Vincent van Gogh to His Brother*, 1927), Messrs. Faber and Faber (T. S. Eliot, *Four Quartets*, 1944), Messrs. Harcourt, Brace & Company Limited (*Collected Poems of E. E. Cummings*, 1935), Messrs. Harper & Brothers (Clarence Streit, *Union Now*, 1949), New Directions ("First All-Vou Chain-poem," *New Directions in Prose & Poetry 1940*), Mr. Arthur Probsthain (A. Forke, *The World-Conception of the Chinese*, 1925), Miss Hilla Rebay (*Non-Objectivity is the Realm of Spirit*, 1939), Random House, Inc. (Karl Shapiro, *Essay on Rime*, 1945, and *Selected Writings of Gertrude Stein*, 1946), Messrs. Routledge and Kegan Paul (Fung Yu-lan, *Spirit of Chinese Philosophy*, 1947, and E. A. Gutkind, *Revolution of Environment*, 1946), Charles Scribners Sons (Rolfe Humphries, *Out of the Jewel*, 1942). I wish more especially to thank the Sisters of the Church and the publishers of the *Queen's Quarterly* and the *Dalhousie Review* for permission to reprint articles as chapters of this book.

A grant from the University of Saskatchewan enabled me to spend the summer of 1951 in Toronto working on the manuscript. The University of Toronto also provided a grant from its Research Fund. Publication has been assisted by the Humanities Research Council of Canada and by the University of Toronto Press through its Publications Fund. Mr. Donald Greene has made useful suggestions about the text of the essay on myth, and Mr. Richard Burgener has taken a helpful interest in the whole project from the beginning. Great thanks are due to Mrs. J. R. McNeily and to Mrs. A. E. Sawyer for preparing a full and accurate typescript of the unpublished material.

But most of all I must thank Mrs. MacCallum for the honour of editing this book, which, had her husband lived, would undoubtedly have been dedicated to her.

W. F. B.

University of Saskatchewan

CONTENTS

INTRODUCTION

I

IT would be ironic in an account of the author of "First and Second Self" if the second or accidental self were allowed to usurp the place of the essential first. Perhaps, however, the biographical data will convey more than is usually the case when it is noted that Reid MacCallum was born in 1897 in Turkey, the son of missionaries; and that he died fifty-one years later, in 1949, while on a brief visit to the monastery of the Cowley Fathers at Bracebridge, Ontario. Little need be added in the way of outward fact except that he graduated from Queen's University, went as a Rhodes Scholar to Oxford, and did further research at Harvard; that he taught for a time at Queen's but spent most of his mature years as Professor of Philosophy in the University of Toronto, where his principal fields of investigation were the philosophy of Kant, French philosophy from Descartes to the present, and aesthetics.

His learning, however, was so wide and unusual that it was impossible for anyone to regard him as merely the "expert" in one or two or three fields. He was tacitly regarded as a sort of honorary member of the English Department; and he served for a year as acting head of the Department of Fine Art. At the time of his death he was using books in Latin, Greek, French, German, Spanish, and Italian, as well as books in English by the score; and he made a close study of philosophers as disparate as Plotinus and Kierkegaard, Nicholas of Cusa and Ernst Cassirer, Descartes and Gabriel Marcel.

But his life was by no means constricted even within this larger field of general scholarship. He took a lively—and not at all academic—interest in contemporary poetry and eagerly awaited the poems and books of certain poets for whom he had a special liking—T. S. Eliot, Archibald MacLeish, W. R. Rodgers, Kathleen Raine, Anne Ridler, Rolfe Humphries, and Robert Finch, who was his personal friend. Three of his own poems were published in *Contemporary Verse* and four others in *Here and Now* under the pseudonym of J. Columbson—

a name suggesting, as his own does, a scion of St. Columbia. He was active in various branches of art over many years, finding his own medium in the use of pastels with considerable satisfaction and success. He was also a leading spirit in getting together a group which came to sing madrigals quite creditably and with great delight. Thus he was equipped for writing a book on aesthetics not only with the mind of a philosopher and an intelligent layman's enjoyment of the arts, but with something also of the artist's and performer's knowledge of the difficulties to be overcome and the rewards of overcoming them. This book was the work on which he was engaged at the time of his death.

By profession he was a teacher. Teaching never came easily to him; and in contrast to the fluency of many academics, his lectures gave the impression of cutting through refractory material. He thought his way through the subject in the class-room and hesitated as long as he needed to find the right word. Some found this style neither restful nor diverting; it was not intended to be; it was intended *not* to be. Others praised it as great teaching though (or because) it broke every rule in the teacher's handbook. Its virtues may be summed up by saying that it "had a contemplative, exploratory character which made it extraordinarily stimulating to thoughtful students, and all the more so in the fact that, like his conversation, it was entirely free from professional ostentation. It was possible for anyone really interested in a subject to discuss it with him easily and rewardingly." How true this last statement is I can readily attest, for at my first meeting with him, in 1945, he allowed me to consume an entire afternoon in stating my self-important projects and opinions, without the least show of impatience. And patience did not come easily either, for he was constitutionally alert and had much to occupy him, but, by an effort of submission which it would not be wrong to call heroic, patience had become second nature to him. He told me shortly before he died that he was planning in the coming summer to study anew the Epistle of St. James—the subject of the only sermon he ever preached—and I think I know the passage he would have taken as addressed to him and to all who live by teaching:

Who is a wise man and endued with knowledge among you? let him shew out of a good conversation his works with meekness of wisdom. But if ye have bitter envying and strife in your hearts, glory not, and lie not against the truth. This wisdom descendeth not from above, but is earthly, sensual, devilish. For where envying and strife is, there is confusion and every evil work. But the wisdom that is from above is first pure, then peaceable, gentle, and easy to be intreated, full of mercy and good fruits, without partiality, and without hypocrisy. And the fruit of righteousness is sown in peace of them that make peace.

The quotation of Scripture is entirely appropriate in speaking of MacCallum as a teacher. After adopting Catholic belief and practice within the Church of England, the question of receiving Holy Orders arose for him, and he sought the advice of the late Archbishop Owen, who recommended that he continue in his lay calling; this he accepted as a ruling. But though he never became a priest, his wisdom was holy wisdom, and there was much in him of the Sage as described in the third essay of this book. Things in the world—clouds, buildings, trees, persons—sprang into more vivid being when he talked of them. And before he said anything, as his long lean contemplative form came in sight, topped by a hat gaily tilted, he made one remember Pascal's words (to use a grave pun which he would have enjoyed), "L'homme n'est qu'un roseau, mais c'est un roseau pensant," a thinking Reid.

II

Certain leading ideas appear and reappear throughout the twenty-five years of MacCallum's scholarly life. His first article, "Leonardo and the Method of Analogy" (1925), defends against logical formalism a way of thinking common and basic to myth, religion, and the arts; and there is not one of the eleven ensuing articles which does not assume and hardly one which does not argue this point of view. It is most sharply stated in the essay on "Art and Science" (1946), which begins with these fighting words:

> Neither art nor religion may be supposed to benefit from adherents who reiterate, "We have no quarrel with science." For however sound it may be in the abstract, this thesis ignores a capital contemporary fact: that in our age the prestige of natural science, and of an aggressive naturalistic "scientism" which the successes of science are supposed to authenticate, is overwhelming to the point where any non-scientific realm or aspect of experience must defend its very right to exist. In the circumstances, "We have no quarrel with science" is a formula of appeasement made in the timid hope that some remote corner of the human spirit may be secured from encroachment, or with the more sinister motive of those who have already sold out to "scientism" and are preparing some such monstrosity as "scientific art" or "the religion of science."

The war is to be waged on two fronts—against the scientism which would deny any autonomy to the arts, and against a defeatism within the arts which opens the gates to the enemy forces. To quote again from the same article:

Even a glance at logical positivism, a current manifestation of this aggressive scientism, would show that there is a quarrel between art and science, and what the threat of domination implies for art. For this school there are only two sorts of significant statement: those which are tautologous developments of a set of postulates, as in mathematics and logic, and those which permit of empirical verification, as in the empirical sciences, where the symbols used admit of being checked in terms of their "referents" or objects. Since the utterances of the artist conform to neither of these conditions, it follows that they are strictly speaking meaningless or nonsensical.

This is a verdict which the artist cannot possibly accept. Thus, the very curious example of surrealism shows him making a technical submission: if all that is left to him is nonsense, let nonsense be deliberately and systematically exploited. Though even in submitting he recants, advancing the desperate claim that in the absurd, the unreal, the insane itself, there is a truth deeper than any accessible to common-sense and science. This exasperated conflict of semanticist and surrealist is the sort of sign of our times which the would-be pacifier or appeaser ignores. Not its least remarkable feature is the interplay, the secret understanding, almost the complicity of the two opponents; for they may be said to agree that intellect, in Bacon's phrase, is a *lumen siccum.* Whenever and as often as intelligence is thus severed from "the infusions of will and feeling," driven to the condition of being a pure dry light, will and feeling can only in their turn become a kind of moist darkness, proliferating with unwholesome growths. Positivism and surrealism seem to be the products of a divorce which both agree to maintain and perpetuate.

MacCallum's defence of art is thus by no means merely another defence of the unconscious, the irrational, the "commotional" side of experience—an activity which, as the foregoing passage shows, all too often is less that of a rearguard than of a fifth column. Following and developing Alain's *Système des beaux-arts*, he wrote in his early article, "Emotion and Pattern in Aesthetic Experience" (1930):

Dreams and revery, because they are unreal, are not aesthetic facts: there is nothing there beyond a "horrid convulsion" of the nerves, a diffused, almost disembodied emotional state. It is, of course, because the dreamer takes his dream too seriously that it is an illusion: he finds in a vague emotional state some indescribable or ineffable meaning. Consider how interesting one's own dreams are (if one were not always forgetting details!) and how tedious those of others. In the endeavour to communicate a dream who can say that he has not been guilty of dressing it up, claiming to have experiences far more interesting than he can be sure of having experienced? The opium eater's disappointingly dull dreams are a case in point. These extravagant and at bottom meaningless fancies mask a mechanical exaltation which is unreal except in the purely physical sense that violence has been done to the body by tearing it out of its normal context of relatedness to the real world. No: dreams, reveries, pure imagination are not even the material of art, for art is fundamentally a social, a common product, and the incommunicable and the irremediably subjective is forever excluded from it. The work of art arises, I repeat, when the sterile process of imagination is brought under control, directed, given an objective pattern of ordered motions about which to integrate and actualize itself.

In fact, his whole endeavour was a general defence of intelligence in all its fields and functions; and the book which was left uncompleted at his death, though usually thought of as the "Book on Aesthetics," actually includes a chapter on myth as a product of intelligence and was to have included one on intelligence in theological thought, while the nature and limits of logical thought were to be implied throughout and perhaps defined. Thus the chapters on the various arts were to be placed in the widest context—as varieties and activities of human intelligence.

In spite, too, of a certain declarative acerbity in some of his unrevised writings, he very often achieved the desired tone of "charitable polemic," and the intention of the work as a whole was irenical: it was an attempt to heal a schism in the soul. The essay on "Art and Science" states some harsh truths, but at the end we feel only "the sharp compassion of the healer's art":

> All that can sensibly be said about the reconciliation of art and science might be put in the form of a couple of medical prescriptions. When an individual, nation, or culture, through prolonged and excessive introversion, threatens to fall into the cataleptic inertia that marks the schizophrenic, the treatment is for him to turn outward, to develop a salutary concern with things in the physical order; a course of science would be to the point. But there is another kind of insanity, marked by excessive extraversion and loss of the sense of self, and exhibiting, as our whole civilization does, a clinical alternation of manic activity and panic depression. There, it seems to me, a sound therapy would be to restore the patient's sense of the authenticity of subjective fact by inducing him to explore the realm of art. Is it really utopian to hope that as the result of repeated catastrophes, mankind will one day recognize the necessity of a healthy balance of inner and outer, subjective and objective fact, art and science?

III

This selection of essays falls naturally into two parts, the unpublished and the published material, and the editorial problem reflects this division.

The unpublished material consisted largely of a sizeable fragment of a book, and it was first thought possible to present it as such. It became apparent, however, that, while painting and poetry were treated at some length, architecture and music were quite untouched, and while a lengthy section was devoted to myth, the section on religion which would have been its companion and culmination remained unwritten; and it was decided that the only possible course would be to present the material as a group of separate though related essays.

The first two of these, "Imitation and Design" and "Poetry and Truth," are printed substantially as written: some details of expression have been altered, but nothing more than—in the editor's opinion—the author would have done if he had seen them in type. This opinion is supported by the fact that the essay on the *Four Quartets*, which had been mimeographed in MacCallum's lifetime, needed hardly to be touched. This essay, though not originally intended as part of the completed book, gives practical illustration to the ideas on poetry in the second essay and has obvious ties with the ground-plan of fourfoldness in the third. Eliot criticism is in a flourishing state, but as a contributor to it, I may give it as my opinion that this is the best thing on the subject.

The third essay, "Myth and Intelligence," presented much the most difficult problem. MacCallum wrote two complete treatments of myth, both in rough draft, one as a lecture to students of psychology, the other as a chapter of the book. They overlapped somewhat in expression, more in subject and intent; the defence of myth and the specimen of mythical thinking were each too good to be sacrificed to the other. They have been, accordingly, combined into one chapter. Naturally, there had to be a good deal of editorial work, but no new ideas have been supplied, and the style of writing has been kept as close as possible to the author's normal use. It has, of course, been impossible to indicate the changes in the text.

The shaping of the essay on myth was perhaps the largest part of the editor's assignment—that and the finding of references. The author left half a dozen page references in his text—enough to indicate that he had intended to annotate the book. Most of the remaining passages of quotation have been identified, but in a few instances I have had to admit failure.

The editorial problem in the second group of essays was one of selection, and here I have followed, with willing agreement, the advice of an informal committee consisting of Professors F. H. Anderson, N. J. Endicott, Robert Finch, T. A. Goudge, and Miss Jessie Macpherson. The text has been touched only to correct misprints and to bring it into typographical and stylistic uniformity with the rest of the book. Footnote references have not been given, since the author published the articles without them.

Some account should be given of the articles whose omission was necessitated by the dimensions agreed on for the volume. The essay on Leonardo, the work of a man still in his twenties, is both remarkably good and remarkably in line with his later work. Strongly and avowedly influenced by Paul Valéry, whose study of Leonardo was in 1925 almost unknown to the English-speaking world, it nevertheless had its own observations to record, both about the mind of Leonardo and about analogy as a form of argument or method of thinking more fruitful of truth than the syllogism can ever be. But where it is original, it develops naturally into the bolder, more adequate and mature statements of the essays presented in this book, and it has therefore not been reprinted.

Though it contains many passages of interest and importance, "Emotion and Pattern in Aesthetic Experience" cannot be accounted a successful piece of writing as a whole; the author cared little for it, and it was not considered for inclusion here. "Unpoetry—Poetry—Metapoetry" was found to have been used, some paragraphs almost verbatim, in the second essay of this book. The gist of the short paper on "Art and Science" has been given in this introduction. The Kierkegaard and the *Waste Land* articles are notable not because they are or attempt to be definitive but because they are lucid expositions of subjects which all too often have called forth turgid and pretentious nonsense. So many full-length studies have appeared since they were written, however, that it was reluctantly decided to pass them over.

As for the articles which it has been found possible to reprint, little need be added to what they say for themselves. The one on the Group of Seven, though not "important," shows something of MacCallum's lifelong interest in contemporary developments in the arts and of his ability to see them in more than a local and temporary context; it is refreshing to find a Canadian critic who does not write as if Tom Thomson invented the art of painting. "Contemporary Aesthetic Theory" is a workmanlike exposition and judicious appraisal of conflicting theories of art. Academic in the best sense, it establishes MacCallum's authority in his field and his right to try his wings in more adventurous flight. "The Idea of Man" is an admirable, an admirably short and deceptively simple treatment of a general subject, the scope and value of philosophy. Not all its readers have been carried along by the argument of "First and Second Self"; a friend of mine, however, whose Montaigne is never put back on the shelf found the contrast of Montaigne and Descartes most illuminating. I am glad to include it because I admire it and because it would be hard for anyone not to be delighted with the "unpretentious pun" with which the article, and this book, ends.

THE PUBLISHED WRITINGS OF REID MacCALLUM

"Leonardo and the Method of Analogy," *Queen's Quarterly*, XXXIII (1925), 178–88.

"Emotion and Pattern in Aesthetic Experience," *The Monist*, XL (1930), 53–73.

"The Group of Seven: A Retrospect," *Queen's Quarterly*, XL (1933), 242–52.

"Contemporary Aesthetic Theory," *University of Toronto Quarterly*, VI (1937), 480–96.

"The Idea of Man," *University of Toronto Quarterly*, XI (1941), 87–96.

"Unpoetry—Poetry—Metapoetry," *University of Toronto Quarterly*, XI (1942), 269–79.

"Kierkegaard and the Levels of Existence," *University of Toronto Quarterly*, XIII (1944), 258–75.

"Art and Science," *College Art Journal*, V (1946), 180–5.

"*The Waste Land* after Twenty-five Years," *Here and Now*, December, 1947, 16–24.

"Coal and Diamonds," *Here and Now*, May, 1948, 12–20.

"Three Poems," *Contemporary Verse*, Winter-Spring, 1948–9. Pseudonym, J. Columbson.

"Four Poems," *Here and Now*, January, 1949, 72–3. Pseudonym, J. Columbson.

Time Lost and Regained: The Theme of Eliot's "Four Quartets" (Toronto: the Sisters of the Church, 1949), mimeo.

"First and Second Self," *Dalhousie Review*, XXIX (1949), 73–84.

In addition to these published works and the substance of the first three essays of this book, Professor MacCallum left five notebooks containing a journal begun in 1939 under the title "*Nulla Dies*" and continued under the title "*Tempora mea in manibus tuis.*"

IMITATION & DESIGN

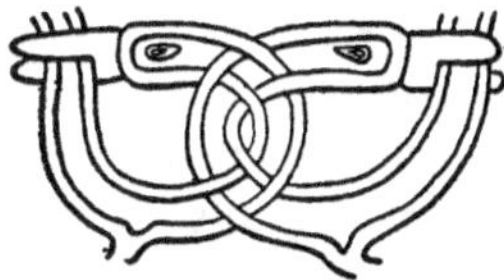

IMITATION & DESIGN

THE first and most spontaneous definition of art is that it is the imitation of nature. Like so many other items of common sense this requires criticism and as it stands is misleading. Like all common sense, too, it has a way of surviving criticism and cropping up in its unregenerate form when you least expect it. And it may be regarded as having permanent value at least in the sense of being prolific of issues and problems, if not of solutions; that is to say, it remains the best starting point for a philosophy of art.

The operative concept contained in the definition is that of likeness, the concept which Plato made such a primary one in his metaphysics, using it in fact to cover the whole relation between the realm of eternal, intelligible essences and the world of physical objects which are defective or imperfect imitations of these forms, at least in the early versions of his theory of Ideas. If later he tended to substitute the term "participation" for "imitation," it was doubtless because the prominence given to the copy relation in his earlier theory led him to examine the concept of likeness, and detect its own dialectical incompleteness. In the *Cratylus* he may be observed pointing out that if words could be indistinguishably like their object, complete twins of what they refer to, they would cease to function as words; we would simply not know which was the word and which the thing.[1] Among the basic conditions of meaning, then, we have to place unlikeness of the sign in respect of what it signifies, or at least a sufficient degree of unlikeness for it to be recognizable as language, not mere physical fact. Again in the *Parmenides*, where the mutual implication of even opposed Forms is recognized and elaborated, we discover that the Forms of sameness and

[1] *Cratylus* 432.

difference are not mutually exclusive.[2] A logic which held rigorously to the principle of contradiction might claim that one thing must be either the same as another, or not the same. A more supple dialectic will note that sameness is by definition different from other Forms, such as straightness, or roundness, or even difference; while the Form of difference is at least identical with itself. Since this is the case Plato denies separateness and absence of communication between Forms.

In practice, that is, in reference to the familiar things and events in the world of sense, this means that likeness is predicable only in correlation with unlikeness, and that it is a matter of degree. The defect of the physical order can no longer be said to lie in its failure to carry likeness to the point of perfect and complete identity with the Forms; such duplication would have achieved only a meaningless sameness. A meaning which can be understood is possible only in terms of some measure of difference, and participation is on the whole a more satisfactory term to cover this situation than imitation.

Applying these considerations to the notion that art is the imitation of nature, we should have to say that the dialectical couple likeness-unlikeness refers us to a whole range of degrees running between the limits of total sameness and complete difference, and that any point on this line may be judged as exhibiting likeness when viewed as approximating to a perfect replica, and at the same time as a case of unlikeness when viewed as approximating to total difference from the object.

Polarities in the Visual Arts

Since the theory of imitation obviously arises in the context of representational art, and is of more difficult application beyond that context, we should in fairness begin by considering it in the realm where it is likely to have the most success, let us say in the field of the art of painting.

This art seems to undergo a pull in two directions at once, one toward, one away from the object (or from nature)—a fact which has been very widely recognized, though differently expressed. Aristotle, dealing with the question of the origin of poetry in Chapter IV of the *Poetics*, attributes it to two innate tendencies of man, the first being a natural instinct to mimic, and the second (though the text here is not unambiguous as in the case of the first instinct) what may be called the instinct for harmony, rhythm, and metre. For Schiller the whole secret of beauty lies in the interplay of two opposed impulses, one toward matter or the sensuous, and one toward form or order; beauty is found in that fusion whereby "form lives in our feeling, and life has

[2] *Parmenides* 139.

form for our understanding"—i.e., in the achievement of "living form."[3] Again, R. A. M. Stevenson, in his essay on Velasquez, points out how the painter must reconcile two interests in a picture, "the facts and impressions of nature on one hand, and, on the other, the beauties and exigencies of the framed pictorial world."[4]

In whatever special terms this double requirement is formulated, as a polarity of the naturalistic and the decorative, the reproductive and the creative, or as the opposition of objective recording and subjective expression, it is clear that the painter is both attracted toward and repelled away from nature, so that his attitude towards it is ambiguous—an attitude of mingled reliance and distrust.

We may accordingly attempt to show the influence of this polarity by means of a curve *AF*, intended to represent the various forms of the

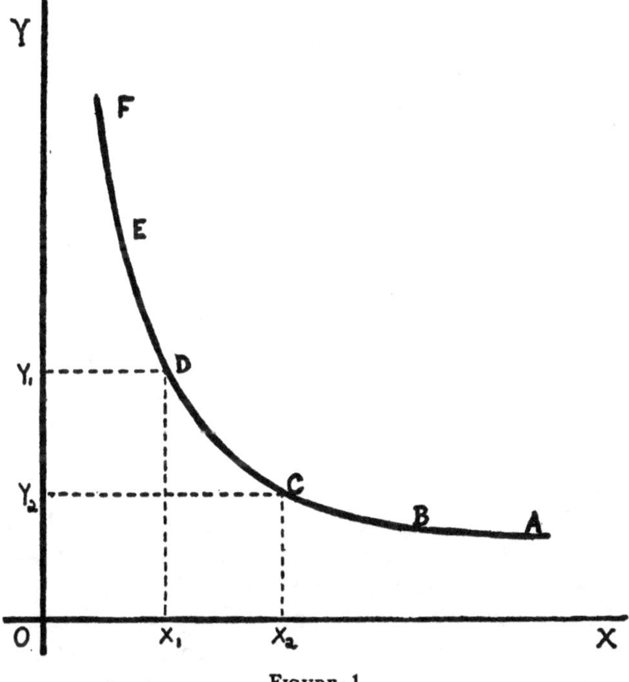

FIGURE 1

art as estimated by reference to the co-ordinates *OX* (approximation to the object of "likeness") and *OY* (approximation to pure pattern, formal decoration), and in which the points *B, C, D, E* mark certain

[3]Schiller, *Letters on the Aesthetical Education of Man,* especially XV and XVIII.

[4]R. A. M. Stevenson, *Velasquez* (London, 1906), 39.

important changes of direction. A hyperbola is chosen as a curve which goes on approaching the co-ordinates, but no matter how far they are extended never meets them. This conveys graphically enough the painter's relation to the two poles whose attraction he undergoes; as either is approached there arises an increasing and finally an insuperable difficulty in attaining it as a goal.

In the *X*, or "object," direction, in the segment *BA*, the impossibility of reproducing first motion, then the true colour and illumination of objects in nature, and lastly the full wealth of form and detail in nature, accumulates to the point where we have to admit that the most photographic literal likeness possible is still a selection from the appearances transposed into another key. At some such point as *A* itself we would, in fact, situate photography, in which the residual aesthetic element, if indeed any is left, consists in actions like the choice and arrangement of the objects to be photographed, or in processes like retouching, which cause the product to differ in some measure from a purely mechanical recording of the facts of nature as they stand. Though the concern with form and pattern be reduced here to the limiting case merely of turning a camera toward one group of objects in preference to another, it still remains operative, no matter how minimally.

At the other extreme, in respect of the "subject" axis *OY*, in the segment *EF* we encounter the impossibility of eliminating all reference to the world of nature. The "non-objective" painter may regard not only the depiction of recognizable objects, however formalized, but even the "likeness" of a third dimension of space produced by perspective rendering of forms, as impurities, the last traces of portraiture, and thereby intrusions of an alien literary element or "story" into what should be pure painting. He will then produce a flat pattern—let us say of coloured circles irregularly distributed against a central background. However he may warn us that it is intended to represent nothing at all, he cannot prevent the instinctive search for perceptual significance from finding some sort of satisfaction. We may think of these circles as toy balloons in the air, or perhaps as a close-up of a section of the Milky Way, thus reintroducing both objects of nature and the third dimension of space. It is impossible to eliminate such perceptual interpretations completely: all an artist can do is to warn us that they are unauthorized, but that is not the same thing.

These extreme cases have their significance for the theoretical assessment of the art, though it may seem to be a limiting and largely negative one.

The segment *BC* might be appropriated to the art of portraiture, extending the term to include all identifiable likeness of people, places, and things. The superiority of OX_2 over OY_2 at the point *C* would indicate that likeness is not only an integral but a predominant condition of this art; whatever other merits a painting may have, if it is not a "likeness" it is not to be classed as a portrait. Yet it is clear that there is a considerable range even here between *B*, which approaches photographic likeness, and *C*; toward the latter, pictures will be less and less immediately identifiable with an original. In the segment *CD* would be located depictions of people, places, etc., which though recognizably such, will not be identifiable with any given originals, having undergone one or another type of modification, transposition, transformation, or "distortion" at the artist's hands. We call these "pictures" not "portraits," though toward *C* it might not be possible to be sure the work was not an individual likeness or portrait. As we approach *D, OX* diminishes notably relatively to *OY*; likeness is on the wane, and in the next segment *DE* formalism has risen to the point of swamping it. Cubism, to mention but one of the numerous programmes of abstraction, resolves the object and its details into geometrical solids so that even the generic resemblance becomes conjectural; or in surrealism we may have, in a canvas which presents curious geometrical solids displayed in depth, no recognizable reference to nature beyond the "likeness" of the third dimension of space itself. With the passage to *EF*, as already indicated, even lineal perspective disappears, though something like it continues to haunt the non-objective painter for a certain distance past *E*, in so far, for instance, as he exploits the mutual distancing of colours whereby red comes forward against green, yellow expands where blue withdraws, etc. But, as we advance, even this ghost of likeness is laid, to leave flat coloured pattern; the art of painting has passed into the art of pure formal design or pattern whose normal existence is carried on in textile, wall-paper, ceramic, and other "minor" arts. Even here, as was said, remote and arbitrary associations with natural forms will be made in spite of every intention to the contrary. Expel nature with a pitchfork, she still comes back.

Objections to Likeness

We shall now attempt to determine more accurately what draws the painter away from likeness by re-examining in the light of historical situations the various stages of deviation from it which we have just surveyed. The objections to likeness can be grouped under four main heads: religious, moral, logical, and aesthetic, each of which will be found to contribute something to the notion we are trying to determine.

A. *The Religious Objection*

The issues here are complicated and enormous; more than once blood has been shed in bitter conflict over the right to make images, or to employ them in worship. We shall thus have to be content with a bare summary of the ideas at work, referring the reader for more ample information to Mr. Edwyn Bevan's fine book *Holy Images*.[5]

The proscription of "graven images" by Hebrews, Zoroastrians, Puritans, Moslems, and some modern Hindus, points to a deep-seated religious hostility toward likeness of which distinct evidence can also be found even among peoples like the Greeks and Romans who made free use of "idols." Its main ground, "I the Lord thy God am a jealous God," is the monotheism characteristic of Judaism and Islam. To permit "graven images" of the Deity, by the physical fact of multiplication alone, encourages a relapse into polytheism. Further (and the implied compliment to the power of the artist is very high) permission to make "any likeness of any thing that is in heaven above, or that is in the earth beneath, or that is in the water under the earth" would expose Israel to a constant menace: it is easy for people to fall into the way of worshipping such works; Aaron's golden calf is only one illustration of the fact.

A second motive of hostility, in which polytheists like the Greeks and Romans could share, is that the sacredness of the divine object gives its embodiment in wood or stone shaped by human hands a sacrilegious character. Horace, who wrote "Once I was a fig-tree, good-for-nothing wood, when the craftsman, after hesitating for a while whether to make me a stool or a Priapus, decided for the god,"[6] could share Isaiah's sense of the absurdity of worshipping a piece of wood, the rest of which had been burned to cook the wood-carver's dinner, though he would do so without the full outraged indignation of the Hebrew.[7] From the Greek, too, significantly, comes the term "palladium," the statue not made by hands, but fallen from heaven. The black stone known as the Kaabah, at Mecca, is presumed to be a meteorite, and can be venerated without danger, for it has the advantage of being a mere black object, having no "similitude" to tempt the faithful into idolatry.

All this indicates that it is the horror of desecration that forms the core of the religious objection to likeness, and it is a danger that becomes greater the more beautiful and striking the work. It was just

[5]Edwyn Bevan, *Holy Images* (London, 1940).
[6]Horace *Satires* I.8.i, quoted by Bevan, *Holy Images*, 21.
[7]Isaiah 44: 16–17.

because Homer was such a great poet that Plato found his accounts of the gods' immoralities specially intolerable. Consider how, according to Byzantine regulations, no icon could be made in sufficient relief to allow an impious person to seize the sacred figure by the nose; or again how at the time of the Renaissance, St. Bernardino of Siena and Savonarola fulminate against the painters' habit of introducing their acquaintances, even their mistresses, into religious pictures in the guise of sacred personages such as Our Lady. In these and countless other cases of attacks and restrictions on art on this logical ground, the basic fear of desecrating the holy by confusing it with the profane stands revealed.

There remains a third powerful motive of hostility, that the maker of likenesses is blasphemously aping the work of the Creator. The Moslem prohibition is supported by the warning that, at the Day of Judgment, the painter will be told to breathe effective life into his works; his inability to do so will make his presumption plain, and he will suffer eternal disgrace in consequence.[8] The Christian fathers speak with the same voice. The artist, according to Clement of Alexandria, "would rob God: he seeks to usurp the Divine prerogative of creation and by means of his plastic or graphic art, pretends to be a maker of animals and plants."[9] Another father says that it is scandalous to marvel at man's work as if it were that of the Creator. The Emperor Constantine, according to Eusebius' account, held that "a gifted sculptor when he has conceived an idea, tries to realize it through his skill; therein in a way he forgets himself: he flatters his own work, honours it as an immortal god, and yet would admit that he, the author and maker of this statue, is a mortal."[10] These samples of a recurrent theme will be enough to illustrate this form of the objection. It, too, contains an important implied tribute to the work of art, as possessing, though without effective life and motion, a quality closely approaching the vitality of animate creation.

Mr. Bevan, reviewing the evidence, shows that, though there is no general use of images in Christian worship till the eighth century, and though Eusebius, writing in the first part of the fourth century, speaks of the general exclusion of likeness of Christ as "well-known," there is no outright prohibition of images of living things, and that, from the time of the tomb-painting of the first century on, there is a continuous

[8]E. W. Lane, *Manners and Customs of the Modern Egyptians* (5th ed., 1871), I, 120; quoted by Bevan, *Holy Images*, 81.

[9]Clement of Alexandria *Stromata* VI.16.147; quoted in Bevan, *Holy Images*, 87.

[10]Eusebius, *The Oration of Constantine,* chap. 4, "On the Error of Idolatrous Worship."

tradition of Christian religious art, and of symbolic representations of the Saviour as, for example, the Good Shepherd.[11]

We may say without exaggeration that the most momentous single fact in the history of European art since the advent of Christianity has been the Christian doctrine of the Incarnation.

That the infinite eternal Being should in humility and self-limitation descend into time and human embodiment, in order to raise fallen nature to a new life, had very definite and inescapable implications for art. It was no longer impossible in theory to make a likeness of God once he had been present within the finite contours of a human body. And since God himself had given the example of how the most ordinary material things could be raised to the plane of sacramental, or holy, existence and significance, the artist was freed from that dualistic fear of matter which we termed, a moment ago, the horror of desecration. No doubt the fear of presumption retains its force in some degree: the Christian artist will not approach the sacred theme lightly nor without prior appeal for the grace he knows he needs; but the point is that orthodoxy not only permits, but in a sense compels him to approach it. The defenders of images against the iconoclasts were, at the same time, defending the faith against a heresy, a form of the Docetist heresy which recurrently denies the full humanity of Christ, regarding his physical body as a kind of illusory manifestation, and consequently his death as something enacted by the impassible Godhead without undergoing the actuality of human agony. The iconoclasts were opposed to depicting Christ because they thought of him as a God who had never really been "made man." The image-breakers of the Reformation exhibit the same unorthodoxy. The Reformers' impulsion *ad fontes*, "back to the sources," worked with such impetus as to carry them well beyond the New Testament and back behind its Founder, to much of the legalistic monotheism of Hebrew Scripture; the hostility of the Puritans to "graven images," like their sabbatarianism, illustrates this legalism. And (as in Byzantium) the party of image-breakers tends toward the heretical confusion of the divine with pure spirit, and of matter with evil, with a consequent dualistic opposition of one to the other. Christian orthodoxy rejects all these statements: it has always maintained that pure spirit may be diabolical; that matter, as a creature of God's making, is basically good; and that the perfect union of divine and human natures in the person of Christ permanently forbids any such dualistic opposition of soul and body as would rule out this union.

[11]Bevan, *Holy Images*, Lecture III, especially p. 100.

Thus the authorization of holy images in the East, at the Second Council of Nicaea in the eighth century, and the corresponding, if later, results of the Council of Trent in the West, were in fact, with characteristic differences between the two, the result of working out the logical consequences of the central doctrine of Christian theology.

B. *The Moral Objection*

In close alliance with religious objections such as these, but detachable from them, is the charge of deceit laid against the maker of likenesses. According to Origen men should be concerned with the reality of each thing, not with things other than the truth which mendaciously assume the appearance of male or female, bird, beast or fish.[12] The Caroline books, the product of Alcuin at the court of Charlemagne, condemn the "vain representation of what is not present as if it were."[13] Plato's objections likewise turn on the moral effect of the versatility he supposes the imitative artist to encourage: people who readily imitate anything and everything do not conform to the principle of justice, which is that each should perform the task for which he is best fitted.

This topic is large and unwieldy. It properly includes the whole adverse criticism of dramatic art and mimicking; the theories (such as Plato's and Tolstoy's) which find the danger of art in the fact that ignoble or weakening and corrupting emotions are easily imitated and induced; indeed, it should include the entire animus against fiction characteristic of the Puritan mind. Much of this criticism will recur in other contexts of our discussion; here it will be sufficient to note that its effect is to encourage non-representational arts, those graphic arts which, tending toward what we have termed the *Y* pole in Figure 1, can be free from the charge of pretending to be what they are not. Whether or not we consider the Puritan view of likeness a sensible one, we must recognize that it has effectively worked, like the religious objections dealt with in the previous section, to draw the artist away from nature.

C. *Logic and Likeness*

But certainly the most influential, the most prolonged and powerful of the forces affecting the art of painting is the mind's reflection upon the nature and possibility of likeness. What does likeness really mean? What does nature really look like? What is the true object, and how can it be known as it is, and what account should the painter take of this knowledge, supposing it to be obtainable? Problems which are

[12] *Ibid.*, 88, following *Contra Celsus* IV.31. [13] *Ibid.*, 147.

both epistemological and metaphysical at once arise when the question is approached from this side; the art of painting becomes inseparable from the venerable philosophical investigation into the distinction of appearance and reality, and will vary with variations in the solution of that problem.

Here we should recur to the stages outlined in Figure 1, starting with the mixed attitude of the portrait painter to his sitter. He is to make a faithful likeness; but if he pushes his fidelity too far, all of a sudden, and without it being quite clear what has happened, the portrait becomes a "slavish" likeness. The problem is why fidelity carried past a certain point should become slavishness, why the very feature for which the artist is commended should turn into the ground on which he is condemned.

We may start light-heartedly with the typical contemporary anecdote. Miss Gertrude Stein ventures to tell Picasso that she doubts whether she resembles his portrait of her very closely. "Never mind," is the reply, "you will." Again, James Joyce's father, scanning one of those economical sketches of his self-exiled son which simplify the face down to a line of cheek, a suggestion of forehead, and the trace of an eyeglass, is heard to say, "So that is James! My, he has changed since I last saw him."

These modern anecdotes differ typically in tone from comparable anecdotes of classical antiquity, where for instance wasps fly in the window to settle on the fruit painted by Apelles, or another painter acknowledges himself defeated when in the morning he goes to remove the curtain he finds covering his picture only to discover that it has been painted there overnight by his rival. This difference in tone conveys well enough that transformation in the popular or common-sense acceptation of the term "likeness" which antiquity itself did so much to bring about. A deceptively illusionistic goal is no longer generally recognized, even in portraiture, though no doubt the notion subsists in a submerged form and still occasionally breaks out in practice, as in the stereoscopic paintings of the Belgian Wiertz in the last century, or in the occasional diorama of today. It subsists in fact at the same level as the museum of waxworks in the sister art of sculpture—a manifestation which is not taken seriously as art even by the general public, but belongs roughly to the context of historical or objective recording of fact, together with news photography, map-making, and journalism.

To see how this attitude toward the portrait is grounded, we have to consider the whole idealistic or idealizing conception of painting, the source of which is to be sought in antiquity itself. It may be introduced by the question, Who is the sitter, anyway, and who is to say what he or she really looks like? Any person's appearance is variable and multiple: is it the face we present first thing in the morning, or in the afternoon, or engaged in conversation, at tennis, at study, in a state of excitement, or in a state of dullness, which is our true face? Though we are bound to admit that each passing expression is ours in fact, we are surely entitled also to repudiate such transitory appearances as the camera often records; we did look like that, we are bound to admit it, the camera does not lie, but we looked like that only for a fraction of a second, for the time of a snapshot. We know, for example, that Nazi propagandists, by the cunning selection of "stills" from the news-reels of Allied statesmen in action or in public speech, gave their people what seemed documentary evidence of the incompetence and idiocy of these statesmen. Break up the living movement and passage of a facial expression into fine enough bits, and they lose all meaning by losing their relation to what preceded and follows. Even the most intelligent and sensitive face could, by this method of fragmentation, be made to look stupid and brutal, though on reintegration in the moving picture as a whole what seemed to be a senseless leer would be recognizable as incidental to the enunciation of some word, to breathing, to the momentary pause when the speaker is about to attack some difficult notion, or to something else of this kind.

The point is that to depict what the person "really looks like" the artist must convey what he really is, his essential character, temperament, or make-up; and this, in turn, is something lasting or enduring, something with a time range extending in both directions from the present moment and indeed, in the most adequate sense, coextensive with the entire life of the sitter. This whole life is like a single long sentence, whose meaning it is required to convey; what we are saying is that to take a single syllable from somewhere out of the middle of the sentence is necessarily to make the whole thing seem meaningless. The true artist is the one who, upon as long study and acquaintance with feature, pose and gesture, thought, feeling, and action as he can manage to acquire, and upon due reflection on this material, i.e., after a process of comparison and sifting in which he brings to bear all the experience he has had of people and their ways, makes, as it were, a pregnant summary of what he has apprehended of this sentence, and putting it into his own words, translating it into his own idiom, gives us a concentrated statement of what it all seems to him to mean. We, in turn, are thus able to conjecture both backward before the beginning of the summary and forward beyond its termination what the complete sentence would be. The analogy is doubtless imperfect, since the fact is that the painter is forced to depict his model in a single appearance, which has no more actual temporal spread than the snapshot, so that what we are given is physically something more like a syllable, or even an isolated letter of the sentence, than an abbreviated summary. And yet the idealizing school is surely right in maintaining that the painter is no more deprived by the instantaneity of his canvas of introducing an ideal temporal dimension of before and after than he is prevented by its flatness from introducing an ideal third dimension of spatial depth. Simmel points out the extraordinary temporal depth of Rembrandt's portraits, and the example is a good one.[14] Or to take events of shorter duration, the same artist has a quick sketch of the beheading of John the Baptist in which the executioner is obviously drawing, and not sheathing his sword—a fact which would be evident even if the figure were isolated from the others so that the observer would not know whether the Baptist were still intact or not. The famous sea-shell on which Botticelli's Venus floats doubtless is dictated by a consideration of this sort. To depict her in the act of rising, contrary to gravity, from the waves, would be impossible; the temporal sequence would be dictated by our awareness of weight, so that she would infallibly seem to be sinking into, not rising from the waves. But the shallowness and modest dimensions of the shell utilize the same experience of gravity to confer on the figure which can be borne by such a frail support a degree of lightness which is fully equivalent to that asserted by the poet in his description of her rising from the foam.

If the skill of the painter is thus, in part, a matter of stretching an instant so as to give it a certain temporal solidity and duration, the art of the portrait painter will not be exempt from the same conditions. They are even more severe, and portraiture correspondingly more difficult, and more rarely successful than painting in general, since it does not represent someone moving in some overt form of action. The movement, as was said, is the movement of a life itself, its line of development, its character and direction. The sitter is traditionally posed in a state of rest, no doubt precisely for this reason; it is here the case with painting as it was, according to Aristotle, the case with poetry, which he explicitly contrasted with history on the grounds that poetry concerns itself not with what such and such a person actually did, but with the kind of thing he might have done or might be likely to do. This is why poetry is said to be more concerned with universals and to be more philosophical than history. In fact the depiction of character in a por-

[14]Georg Simmel, *Rembrandt* (Munich, 1925), opening chapters.

trait necessarily implies a temporal reference, for character means virtual action, the way you suppose it likely that a given person may behave in the usual situations of life; which, again, in the sister art of poetry, explains how Aristotle was able to say that action is the first requirement in tragic poetry and to deny what we are inclined to suppose today, that the plot of action is merely a means for exhibiting character.[15] This dramatic element in the art of portraiture may be a subdued one, yet if these considerations are accepted, we shall have to recognize its presence. The portrait painter, in fact, succeeds in the measure that his portrait can be treated as conveying some kind of climax or focal stage in a life which gathers up into a moment as much as possible of what precedes, and projects the whole forward in what may, dramatically speaking, be called a foreseeable *dénouement*.

Consequently, as regards the relation between the sitter and the painter in search of a "true" likeness, we find ourselves at quite a distance from any preliminary notion, such as common sense suggests, of a literal charting of actual facial contours—an activity essentially comparable to that of the map-maker. To say that the real person lies behind, and is not to be identified with any of his actual manifestations is, of course, to indulge in metaphysics. Yet the relevance to painting of this distinction of the real and the actual is borne out by the whole idealizing trend in the art of the West. The real, which is contrasted with the fleeting actuality, is constituted by an "ideal" content; clearly the true character of a person is something to be formulated in terms of "ideas," not something to be seen by the eye. But since the painter can only address the mind through the eye, he must express the ideal in the actual, the intelligible reality in a sensible appearance. This requirement states in a general way the driving force behind the whole idealizing movement; it has frequently been formulated as the paradox that the great portrait will be more like the model than he is himself.[16]

We have already noted that this deviation from literal likeness is to be traced back to antiquity itself, especially to the critical examination of *mimesis* by Plato and Aristotle; the underlying notion of "rivalry with nature" remains firm, but it takes on "more philosophical" meanings which we shall proceed to examine in turn. It should be remarked, initially, however, that probably the best grounds for dissatisfaction with the actual are those we have just been examining: its instantaneity; its lack of "temporal depth," whereby the painter's task becomes that of gathering all that lies dispersed, scattered, and fragmentary,

[15]*Poetics* VI.12–13.
[16]As by Alain in his *Système des beaux-arts* (Paris, 1926).

everything that the actual only hints at, or approximates to, or vitiates by its momentariness, into a single focus where it exists in concentration, climactically.

In the first instance the improvement upon nature takes the form of naïve *selectionism*; discontent with the actual is based on nature's failure ever to combine the finest features all together in the same face. So the artist studies nature just to pick out the most "beautiful" single details; these he then combines into a whole which, as such, has no counterpart anywhere. Selectionism attempts to escape slavish copying, and to make room for the creative originality of the artist; but since it remains imitation-bound with respect to the details, and conceives the artist's activity on the analogy of mechanical "contraption"—viz., the assembling of pre-existing parts—the attempt is a feeble one. Many contemporaries who consider that they escape imitationism automatically by paying tribute to the artist's acts of selection and omission and rearrangement, might be warned by this that selectionism can be nearly as naïve as what it is intended to replace. Map-makers too select and omit; photographers assemble and rearrange. It is clear that the painter's art must involve more drastic forms of action, that "rivalry with nature" must be more serious than this.

Accordingly, the theory at a further remove treats the artist's activity as a radical transformation of the materials of vision provided in nature. Thus in terms of eighteenth-century classicism, as represented by Reynolds' discussion of the grand style, the artist's study of nature has the purpose of discovering what any set of objects has in common, and therefore what each in particular lacks. "By this means, he acquires a just idea of beautiful forms; he corrects Nature by herself, her imperfect state by her more perfect. His eye being enabled to distinguish the accidental deficiencies, excrescences, and deformities of things, from their general figures, he makes out an abstract idea of their forms more perfect than any one original; and, what may seem a paradox, he learns to design naturally by drawing his figures unlike to any one object."[17] "Thus it is from a reiterated experience, and a close comparison of the objects in Nature, that an artist becomes possessed of the idea of that central form, if I may so express it, from which every deviation is deformity."[18] Clearly we have much more here than the selectionist's assertion that complete resemblance is an impossibility: we have some kind of positive justification of "drawing figures unlike" the given object.

[17]Roger Fry, ed., *Sir Joshua Reynolds: Discourses* (London, 1905), 54.
[18]*Ibid.*, 55.

What authorizes this degree of dissatisfaction with the natural is the fact that the painter is "addressing the mind, not the eye." It is his intellect which must make its contribution to the painting, and the characteristic operation of intellect is to compare objects of sense and abstract from them what they have in common. This intellectualistic view, which we shall call *conceptualism*, assimilates art as closely as possible to the logical operation of abstraction, the formation of class-concepts, and generic definition.

Its weakness is apparent in the fact that such logical and scientific operations aim at a state of universalization in which images would have no place at all; their direction is totally anti-pictorial, and a canvas which "depicted" a logical universal such as *the triangle* which is neither scalene, equilateral, nor isosceles would remain as blank as the concept itself. It is only fair to say, then, that what Reynolds intended was some kind of generalized image, not actually a depiction of a universal. What that implies, however, is nearly as awkward, pictorially speaking: its clearest illustration would be the composite photograph of a number of figures all posed in the same way and taken to the same scale: the result of which would, of course, be to determine an average outline "from which every deviation is deformity," in however slight a degree. Though blankness, in the sense of complete absence of particular detail, is avoided in this way, the average outline still being a particular concrete shape, yet in the averaging process individual differences are being smothered, and the result, though by no means completely, will be relatively blank.

The vice of conceptualism is to confuse the ideal with the statistical mean. It is easy to fall into this error, since an example of perfect conformity to the average may not exist at all, and a case approaching it closely would be both "extremely," even "ideally" average, and also very rare. But it would be just as hard to find a man with absolutely average intelligence, or morality, and we know quite well that if found he could not be regarded as a paragon of wisdom and goodness; the ideals of intelligence and moral attainment escape statistical determination.

A further observation may be permitted since the point is of great importance, not only with respect to the various common-sense schools that influenced the eighteenth century so profoundly, but in the theory of knowledge generally, and as it affects aesthetics. Though the ideal approached by the intellectual or moral genius is an abnormality in respect of the statistical mean, there is not an entire discrepancy between them. Einstein or Newton, bound down to the average intellectual performance of common sense, would be frustrated; yet what the genius achieves must be capable of some degree of communication to the average intelligence. Common-sense opinion is always undergoing transformation and correction at the hands of scientific investigators. The mean, while it is not the outstanding, should be regarded as involving a more modest version of the same equipment.

Similarly in the case of beauty there are two standards of reference implied, and it would be a mistake to regard them as non-communicating. The sound element in Reynolds' position is that what we might agree to call exceptional physical beauty, the beauty of a Helen or a Cleopatra, cannot deviate too far from the "common" outline; for there is a point beyond which deformity, that is irregularity, is inconsistent with beauty. His mistake lies in his failure to see that the mean only secures regularity, and precisely in the sense in which we often properly speak of a face with regular features as vapid and empty. The qualities such as vivacity, expressiveness, vitality, in terms of which the judgment of beauty is made, would certainly be termed "subjective" by the statistician; it is doubtful whether they submit to measurement at all. At any rate the lover takes it for granted that his mistress's face and form do not deviate greatly from the human mean. This is not what interests him, but "a majestic air, a sprightly look, an Amazon bold grace," something individually and uniquely distinctive. As such it will, on the scale of purely physical measurements, be irregular, a "deformity" in Reynolds' sense of the term.

The mistake of conceptualism is to confuse class-concept and ideal, the mean and the optimal, the "regular" and the "expressive." The Platonist would go on to say, it is to confuse the physical and measurable with the non-physical or purely logical essences that make measurement possible, and to confuse inward and invisible realities with their outward and visible expressions. Accordingly we pass to what should be called the properly idealist transformation of the theory of imitation, where the artist's "rivalry with nature" implies access to those essences and ideal forms which nature may be supposed to aim at, and never quite successfully embody, in her productions. Being less hampered by the obduracy of matter than nature is, for after all he does not have to produce a living creature but only the likeness of one, the painter may realize nature's "intention" more adequately than she herself succeeds in doing. This view is obviously Platonism—or better, neo-platonism, since Plato in deliberate disparagement confined the artist to making likenesses of individual objects and disallowed that, as artist, his intellect had access to the archetypes of nature's workshop.

In modern times this view is taken by Schopenhauer,[19] who held that the artist displays "Platonic Ideas" for our contemplation. These he distinguished sharply from class-concepts: they were individualized ideals, whereas concepts were generic averages; they conveyed things to us whereas concepts dealt merely in relations; a Platonic Idea was a *unitas ante rem*, whereas a concept reached by abstraction is a *unitas post rem*. From all this it followed not only that the artist "improved on nature," but in so doing improved on science too, to the point of supplying us with the only purely theoretical, purely disinterested truth available to man. For concepts, through which science is built up, are also thoroughly pragmatic; they are vistas of action, projects of pursuit or avoidance which neglect theory, i.e., the contemplation of things as they are in themselves, in favour of practice, i.e., things as virtual promises or menaces to our living.

Intuitionism is the proper title for this version of the theory of imitation. From Plato himself on, the most obstinate feature of Platonism has been the denial that ideas, ideals, forms, essences, or whatever they may be termed, can be arrived at by comparison and abstraction from a plurality of particular sensible objects. Whether our access to them be described in terms of reminiscence, illumination, or mental vision, it is equally an intuitive mode of apprehension, which bypasses the discursive operations of intellect. To place pairs of objects together and arrange them in order of increasing similarity of size would for the Platonist be an absurd way of pretending to arrive at the so-called "limiting" notion of perfect equality. Equality, everyone must agree, has no known or at least knowable physical instances; to claim to approach it as the limit of approximation to a series of physical comparisons is to forget what should be obvious, that unless we were already in possession of the idea of equality it could never occur to us to judge that any two objects are unequal, in any degree.

Intuitionism, in antiquity, is firmly formulated by Plotinus. Let us be quite clear, he says, "that the arts do not directly imitate visible objects, but rise to the reasons from which the natural object issues; let us add that they make many things of their own: they remedy the defects of things, because they possess beauty. Phidias made his Zeus without regard to any sensible model: he imagined Zeus as he would be if he consented to appear before our eyes."[20] This echoes Cicero's statement in the *Orator*, that when Phidias was carving a Zeus or an Athene he did not study a model which he should imitate. Rather,

[19]Arthur Schopenhauer, *The World as Will and Idea*, Book III.
[20]Plotinus *Enneads* V.8.1.

there was an exalted type of beauty residing in his own mind; and fixing his whole attention upon this, he used his skill and dexterity to reproduce it.[21] And for a practical version of the same approach we can leap across twenty centuries to the nineteenth-century British artist who frequently remarked that in painting ladies' portraits he used to make as beautiful a face as he could and then give it a likeness to the sitter, working down from this beautiful state till the bystanders should cry out, "Oh, I see a likeness coming!"—whereupon he would stop, and never venture to make it more like.

The "central form" which, in the previous case, was treated as ascertainable by abstraction from particulars has clearly been reinterpreted as something which, though not incommensurable with particulars, is certainly not derivable from them. By the same token aesthetic dissatisfaction with the actual becomes still more marked.

The principle affecting these successive extensions of the notion of an artistic "rivalry with nature" is that the artist is in search of truth. They are all cognitive aesthetic theories, in which the term "beauty" is understood to mean "truth." In demanding correctness, common sense is merely transposing its naïve copy-theory from the order of knowledge to that of art. This is the point of view of the map-maker, for whom truth means just the point-for-point correspondence between the actual measured contours of a hill and the variations of the contour-line on his sheet; and it is no more adequate as a theory of truth than as a theory of beauty. As the earlier discussion of likeness showed, it is because of the difference between lines on paper and the actual hill that the former can serve as a sign and guide to the latter. If the truth of the map lay simply in its correspondence to the hill, it would be increased by transferring it from paper to clay, and be completed by enlarging the dimensions of the scale-model till they attain those of the hill itself; but this would leave you not with a map and a hill, but with two "identical" hills.

Conceptualism modifies common sense by recognizing that truth is a product of the mind's activity, not an affair of likeness between one sense-object and another. It results not from a mere comparison of sense-objects, but from the operation of abstraction which introduces into sense-experience categories and classification schemes of the mind's own construction. The coherence and consistency of these schemes and of the details ordered by means of them thus tends to take the lead over likeness or correctness or representation as the test, and therefore the meaning, of truth.

[21]Cicero *Orator* II.9.

With intuitionism this emphasis on truth as a mental and not a sensory product gains further ground. Accordingly the theory of truth is again transformed; the test is now self-evidence, the claim is that what is revealed to thought as by a direct inner illumination cannot help but be the case; apprehension of it is as direct and immediate as sensation, but as universal as abstraction, though intuition is something different from either.

There remains a final extension in which the artist vies with nature, not in respect of her intentions or her products, but in respect of the creative power and energy she displays, for as we have moved through these stages, the term "nature" itself has been insensibly changing. The notion of ideal forms which nature "intends" to realize, of "archetypes of nature's workshop," just examined, with its implicit personification of the powers of generation, already points us in this direction. The Nature from which the pronoun "she" is never quite detachable, differs from nature as the given state of empirical fact, as productive force differs from product and by-product. This transformation was already implicit in Plotinus' phrase that the arts remedy the defects of things "because they possess beauty."[22] If art makes its product beautiful by conforming it to the idea of what it wishes to create, he explains, "art is itself of a greatly superior and truer beauty . . . the beauty of art is much greater than that which is found in the external object." For the further beauty spreads into space and into matter, the weaker it grows; and the more inferior it becomes to that beauty which has remained in unity: whatever scatters, departs from itself, whether it be physical vigour, or force in general, or beauty; and the first agent, taken in itself, must always be superior to its product. It is music, not its absence, which makes the musician; and music in objects of sense is created by a music which is anterior to them. "It is the beautifying," says Shaftesbury, "not the beautified, which is truly beautiful."[23]

The idea of likeness could hardly be attenuated any further without disappearing: a competition with nature which has become a matching of energies could be used to justify expressionist, surrealist, or non-objective painting, or any other form of art localizable toward the *Y* co-ordinate in Figure 1. The surrealist, for one, is given full authorization to ignore the world of our ordinary experience, since he is engaged in the pictorial creation of a world of his own; as long as this pictorial world has its own inner consistency, its own laws, its own

22Plotinus *Enneads* V.8.1.

23Shaftesbury, "The Moralists," *Characteristics*, ed. J. M. Robertson (London, 1900), II.131.

fertility of detail and form, all is well. Just as the third ground of religious objection stated, the distinguishing fact about the painter is that he is a creator—even a creator of possible worlds alternative to this actual one; a Prometheus, Shaftesbury says, under Jove.[24]

With the attenuation of likeness toward the vanishing point at this stage, we are naturally impelled to ask whether there is a parallel transformation in the concept of truth, beyond the intuitionist version just considered.

I think it could be maintained that there is. The whole logical development away from likeness, that is, the whole attempt to view the efforts of the artist as a search for truth, implies that theories of knowledge, too, could be laid out along our hyperbolic curve, that in respect of truth, too, the mind functions somewhere between two unattainable poles—between pure invention, construction, the *made* on one hand, and pure discovery, recording, the *given* on the other. Toward the *Y* co-ordinate, that of thought, knowledge tends more and more (though never completely) to be the elaboration of ideal thought-forms, as in mathematics and logic. Toward the *X* co-ordinate, that of sense-experience, it tends (but never completely attains) to "adequation with things"—a purely objective recording of fact, as in historical and descriptive science.

Accordingly, we may expect to find, in the same direction as intuitionism, but carrying its tendency to a more extreme point, a version of the theory of truth comparable to that of the abstractionist, surrealist, or non-objectivist in art.

Positivism and pragmatism between them supply this counterpart. By the pragmatist truth is energetically viewed as a creative display of activity which works. The choice of one set of postulates rather than another is always open; the thing is to elaborate the set and see how well it works in terms of fitting a given body of facts together, and enabling prediction in practice; the set that works best is thereby made true, i.e. verified. As the pragmatist is fond of saying in his wild, surrealistic way, if the rules of chess proved more serviceable and convenient than any other set of rules in dealing with the motions of the stars, then chess would supply astronomical truth.

Positivism also emphasizes the conventional, that is, the arbitrary and deliberate element in thought. The thinker is free to construct any world he likes, "worlds" being constructed nominalistically as linguistic constructions governed by a syntax. As long as a proposition conforms to the conventions stipulated by acts of definition, no exception can be taken to it. Of course the notion of verification in experience still plays

[24]*Characteristics*, II, 15–16.

a part in this conception of knowledge, but a severely reduced one; semanticists differ among themselves as to its role, but show a common tendency to reduce it to "coincidence," i.e., measurements, pointer-readings and the like. Ultimately, along this nominalistic line of development, you come to the fact that the data of sense are strictly ineffable: to quote one of them, "questions hitherto thought to be substantial are seen to be really only questions as to what language we choose to employ." Again, "No non-linguistic fact enables us to choose one language as more adequate than another."[25] To use words at all, to name "blue," "big," or "sweet," is to leave the realm of the given for that of language, and that is to fall back upon the "convenient conventions" of the language to give your statement significance. What, in common-sense realism, toward the *X* co-ordinate was an attempt to construct as accurate a duplicate as possible of an independent world has become an attempt to order the statements in a language as consistently as possible; only a residual "reference to nature" remains.

These brief, and considering the complication of the subject, superficial remarks on current developments in the theory of truth are intended to suggest that there are real affinities between, say, the syntacticist or semanticist and the surrealist: both emphasize the constructive activity of the mind, the arbitrariness of the choice of postulates, or what is the same thing, the perhaps limitless possibilities of substituting one set of postulates for another while yet developing each in internal consistency into a "world" of its own. In each the notion of truth has been carried so far in the subjective direction that it threatens to lose its plain connotation, as when Schlick, for example, asserts that meaning and verifiability do not depend on experience, but are determined by purely logical possibilities.[26] Any surrealist could sign his name to this statement. It is only fair to add that this school fights shy of the word "truth," which it regards as emotive, preferring terms more fitting to shifting circumstances, such as verifiability, meaning, correctness, or accuracy.

D. *Aesthetic Dissatisfaction with the Actual*

The grounds so far adduced will seem in varying degrees alien to the artist. As artist he is not likely to complain that a literal likeness is a piece of impiety, presumptuousness, lying deceit, or unreality; he is likely to call it just dull and insipid.

Of course it is possible for a painter himself to be dull. It was a fashionable portrait painter, president of an academy, who was heard

[25]The editor has been unable to identify these passages.

[26]Moritz Schlick, "Meaning and Verification," *Gesammelte Aufsätze* (Vienna, 1938) 348.

to observe that anyone could see that Chirico knew nothing about horses; to sit on one of Chirico's horses would be to break its back. But such cases can be ignored, except as warnings against supposing that all painters are artists; the obvious reply was to point out that what Chirico paints is pictures not horses, and that pictures are not things to sit on, but to look at.

In other words the artist is one who from the first is well aware of the "exigencies of the framed pictorial world," and of how easily the actual can violate or fail to conform to them. It is then his preoccupation with form and design that leads him away from the letter of likeness. The point does not need to be laboured; it is simply what was just said, Chirico does not paint horses but pictures. Or, if you prefer, it was the gardeners in *Alice in Wonderland* who painted roses; William Sampson paints not roses but pictures.

What makes it possible to say this sensibly and not sophistically (as it first sounds to the ear of common sense) is that a picture is in itself a composition, or design, or pattern which can be judged on its merits as such, abstracted from any reference to nature. Its excellence will be a function of the formal relationships obtaining between various shapes and colours, variously disposed, repeated, inverted, opposed; of the organization of a field of forms in such a way as to obtain the entire unity of the whole; of hierarchic subordination of the various details to one another in due proportion to their intrinsic interest as shapes and colours, so that each takes account of all the rest and all together lead the eye easily to some dominant, climactic, or focal point from which the pattern as a whole is best apprehended, and so that the "blanks" or empty places in the design (corresponding roughly to the intervals of silence between the notes of a melody) are adequately and harmoniously related to the filled spaces—caught up, as it were, and dominated by the action of the pattern even in those parts of its "field of force" where it is not physically present: these are some of the immensely complicated and difficult and, to the artist, immensely interesting "exigencies" which make the picture an autonomous entity, something *sui generis*, a picture and not a horse, or a woman, or a hill.

But it might be objected, nature is full of patterns. From the snowflake down at the microscopic level, from the mustard seed and gnat up, at the macroscopic level, and on the cosmic scale of the telescope too, she presents a continuous and marvellous spectacle of structures of inexhaustible variety. This is perfectly true, and we shall shortly be appealing to this fact in justification of the rule that the painter can never afford to eliminate all "reference to nature" from his work. But still there is ground for aesthetic dissatisfaction with the actual.

To appreciate this, we should try to formulate the discrepancy between form in nature and form in painting. We might begin with a factor introduced by Plotinus' concern with the source of form, the form-giving energy and act, and noticed by artists like Leonardo da Vinci who are more or less tinged with neo-platonism.

"The soul," says Leonardo, "which rules and governs the body constitutes our judgment before it is our judgment. Thus it has determined every contour of the man, judging it right to endow him with a long or a short or a snub nose, and similarly it has determined his height and shape; and this judgment is of such power that it moves the painter's arm, causing him to make a replica of himself, for it appears to this soul that that is the correct way of shaping man and that any other way of doing so is incorrect."[27]

This is not the place to discuss the nature of the organizing forces at work directing the development of the embryo—a fairly mysterious circumstance at best. It would sufficiently indicate what Leonardo means by "our judgment before it is our judgment" to refer to the modern theory of Unconscious Mind; beyond the moving spotlight of consciousness we not only detect a penumbra of half-conscious awareness, but glimpse a periphery of pre-consciousness or unconsciousness which the spotlight never manages to illuminate directly. Presumably, the neo-platonist maintains, intelligence in its conscious form would not issue from the development of the body, had it not in some broader sense presided over this development; nor can we, Plotinus asserts, conceive this organizing intelligence on the model of the conscious intellect which it produces, the intellect that first thinks of all the parts it is going to need, and then by means of hands and tools undertakes to realize them effectively. The shaping force works "without intermediary"; by the mere fact of its presence to matter, the entire form which "first exists elsewhere"—i.e., in the "intelligible" realm, the realm of forms—brings into existence "a copy or image of itself."[28]

Whatever we may think of this particular knot of metaphysical, biological, and psychological issues, the contention in regard to the painter is quite clear; by something like the physical law of heredity, he tends to reproduce himself in his works. If he is gaunt, like El Greco, or squat like Goya, or plump and florid like Rubens, so will his figures be. Stripping the term of its adverse moral connotation, we may say there is a native and unconscious egoism in the artist's outlook, by virtue of which he projects himself upon the world.

Since likeness is the category to which the painter's thinking spon-

[27]The editor has not found this passage in Leonardo's *Notebooks.*
[28]Plotinus *Enneads* V.8.7.

taneously turns, we can see how natural it is that Leonardo should view the situation as a struggle between competing likenesses—a manifest and intended likeness to the object and a latent unconscious likeness to the artist. But a wider view of the facts would lead us to detect this personal element not only in portrait and figure paintings, but in landscape, in abstract and even in non-objective painting, where to describe it in terms of physical resemblance to the painter would be absurd.

As we move in Figure 1 along the various divisions leading to *F*, we are not in fact passing from the imitation of natural objects to the copying of structural patterns equally given in nature. As we said at the time, the movement is away from the reduplication of the given altogether, away from the passive recording of objective fact toward the elaboration of subjectively initiated form. Since the initiative to such activity is provided by the pressure of feeling, sentiment, or emotion, and since this is a pressure toward the outward manifestation of an inner state, we may enlarge the notion that every painting is a "portrait of the artist" in this sense: in the sense not of physical resemblance but of personally expressive quality.

Here, rather than in the technical impossibility of reaching the *X* co-ordinate, that is of carrying resemblance to the limit, we may locate the attraction which draws the painter decisively away toward *Y*. The fact which we required to distinguish aesthetic from natural form is now in our possession: it is the fact that the formal "exigencies of the framed pictorial world" are exigencies of expression, and the artist's fascinated concern with pattern in its endless variety is a concern with the modalities of feeling and expression.

Thus, to take the simplest instance, the rhythmic trace left by the gesture of the hand that holds a brush or pencil not only betrays whether the movement was abrupt, cursive, leisurely, punctual, cautious, iterative, continuous, and so on through the countless distinctive qualities of motion, but also it tends to reveal what kind of person left the trace, what normal emotional make-up, or temperament, was his, whether timid, aggressive, orderly, scatter-brained, restrictive, expensive, stolid, nervous, and so on; qualities which each of us, in some degree, is accustomed to estimate from the formal pattern of any specimen of handwriting. Or again, temporary moods or states of intense feeling may be given away by patterns. If the "doodler's" telephone pad shows on one occasion a design of straight and broken lines criss-crossing in sharply angular fashion, and on another a more open pattern of swinging curves, we may infer that the second conversation has been pleasanter than the first. Not that we are able to tell whether he had been perplexed or angry or perhaps impatient on the first occasion, for the "doodling" is an event at a rather elementary, unconscious level of expression; but it is expressive, and thereby reveals personal state and mood as infallibly as would the overheard intonations of the voice, supposing the words themselves to be indistinguishable.

When the painter is dissatisfied with the actual structures and forms, and "corrects," or, if you prefer, "distorts" what stands before him, he can say that he does so because nature actually has no "moods" but only seems to have. Natural forms stimulate without satisfying the human need of expression, so that the correction or distortion takes place in the interest of bringing to free expression some "mood of nature" which is evasively visible to the artist. To describe more literally what happens, some shape or configuration of shapes in nature serves the painter as a cue; in his mood, grave or gay or whatever its tone, that particular configuration is recognized as fitting; for a mood, like a question, is something very likely to precipitate some kind of answer. But such a cue is only a starting point; to develop it and realize to the full its expressive possibilities is to make precisely the transition from natural to aesthetic form.

It may be added that another aesthetic factor modifying the tendency to likeness is the element of style, artistic convention, or taste. It is quite true, as any history of painting will prove, that each period has distinctive common features of style, forming the general convention of painting at the time, and powerfully affecting the work of all artists—even of the innovators who bring about a change of taste. Examples are endless. If we look at sketch-portraits of European subjects made by Easter Islanders accustomed to work within a Polynesian convention of sacred art where the god is a hawk-like bird figure, the influence of the convention on the portraits will be sensible enough to our eyes to make it seem most unlikely that the sketches can have resembled the sitters. Yet the natives will unanimously admire the likeness which the subjects themselves find it hard to detect at all. What a Chinese, a Byzantine, a man of the Renaissance or of the Baroque period sees before him is certainly determined in part by the conventions of representation holding at the period—a fact which is the basis of the paradoxical remark recurring every so often in the history of aesthetics, that it is nature which copies art, rather than art nature. If Renaissance painting shows a general tendency to elaborate the separate details each for itself in such a way that each, if cut out from the canvas, would be a complete picture in itself, whereas in the Baroque period interest in details is sacrificed to a total effect so that such a severed part would be largely meaningless, these differences in convention bespeak differences in vision. People are taught to see different things, and to see them differently, as a result of the collective effort of different schools of art. Thus, after the cubist movement had established its conventions, one was likely to notice the patterns of crossing, reinforced, or parallel shadows cast by objects in a room illuminated by several sources of light simultaneously; or, with the emergence of surrealism, little casual incongruities would attract the eye which before would have passed largely unperceived: in a broken-down joint-establishment, a combined saddler's and jeweller's shop, for example, the sudden spectacle of the jeweller standing by the shop-window examining the works of a watch through his glass, while the head of the saddler's wooden horse looks over his shoulder.

This conventional, that is to say, agreed and collective influence belongs with the personally expressive factor to the formal side of the art. It is a convention or mode of transposing the forms and colours of nature into aesthetic forms. A closer inspection of such formal conventions will, however, reveal that they too spring from the same source and have the same expressive function as the individual artist's manipulation of pattern. Their apparent impersonality is due to the fact that they express widespread collective attitudes and feelings, which can be called general, not because there is some overruling "spirit of the age," but simply because they are very widely diffused, and shared by the majority of individuals at the time—in exactly the same way, that is, as a given age will have its characteristic set of beliefs and opinions. The rigid, separate, hierarchic, and highly formalized disposition of figures in a Byzantine painting or mosaic betokens a Byzantine temper, for example, which has every kind of affinity with the beliefs and institutions of the Byzantine world. There is little that could be called gratuitous or a matter of pure caprice in the major revolutions of taste that result in sweeping changes in artistic convention, since every age seeks and finds for itself modes of expression appropriate to its own peculiar outlook at that juncture in time. The factor we are discussing is merely the factor of style in its general sense, as contrasted with personal or individual style, and we must take precautions against supposing that the former can be opposed to the latter. The impersonal or "period" style is, in the first instance, the product of individual artists, there being nowhere else for it to come from, no sense in which society itself is an artist. But the person who happens to "hit off" the most common attitudes and feelings of his time, or better, those which it could generally be said to aspire toward and require, will summon into activity a host of others. Often the resulting elaboration of individual styles into a common style is a surprisingly rapid affair, a kind of precipitation in which a small group of men, or even one man, has played the role of catalyst.

Logical and Aesthetic Objections Considered

If there are so many influences soliciting the painter to abandon likeness, why should he make any effort to retain or cultivate it? It seems to follow from all we have said that, unless some real defence of likeness is possible, we shall find ourselves firmly clasped in the embrace of the "non-objective" or "abstract" artist.

The question not yet squarely faced is as to where, on our graph, we should locate the optimal range of performance. It is at the same time the question as to which of the two factors, if either, we should assign primacy. Since this issue is a delicate one, we may begin by outlining the alternatives in an abstract way.

Starting from the already noted properties of the hyperbola, (1) the non-objective painter will assert the primacy of expressive design and make it the all-inclusive term, pointing out that however closely the curve approaches X it will always be possible to drop a perpendicular to OY, and that this is to measure off along OY some appreciable degree of formal pattern, however slight. This argument has the effect of placing the optimum well toward F and the Y co-ordinate, where likeness, reducible toward a vanishing point, tends to become an irrelevance. Freed from alien intrusion, purified of everything extrinsic, painting, the abstractionist claims, is now in a position to be aware of itself, of its essential resources and of its creative possibilities.

But (2) by purity of reasoning it should be possible for the imitationist to argue in the same way: likeness too is an all-inclusive term covering the whole art from end to end; and no matter how close it approaches to pure design, the perpendicular dropped to OX and the distance measured off along it indicate an uneliminable objective reference. It is open to him to claim the primacy of likeness over form, and to displace the optimal range well in the direction of A, treating design as an extrinsic disturbance, an irrelevance to be reduced toward the vanishing point. Let the painter go on with his job, the making of likeness, and forget about decoration, expression, and all such fancy notions.

With the first two positions the whole problem of painting is merely laid wide open again. We have seen every reason to reject the philistinism of the second, and we shall shortly add to the good grounds already discovered for distrusting the sophistication of the first. A compromise position (3) would deny primacy to either factor. It would now be incorrect to say either that a picture is first of all a likeness and then may also be a decorative pattern, or to say that it is first of all an expressive design and then on top of that may bear a resemblance to something; it is "first of all" both a likeness and a design. The effect of this is to push the optimal range from either extreme toward the centre of the curve where it most nearly approaches *O*, a solution commended by the fact that it shows a touch of common-sense moderation. Yet we are not to forget so soon our misgivings about the "meanness" of the mean, and the mediocrity of the mere averaged compromise. It is also common sense to call this solution indecision and fence-sitting. "Make up your mind! Commit yourself! No judicious indifference!" howl enraged extremists from both directions at once. And indeed, to say that each of two opposed forces is all-inclusive (though it obviously excludes the other) is to get into a serious logical dilemma; further, to assert that neither has any degree of superiority over the other, is like trying to find a point of indifference or equilibrium between inhalation and exhalation, which can only mean holding your breath—a possible compromise, but not for long. This image is a good one to describe the history of painting which, from as far back as we can go, even in prehistory, shows alternations of naturalistic and formalizing phases; yet clearly the living rhythms of historical process only provide evidence of tension, of the existence of a problem, material toward its theoretical solution, not the solution itself; for it is no solution to assign a temporary pre-eminence now to one party and now to its opponent.

And so we return again to the question of primacy—that is, the question of emphasis, which is always the crucial issue. The remaining alternative (4), and the best one, is supplied by a fact which all the positions (1), (2), and (3), ignore, viz., that in any polar opposition whatever, one of the poles must be regarded as positive, the other negative; thus, from the point of view of the organism, to take air into the lungs is a positive act of appropriation; to expel it is an act of elimination and rejection, and therefore negative. Position (1), though it asserts the primacy of form and thus technically recognizes the existence of a positive pole, wishes to eliminate the negative, and with it the polarity itself—it is something like the frog's project in Aesop's fable, that of uninterrupted self-inflation; (2) also tries to ignore the polarity, so that it presents a kind of programme of sustained exhalation and eflation; (3), we already said, is the senseless scheme of just not breathing. Accordingly (4) will be the position which combines polarity with primacy; and there ought to be no question to which of the competing forces this relative superiority is to be attributed. It is the active, shaping, expressive form-giving function which is authentically *art*, the positive pole; with equal vigour we should assert that resemblance and representation are not to be reduced to the vanishing point. They play, not as position (1) asserts, a residual role, in the sense that they cannot quite be got rid of, but an essential, if negative, role in the art of painting. The upshot of (4) in terms of the location of the optimum is to place it not toward *O*, at the point where we might suppose each attraction to be at the exact maximum consistent with the greatest possible degree of the other, but somewhat off-centre, toward *Y*, where the relative primacy of pattern can be maintained. What this means in actual pictorial terms is not so easy to state: non-objectivism, abstractionism, surrealism would be definitely condemned in one direction; photographic literalism, "selectionism," and probably the type of impressionism inspired by scientific theories of perception in the other. There is still a sufficient gap to leave the practical consequences of our investigation uncomfortably vague. Is the formalizing Byzantine convention nearer this optimum than, say, Renaissance naturalism? I suspect so; but in general, not always or in any instance. Is the antique stylized Dorian sculpture closer to it than the incipient Hellenism of the age of Phidias? Again I suspect so, though it would be difficult to make the statement good in such a sweeping form as this. Yet we may still be satisfied that our account is substantially correct without being able to apply it this far in specific detail. It is sufficient to liken the painter's attack on his problem to a "pincers movement" in which, as in sound strategy, one pincer, that of form, is developed with greater force and impetus, serving as hammer to the other's anvil.

The defence of likeness on which we are engaged requires some reconsideration of the main points already discussed. And first of all a reconsideration of the whole logical issue. We have seen how profoundly the cognitive theory of art modifies the common-sense definition from which it takes its departure, and this in respect of both its terms; "nature," from signifying the immediately given appearance to sense, becomes a system of intelligible concepts, or of laws, or of intuited essences, or even of purely linguistic conventions; "imitation," from simple transcription and recording of given facts of sense, becomes a progressively more active, reflective operation, whether of selection, discursive abstraction, intuitive apprehension, or prescriptive postulation. Therewith the requirement of likeness is both broadened and toned down, becoming at last a functional likeness in rivalry with nature's display of vitality and fertility of form.

The reader is reminded of this development because he may now recognize that its results are rather different from what the parties to it intended. Cognitive, or using the word loosely, logical, motives guided the search for a "true" likeness. But what it terminated in turns out to be decisively subjective: the primacy of aesthetic over natural form, of expression over representation, of rhythmic pattern over objective order and structure. We are now to look back over the path by which we came and ask whether "truth to nature" retains any meaning at all.

It would seem sensible to note that unless painting makes some sort of assertion, and in no metaphorical sense, the use of terms like truth and error is strictly indefensible. Nothing but assertion and denial can be true or false. Is painting then really a language, by which information can be conveyed?

If it is, we may agree that the first thing the framed canvas asserts is something like "This is a picture"—i.e., a whole formal design, framed precisely in order to isolate it in its self-contained wholeness, to cut it off from the surrounding physical objects, whose relations to it and interaction with it the frame warns us to disregard. It is an initial assertion to the effect that this is an aesthetic, not a physical object. And the implication is that it should first of all *look painted*, before it *looks like* anything else.

In the second instance it asserts something such as "This is how I, the artist, feel." Or, if you prefer, impersonally, "This is a feeling, a human state." We should be careful not to confuse expression in this emotional sense with logical expression in propositional form, or with, say, mathematical "expression"; yet all of these share the quality of being utterances, linguistic facts in the most general sense.

The real trouble begins when we pass to a third, objective order of statement which the canvas may be supposed to imply. Does the painter mean to assert when he traces certain contours on the canvas, "These are autumn leaves and fruits; this is a hill; this is a woman's breast"? Certainly. Yet the frame, the paint, the design, everything unites to add "not really." The painting is only a likeness, an image; not a truth but a seeming truth, a verisimilitude, and hence, from the point of view of logical and objective or scientific assessment, a hopelessly ambiguous creature indeed.

The cognitive development of which the reader has just been reminded was motivated by the search for a "true" likeness. Now, no matter what standard of truth is applied—perceptual "correctness," conformity to the average, intuitive self-evidence, pragmatic "working," or consistency among prescriptive definitions—it is clear that such a search ignores the negative sign, the "not really," by which the picture-frame marks the represented world off as something apart, an imagined or mock-objective world. If likeness is seeming, semblance, is not the very idea of "true" likeness a logical will-o'-the-wisp?

But then the other element of likeness asserts itself. Unless the painting is a semblance of *what is*, it is no likeness; and what is, is to be determined by reflection on experience, by science, by logic, by the whole cognitive enterprise which culminates in metaphysics. The first two syllables of the word "verisimilitude" refer us to the objective truth which the whole word removes from sight; the strong word *is* cannot be overlooked if the painting is allowed to say, "This *is* a kneeling woman, though of course not really." Are we thereupon forced to admit the relevance of those things whose relevance we have just denied?

At this juncture we may remind ourselves again of what a solution such as (4) commits us to. In a "pincers movement" nothing but uncertainty can result from examining one branch of the movement in isolation. It is particularly true that the subordinate, relatively passive, or "negative" movement is liable to misinterpretation. Strategically, I suppose, this fact is specially exploited by the attacker: the enemy must be in doubt for some time as to which flanking movement is the main attack; and the object is to mislead him into mistaking the minor for the major effort. The disaster of utter theoretical confusion is similarly invited if we overlook the negative sign attaching to the representational factor in painting and suppose that the search for truth or the avoidance of contradiction and error could be the main impelling force in the art. But when we reintegrate likeness into the whole strategic plan, in due subordination to the dominating aim of expression, we find that the perplexing ambiguity of the negative loses its force and that thinking can be assigned a genuine role in the art of painting.

While patterns are the main resource of the painter, and his primary object is to stir us by their rhythmic elaboration, this is by no means the whole story; representation, his auxiliary or supplementary resource, enables him to accomplish this object much more effectively and with greater precision and sureness.

Nature, it is hardly necessary to say, is full of varicoloured things of various shapes which either disturb, or excite, or allure, or calm us. By deliberate allusion to these things the painter can enrich his design with endless associations of felt quality derived from our familiar experience of these things—their warmth or chill, serenity or menace, forcefulness, impotence, austerity, grace, singleness and solidity, manifoldness, slipperiness, and so on indefinitely: qualities, it should be noted which, though half-sensuous, are at the same time half-personal, or moral, in the sense of being directly transposable in terms of human character or characteristic.

No doubt the fact that these are associations is what makes them objectionable to the non-objectivist, abstractionist, or art-for-art's-saker—for convenience, call him the aesthetic Puritan since he too would like to destroy images. So let us examine a particular case, indicated in the well-known slogan of the nineteenth-century "art-for-art's-sake" painters: "A cabbage is as good as a Madonna."

This is true, in the primary, formalist sense, that one natural structure is as likely as another to supply the painter with the appropriate "cue" that precipitates his designing activity. But the slogan is false and perverse in the context of his whole task and the fullest employment of all his resources. Even for one not brought up in the Christian tradition, for whom the religious associations of the Madonna would be absent, the complex of ideas and deep-lying affective resonances clustering about the spectacle of the mother and child make it incomparably more striking and powerful material, potentially immensely more moving than the cabbage could ever be.

To the Puritan all this is impure—a "story," we said before, a set of extraneous, non-aesthetic, extrinsic, adventitious associations, and so contemptible. If the Puritan means just that such subject-matter is not of itself enough to ensure that the work of art will be a good one, he is of course again quite right. A vapid sentimental depiction of motherhood, feeble in design and photographic in its naturalism, is objectionable. But where the design is fine and firm, the composition simple, strong, and single, the colour internally consistent in scale and disposition, and where what we called the dimension of temporal depth is present, who can doubt that the result will be more moving if it is the likeness of a Madonna, not of a cabbage or of something which might as well be a cabbage as a Madonna?

The Puritan's self-denying ordinance can be approved as a measure of discipline. It drives the painter back to the authentic technical fundamentals of his art; it is a service to require him to engage first of all in purely technical exercises and explorations. But it is as great a disservice to restrict him to them and rob him permanently of half his available resources of expression.

The aesthetic justification of likeness which we are making here is that the extrinsic associations which representation exploits can greatly intensify, specify, and sharpen the expression of feeling. By itself, taken in abstraction from pattern, or when supposed to be the primary thing in painting, likeness will not have this effect. It is a condition, but not a sufficient condition, of full success in the art. The justification is not a cognitive, objectively directed, theoretical one, but a properly aesthetic defence, given in terms of feeling.

Thus fortified, we may return to the "logical" issue, the question of the place of intellection, and of objective truth, in painting. Our aim will be to show that likeness is a vehicle of meaning of a special kind and therefore that its elimination would deprive the art of significance.

Let us begin with a simple illustration. In Figure 2 we witness the budding of a rhythmic pattern into representation. It is a detail from one of those endlessly interwoven designs in the Book of Kells in which

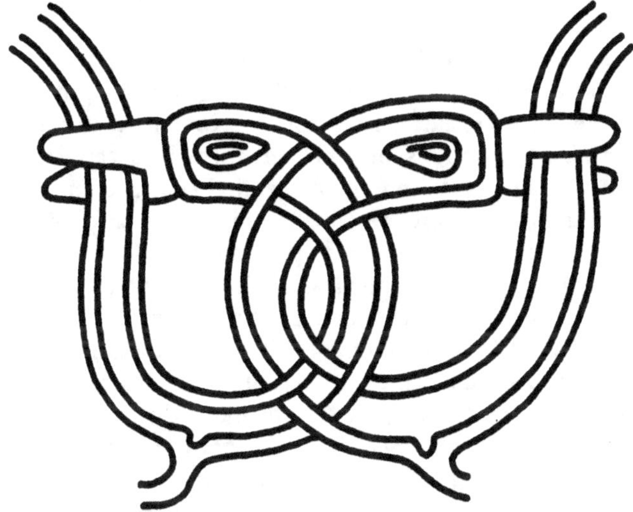

FIGURE 2

interlaced double ribbons pursue each other in alternate crossings so that where the left-hand ribbon crosses over, the right one must cross under. In the intricacy of I do not know how many thousands of such crossings (each of which has been painstakingly scrutinized) there does not occur a single hesitation, correction, or wrong crossing—in itself an astonishing technical fact as anyone will admit who has tried to work out even a simple pattern of this kind. In the circumstances it cannot be anything but deliberate that the bottom lines of the birds' bills are broken between the outside borders of the ribbons. The rhythm of under and over is being projected into the terminal points of the design; but since this is representation also, the double ribbon suddenly becomes solid, a neck, something which can be held in a bill and bitten. Likeness here spreads back from the focal point where it originates, revising the formal pattern. You have only to imagine it spreading further, over the whole surface, to envisage how profoundly representation can transform design; how essentially different a resource it is from design; and how essentially negative it is, from the designer's point of view; something which upsets and requires modification of any preconceived pattern, and may do so to the point where the pattern is either lost to sight or effectively disintegrated. One reason for placing the optimal range slightly to the *Y* side and not directly opposite *O* in Figure 1 was just that, in this way, design visibly dominates and remains in charge, controlling the potentially disruptive force of its antagonist (which is at the same time its collaborator).

The moral of this little instance of the concern with truth to nature may be reinforced by pointing out the difference between a design (Fig. 2) and a diagram (Fig. 1). In the diagram thought has charge, and a perceptual material of lines and curves is used to hold together a group of abstract notions, and present them in a certain order and connection; a diagram is a purely intellectual construction whose merit will depend upon the degree to which it stimulates or satisfies thought. As diagram it has no intrinsic interest whatever—or if it has, it will be unintentionally: it is intended as an instrument of thought in the search for truth and nothing more. In the design, on the other hand, not intellection but feeling has charge; it is not something to think with but something to see and enjoy, something to be felt and experienced.

Current usage, in terming these schematic duck-heads "abstract," correctly implies that the design is not without an intellectual ingredient. They could with equal justice be called diagrammatic, in the sense in which, in Schopenhauer's view already outlined, all perception involves conceptual thinking as well as sensory stimulation and is a process in which thought provides diagrammatic outlines of the various "kinds" of thing familiar to us, the given object being judged as of this or that "kind"—a summary process, one of labelling and pigeonholing, with a severely practical goal; for conceptualization of the given has the immediate effect of drawing off our interest from the unique visual appearance and channelling it upon the "kind," that is upon the more or less tidy ordering of schemes of action.

Our design is then, after all, a diagram. The presence of thought, of observation and reflection, declares itself in the fact that we say "duck" rather than "eagle" or "stork"; but in subordination to design this diagrammatic reference to nature has quite a different character than it would have if it played the dominant role; it is a passing and sidelong reference, without the cognitive future inherent in the perception of actual objects. Where it is really ducks you are perceiving or even biologists' diagrams of duck-structure, you may hope to add indefinitely to your knowledge as you study perhaps the laws of their flight or their habits of migration; study of these "imagined" ducks would be more likely to add to your knowledge of Irish monks, and through them of mankind, than to that of a given bird-species. A sympathetic consideration of the rolling and twisting pattern of interlacings; of the fitness of drawing attention to the point where the movement is tied by the clip-like grasp of birds' beaks; even, since the grasp of any living thing is temporary and precarious, the fact that this termination is not really an end or arrest of movement, only an attempt to contain and partially restrict it within certain limits—all this is very nearly symbolic. The artist's attitude to change, his sense of life as something at once unfathomably complex and infallibly precise and ceaselessly changing direction, his aversion to the static and cubic and immobile, all symbolically speaking lie just below the surface of his design: they are there to be read by anyone, yet they are not conceptually stated, making the design a diagram or a piece of philosophical commentary; they are present as concrete feeling in a design which makes a controlled use of certain diagrammatic materials.

"A more philosophical thing than history"[29]: Aristotle's assessment of the intellectual element in poetic art implies that verisimilitude is worth something in itself, and even that it is worth more than truth to objective fact; and again worth it in itself, not just as a stepping-stone or a ladder leading from historical fact to a universal philosophical meaning.

In detecting such symbolic meanings as these we are perhaps on the track of such a worth—not philosophical, since there is no play of concepts in the design, and whatever the work is, it is certainly not an argument or a demonstration of anything; the abstract paraphrase of its symbolism just given can pretend neither to finality nor to exhaustiveness. If it does not have philosophical status, neither has it status as a record of fact, a piece of natural history. We shall content ourselves for the time with calling it a symbol and, like all true symbols, a revelation of the human person.

But our example may have consequences for the general theory of painting, and particularly for the problem under hand, of determining the genuine role of thought, truth, and intelligence in the art.

We have repeatedly said that the reference to nature is a subordinate,

[29]*Poetics* IX.3.

a supplementary, or a negative, resource, the anvil to the hammer of rhythmic pattern—its antagonist in the sense that it will modify any preconceived design, its collaborator in the sense that it can introduce associated sense qualities of kinds to enhance the expressive force of the work as a whole.

We now suggest that the key to the whole intricate problem may lie in the fact that the objective reference in painting is not simple, or single, but double in function, one significance being contained, as it were, within the other. As a likeness the painting is an ordinary directional sign, indicator, or signal—functioning as the arrow, the highway road-sign, the barber's pole, or the sign-painter's foaming tankard do, to direct us to places or persons, to identify things and occasions. At the non-aesthetic limit of photography this is the sort of meaning that likeness can have: it may be accepted in a court of law as identification of the presence of a given person at a given place and time; or, as employed by the snapshot-taking tourist, it may have the trivial subjective value of stimulating the memory of those who were, or the envy of those who were not, there. All this is perfectly plain sailing, and common sense contents itself, not unnaturally, with an interpretation which is so straightforward and simple.

Yet the immense pains bestowed by generations of men on their art, and the veneration (hardly too strong a word) in which the great masters are held, cannot reasonably be attributed merely to their technical dexterity in catching likenesses, but seem to show that there is a more serious meaning to be found in their works. The type of signification through which this additional meaning is given we have called symbolism, to prevent confusion with the indicative function; the latter is present, to be sure, in the representation, likeness, or image; but we shall deny that being an image is equivalent to being a symbol. The symbolic function is the additional one to which the true painter tempers likeness. Its referent exists nowhere in the physical order, but in the inner life of feeling and thought. On the first, or indicative, line of signification intelligence requires, for instance, that objective correlations be respected, that figures in a winter landscape be warmly dressed, and so on. On the second, or symbolic, line these expectations may quite well be disregarded. When, in spite of physical effects of fire, Blake depicts a resplendent figure sheathed in flames, it is understood at once that this is a visitant from another world, or that the flames are "symbolic"—a mental and spiritual incandescence. Language, of course, takes the same liberty when it speaks of one "burning" with love, or another "frozen" with fear. Lest we be thought to be giving the surrealist more than his due at this point, it may be remarked that this liberty descends to licence when, at a level corresponding to the pun, the painter depicts the human chest as containing drawers, some half-open to display the contents.

But ignoring for the moment the special problem set by the case of symbolism run wild, it may be well to reflect that if we supposed the use of intelligence in painting to be in the indicative function alone, we would be slipping back into imitation-theory. We may remind ourselves of our warning to the contemporary "selectionist": a change from a naïve to a sophisticated and technical vocabulary does not necessarily mean a change in the underlying theory. To assert that "objective correlations are to be respected" is, in effect, just another way of saying "the painter should copy nature," with the additional misleading suggestion that the refined correlations established by laboratory science—say the laws of chemical synthesis or the laws of electromagnetic action—should be known and observed by the painter, whereas none of them has any essential relevance to his art.

If the sign which points to and identifies an object is called an indicator, the additional function given it by science is that of stating the observed correlations between one thing or event and another. As we need a name for this type of signification, let us say that in scientific use an indicator becomes a symptom, as the fact indicated as a temperature of 103° on the thermometer will in medical science be interpreted according to circumstances as a symptom of measles, or pneumonia, or the like. The symptomatic significance conferred on indicative signs has the effect of systematizing our expectations on the basis of what has happened before (and the assumption that the future will be like it). It is not nature, of course, that expects heat to accompany flame, but we; nature *gives* no signs whatever, it is we who *take* one thing as the sign of another and build up the sciences by ordering these signs systematically.

In the texture of objective correlations thus woven by scientific intellect, the category of likeness can be said to play only an imitating or simulating role, as it does in the abstractive process of sorting "like" instances into "kinds," and therefore in the indicative function as well. It is proper to the preliminary imaginative phase which scientific discovery, like any other mental effort, must go through. Thus, to notice a resemblance in the way a ball rebounds, an echo replies, and a beam of light is reflected, would be the first step in discovering the sine law. But likeness or resemblance lacks precision and rigour; it is ambiguous and indefinitely approximate, a qualitative similarity merely, which may objectively speaking mean nothing at all: the test is whether the relation in the three cases admits identical quantitative formulation. With measurement and quantitative precision we pass from guesswork to knowledge, from the imaginative preliminaries to the intellectual elaboration of scientific truth.

While likeness as an indicative sign is certainly an intellectual instrument, its cognitive functions, as indicative, are limited to acts of identification and recognition. In the vast possibilities of knowledge opened up by the symptomatic function, on the other hand, likeness plays a role which is logically suspect and requires the closest criticism. Guesswork is more often than not mistaken; imagination requires the severest control if it is not to get out of bounds, and the mind which allows itself to be led by unexamined resemblance is certain to be misled.

In the other order, that of subjects, with which painting is concerned, where indicative signs serve as vehicles not of symptomatic but of symbolic meaning, the case is far otherwise; here likeness is a category of first-rate importance and is, in one form or another, basic to the structure of every sign given by one person to another and the prime agent of signification. Examples of its human, non-scientific import crowd to mind. In primitive sympathetic magic, for instance, the one possessing a likeness of a person has a certain power over him and may damage him through deforming the image in any part. This is a primitive version of the truth which is the caricaturist's stock in trade; without a telling likeness the caricature falls flat; with it, the artist's malice can work havoc in almost any direction he pleases. Or in a quite different realm, that of religion, we discover the guiding principle that man was made *in the image and likeness of God*. In its Christian version this of course means that in his possession of intellect, imagination, and will, man's conscious life exhibits triplicity and unity, though neither perfectly. The defacing of this Image through sin is the Christian diagnosis of the internal disintegration and conflict from which we suffer, and the most profound view of life's meaning ever taken is that which finds it in the restoration of this defaced Image. Along with this and in the same context belongs the *Imitatio Christi* which, in one form or another, has been the guiding principle of Christians through all the generations. In the less ultimate context of the influence of example in education, in all sorts of manual training and skill, in the formation of character (I am thinking not necessarily of hero-worship but of all those movements of admiration by which we come to shape our ways of acting and feeling and thinking toward striking models of human goodness or excellence), in the whole of this human order, the power of imitation and the importance of likeness are endless and almost impossible to overestimate. Even the young mother's desire for a son "exactly like" his father shows how profoundly likeness can be bound up with and summarize, so to speak, the whole complex movement of the life of affection. And so forth. These are scattered illustrations of the effectiveness of likeness and of the desire to *be* like or to *make* like; desire is a feeble word for what may be a consuming passion. They will perhaps be enough to confirm the claim that this category is of major significance in the human order: magic, religion, love, admiration, affection—the key words in the summary—all point in the same direction, toward the most intimate region of subjective fact, toward the inalienable, and probably unfathomable, privacy from which, as water from beneath a mountain rock, decision, motive, longing, desire, passion, idea, reflection, image, constantly well.

The aesthetic symbol, it will be here maintained, like the symbols employed by the mystic, does not admit of verification in the ordinary sense of checking the reference it makes by direct inspection of the object it refers to. No doubt there are direct mystical experiences, but they are open only to those to whom they occur and cannot be verified by any sort of direct sensuous inspection. The mystic can only try to picture his experience in such recurrent images as that of the sun's light caught and held in a mirror or precious stone, which has done duty all over the world to express the soul's right relation to God,[30] but the experience thus symbolized remains its own authentication: for there is no perception of God except precisely to the worshipping soul; what would be required to be able to verify the mystic's report, an independent impersonal objective experience of God, is a kind of contradiction in terms. Similarly with the aesthetic symbol. Its manifest reference in the outer world (its indicative referent, together with whatever symptomatic reference the artist may choose to incorporate) is verifiable, just as the fact that a mirror or a jewel catches and holds a miniature image of the sun, is verifiable: and with as little relevance to the latent reference which is to the depths of human feeling and the springs of the life of consciousness; this reference cannot itself be checked by independent and impersonal observation. The parallel might mislead by suggesting too much: aesthetic experience is not a form of mystical awareness, its reference being still to the created order in so far as within it there are centres of mental and emotional and

[30]It is of frequent use in St. Paul, cf. 2 Cor. 3:18: It is given to us all to catch the glory of the Lord as in a mirror, with faces unveiled and so we become transfigured into the same likeness, borrowing glory from that glory.

voluntary energy, i.e., persons; and mystical experience is not a form of aesthetic self-enjoyment (the term is intended here without disparagement to signify acquaintance with the active centre) but a surrender of the self to something, as the mystic never tires of asserting, wholly transcending the created order. If there is good reason to speak of symbolic thinking in both cases, it is again because there is no other way of exhibiting the facts experienced than indirectly through some physical likeness. The data of the senses, too, we have suggested, are ineffable in their own way: there comes a point when we can only point, or make indicative noises like "this," and where the most concrete words, "iron" or "water," are recognized as abstractions, ideas of our own making, concepts, signs, not actual entities. However, though it is impossible for us to know the reality of things nakedly and stripped of all the signs, and though the attempts to put *this*, the given experience, the actual entity, into words at once changes it, universalizes it, makes it not a "this," but a "kind" woven into a whole mental texture of related "kinds," the independent verification of any statement about the outer world is possible. Thus when someone tells me that iron always sinks or always floats, I can drop a crowbar in the pond to see whether placing it on water is in fact a symptom or signal for iron to sink or not. By repetition I can establish not just that it sometimes sinks, but that it has sunk each time I have tried, which of course is not the same as always. I am launched on the process of empirical verification in which an abstract mental or theoretical proposition is validated by the senses. Nothing comparable can be expected with the proposition, "God is the light of the soul," or with the latent assertion in a painting; each of these, however pictorially rich, we have to translate in the verbally impoverished form, "Here is a state of human feeling." No doubt both refer to experiences which others may or may not have enjoyed, but they are not experiences of external sense. The man who finds nothing in his consciousness to which to attach the word "soul," or the phrase, "light of the soul," like the man whom the picture leaves unmoved, can only say "No"; and there is no objective empirical process, no microscopic or telescopic extension of sense, no mathematical and quantitative logical process of demonstration by which to convince him. The mystic or the artist can only in turn say, "Yes, I find this, I am sure of this, this is so." What we are describing as symbolic reference cannot then escape from the possibility of disagreement, whereas symptomatic reference is called objective precisely because no matter who drops the crowbar into the pond, he will find the same thing.

In the case of painting, as in the case of religion, who the subject is matters enormously; something like a sounding of conscious subjectivity itself is being taken, the sounding line and what it records alike are visible only to the person taking the sounding, and we are entirely dependent on his skill and accuracy in reporting what he has found.

These are all matters which will receive further light when we come to discuss poetry; meantime the conclusion of this prolonged examination of the place of intelligence, of thought, of truth, in the art of painting may be restated. An objective, an indicative reference to nature is a condition of the painting possessing full symbolic significance. Without it, even though formal pattern and rhythm are directly expressive of inner states and feelings, we would to a large extent be confronted with the mere fact of feeling, as when someone tells us he is miserable or happy—statements which are hardly very infectious unless we chance to have the same or similar causes to be miserable or happy. With the painter's reference to nature, as it were, the same causes are supplied. Thus our use of the term "symbolic" differs unexpectedly from current usage which would readily qualify a piece of thoroughly abstract design as "symbolic" because what it is intended to signify is not at all apparent. The real trouble with such work is that it is not symbolic, or not yet, or not fully symbolic; more is required if it is not to remain, like an abortively sketched gesture, merely evidence that someone intended and started to give a sign. And as the full gesture will always be found to signify through likeness—the shrug by lifting an imaginary weight of doubt or ignorance to give the shoulders a momentary rest, the emphasizing fist by borrowing from the boxer, the Frenchman's accusing wrist-movement by imitation of the fencer in the act of pinning down his opponent—so it is in painting: to fill out what is missing, to give the sign intended, some reference to nature is needed; some degree of deliberately exploited likeness; some marriage between the rhythmic and formal instinct which would reveal all and cannot and the instinct for likeness and passive imitation which does not will to reveal anything, but in this marriage becomes the agency of revelation, the giver of the sign, the bearer of life and meaning other than its own.

There are, of course, other more strictly aesthetic reasons why the pictorial reference to nature will remain an integral part of the art of painting in spite of the various motives of discontent with it and the various movements that attempt to eliminate it.

For one thing, it is an additional difficulty to be overcome. It may be argued, of course, that an abstract or a non-objective painting is not so easy to produce as an uninstructed public assumes. This is true: great technical skill often goes into such "exercises." It is true too that there can be a superficial and fatal facility in catching the look of things which, like the forger's skill at signatures, can be a very dubious gift. Painting since the discovery of the camera has no excuse for counterfeiting nature. But, in terms of the account given here in which painting is the fusion and mutual modification of form and likeness with as nearly an equal emphasis on each as is consistent with the primacy of form, the statement that likeness is an additional difficulty deliberately assumed would be a correct assessment.

Why is this an advantage, permanently securing the place of objective or indicative reference in the art? The answer is best given in terms of materials and their resistance to being worked. The non-practitioner easily supposes that a list of materials—from, say, granite down through marble and wood to clay—will supply more and more favourable conditions for the sculptor's realization of what he intends. In a sense this is true: a preconceived idea is more likely to emerge without modification where the material used is extremely plastic and unresisting. Yet an artist finds it something of a nightmare to contemplate the limiting case of this series—a medium so responsive to his will, some ectoplasm so unresisting that it will take and change shape even without manipulation, simply by fiat. For the artist knows and respects the antagonism, the negativism, the unpredictable resistances and yieldings of his materials; and though they may wreck many a promising work, he remembers well enough that when he has been most satisfied with his work, when it has turned out better than he expected, when he has done better than he knew he could do, the result is largely attributable to this sort of loyal opposition on the part of his materials. Unexpected difficulties, unforeseeable knots and anfractuosities of graining have made him modify his intention as he worked; and where the solution is a happy one he will be the first to admit that it never would have occurred to him without the collaboration of this antagonism. It was William Morris who, noting the whims and idiosyncrasies of the dyer's materials, remarked that it was not very long before the dyer learned to call his vat, "she."

It may not seem evident that "reference to nature" belongs with the peculiarities of paints, brushes, and grounds to the material side of painting; yet this technical justification of its presence ought not to be disparaged. In fact, difficult though it may be to produce a good abstract design, it is certainly easier than to effect that significant marriage of form and likeness, subjective and objective, active form-giving and passive receptivity, which we have demanded throughout this essay.

The antagonistic character of the two has already been pointed out and concretely illustrated; it is the *tour de force* of good painting to transform this into co-operation, and the good fortune by which this is achieved is a matter of turning unforeseen obstacles of representation to formal and rhythmic advantage, precisely as in the case of material resistances. The artist knows better than to attempt the impossibly difficult but is generally aware that the unduly easy is a more pervasive and serious danger to his art. He has an authentic sense of the true nature of freedom, at least as far as art is concerned: it is not the absence of restraint, the line of least resistance, evasion, but is found in the willing acceptance of discipline, and by seeking out what is difficult and encountering and overcoming its opposition.

Another way of putting what is I suppose the same point is to say that the human imagination requires a sort of nourishment of natural forms if it is to retain its aesthetic energy. When an artist leaves the open air for the studio and, supposing that he has accumulated enough capital of form and colour to dispense with all future study and observation of nature, finally abandons representation entirely for formal pattern, we may soon perceive what a sterile, what a mechanical thing unaided pictorial imagination is. The apparent responsiveness of nature to the artist's mood is, as we have already said, evidence of her inexhaustible fertility of forms and configurations. No matter what preoccupies the mind, some appropriate cue will present itself in the visual world which, when fastened upon and developed by the artist, will express his state more adequately than would have been the case with a pattern extracted from his own imagination. This coincidence of a preoccupation with a state of surrounding fact, amounting almost to the status of question and answer, is the type of all those happy accidents which cannot enter beforehand into the artist's calculations in detail, for he does not know what they will be, though he learns to expect them. It is a kind of occurrence closely related to those which link poetry and divination. The artist who turns down the wager of providing a reference to nature is cutting himself free not only from inevitable difficulties but at the same time from inimitable gifts and, as it were, acts of grace.

It has been our object in this lengthy section to show how the primacy of form requires, as its substantiation and for the full deployment of the resources of the painter, a very appreciable degree of representation, likeness, resemblance to nature. Naturally, our concern has throughout been with the cognitive and aesthetic objections to likeness whose force we may now take to be mitigated to the point required by our definition.

Moral and Religious Objections Considered

It remains, however, to say something to moderate similarly the objections that likeness is a lie and a piece of godlessness. If, to an age like ours where religion and morality are in decline, these objections seem to lack any ground or force, so much the worse for the age. Whatever has at any time been taken seriously enough for men to fight over remains a serious human issue, even though the date and the shape of the issue have been changed with the passage of time.

The moral question is that of honesty, a difficult virtue to acquire or assess. An illustration of its difficulty is the position of the art-for-art's-sake school which took the simple, if convenient, line that art has nothing at all to do with morality, that it would be about as sensible to require virtue of a cone or triangle as of a painting or a poem. Meantime, however, the virtue of honesty or sincerity remained to plague them; it was this moral quality, the artist's integrity as an artist, which alone mattered, and mattered supremely. It does not seem to have occurred to them to ask whether fidelity to one's art is a purely aesthetic ideal—as it certainly is not, since the artist is also a man and is being asked to rule his whole life by this single star. Nor do they seem to have asked how this solitary virtue is to be maintained in company with the vices which in this view either did not matter or were positively beneficial to artistic creation—pride, malice, debauchery, intemperance, and envy.

For the time being it is enough to say that it is a matter of some delicacy to lay the charge of dishonesty against a painter. In its contemporary form this charge probably applies to facile copying of the surface appearances of things, in which context we, a moment ago, spoke of the counterfeiter and his unfortunate skill. There is deception in such work, but in the sense that it pretends to have a human significance which it lacks, not in the sense that it pretends to be an actual scene or person when it is "only a picture." The counterfeit painting is not necessarily a copy of an old master: it may be copied straight from nature.

Nor is it so easy to escape from this form of dishonesty as the aesthetic Puritan supposes. To his fiercely iconoclastic mind, as we saw, any taint of naturalism is dishonesty—a reliance on a non-pictorial "literary" interest, on a story, something dragged in to disguise and overlay poverty of design and lack of intrinsic expressiveness. We agreed with him thoroughly where what we have just called counterfeit ware is concerned, but saw reason to reject his own opposed extreme position. Our decision is reinforced when we find apologies for it such as the following:

Non-objective pictures contain no intellectual subject nor any similarity to any known object. Colors, forms, and themes are combined by measurement of line and interval to create a unit of rhythm and beauty. It does not represent anything, and no form is supposed to look like anything known in nature. It is like music; it means nothing. It must be felt to be liked. With time given to their influence a sudden initiation and appreciation happens even to those who at first could not respond to them at all. It is their spiritual life which gets hold of all who live with them.

In amplification the folder goes on to state:

To see such a picture often results in the elevating influence which this important art brings to humanity with the development of its intuitive capacity for personal leadership, and cosmic reaction. The Non-objective painting therefore is far superior to all others through its influential potentiality, educational power, and cultural value. Contrary to abstract paintings which are submitted to earthly inspirations the Non-objective painting reflects the austerity of the beyond.[31]

It would be easy enough to laugh this away as the claptrap of promotional jargon; only its author probably believes what she has said; and it is typical of the claims made by this school. The possibilities of pretending to be what one is not, of deceiving oneself and others, limitless enough though they are in the nature of man's heart, receive an extra impetus wherever he is invited to suppose himself a pure disembodied spirit. Unexpectedly the religious motive turns up here validly, not against images, but against their rejection. It is not after all only the making of likenesses which is idolatrous and a usurpation of the Creator's prerogatives. The Puritan's rejection of the "earthly," of matter, of physical nature and body is first of all dishonest, as any pretence to be a pure spirit on the part of a creature who is obviously embodied must always be; but by the same token it is presumptuous, a claim to a god-like status, to pure creative autonomy, evident in the phrases "cosmic reaction" and "austerity of the beyond." Man's capacities of creativeness as an embodied spirit, though real, are vastly humbler than this and do not include creation *ex nihilo*. And it is, religiously speaking, certainly idolatrous to set man up this high, and to credit poor childish scrawls and scribbles—whatever technical competence they show they deserve no more exalted description than this in a "cosmic" context—with the astounding power to redeem, by sudden conversion or initiation, and presumably to save mankind, by developing our "intuitive capacity for personal leadership."

Religious and aesthetic Puritanism, though of course distinct, do exhibit remarkable parallels. The basic one is the dialectical revenge

[31]Quoted from the folder *Non-Objectivity is the Realm of Spirit*, by Hilla Rebay, put out by the Guggenheim Museum of Non-Objective Painting in New York.

taken by the material and bodily on those who pretend to possess the "purity" which embodied spirits cannot achieve; it is a revenge apparent in the aura of hypocrisy surrounding the Puritan's strait-laced manners and morals; in the graceless, domineering lines of his physical surroundings, from his household furniture to his cities. It is most of all evident in the cruel, unlovely power-system which he imposes on industry in the name of a religious vocation to trade, and in an almost monastic asceticism in the amassing of a capital which he would think sinful to spend on himself. The fact is that while, even by, professing a pure spirituality, Puritan England built up a most imposing system of material power. A reminder of such a fact as that peeps out at us in the word "leadership" from the Non-Objective prospectus quoted.

The moral defence of likeness must be made along the lines of the definition of painting we have reached. Surface illusionism is a cheat, not because it gives us images, but because it claims the status and significance of a work of art: it is rather like a book printed in characters which have no meaning in any tongue. Non-representational art is more like the waste of expensive materials and the best typography on a volume of nursery rhymes—or, what is an exact parallel, on a volume of Dadaist verse. It cheats in the more dangerous sense of pitching its claims for what it has to say impossibly high, like a merchant who deceives as to the worth of his goods. Honesty, like beauty in painting, is a matter of accepting the humbling limitation of likeness, as well as the challenge of making this likeness speak with fire, and with a vigorous voice never heard in the world before. For these are the conditions of fully expressive, personal sign-giving, or symbolic utterance.

An illustration from the field of architectural imitation will perhaps confirm these statements. Richard Krautheimer shows that the Anastasis, the Church of the Holy Sepulchre at Jerusalem, was the original model of all those medieval European churches on a round or octagonal plan (such as that of the Baptistery at Pisa, the Church of Lanleff near Caen, and countless others), which were originally dedications to the Holy Sepulchre or to the Resurrection itself.[32] That in such foundations it was felt necessary to identify the new building with its original he makes clear by producing records that men at different times were sent to Jerusalem to study and measure this famous church on the spot. The building put up on their return, however, might have eight or more sides instead of being round; the number of pillars might be

[32]Richard Krautheimer, "Introduction to an 'Iconography of Mediaeval Architecture,'" *Journal of the Warburg Institute*, V (1942), 1–33, especially 5 ff.

varied, or they might be left out altogether. They might limit the upper storey, alter the shape and proportions in any way they like. In at least one case two measurements taken from the Anastasis are recorded in the form of straight lines engraved on the stone floor of the church.

The author points out that what looks to the modern like incompetence and vagary made very good sense to the medieval mind. To establish the identity in spirit and dedication with the model at Jerusalem it would be enough if a few general resemblances were carried across, and this evidently mattered, or why go to the trouble and expense of crossing the sea? But the church you build is to be a complete thing in itself and to have its own history. You will then avoid aping the Anastasis in every detail; for a thing to be beautiful it must be itself. Hence the family resemblance between these daughters of the same mother, none of which is a replica of any other. We may find a characteristic expression of medieval aesthetic theory in a twelfth-century monk who said that since beauty is a quality of being, each thing should be itself as fully as possible, that a thing is ugly to the extent that it lacks anything natural to it, and that even if it lack nothing it is ugly if it tries to copy another such being.

To the modern, for whom spirit and dedication have little meaning, a copy is an exact, meticulous reproduction. Thus the letter of the Parthenon was at least twice transferred in stone, to the Calton Hill in Edinburgh (the Athens of the North) and to Nashville, Tennessee, where it serves as a museum. They might as well be banks for all the sense of the building's significance displayed by the transportation. If the medieval man plays fast and loose with the letter, it is because he respects and understands the spirit of the building. We, who respect the letter, yet treat it illiterately, as do the ignorant of whom the neo-platonist Porphyry speaks, who suppose that the pillars of the temple are merely wood and stone just as they suppose that the words in a book are merely black marks on paper. In this case the relation of likeness holds, not between a work of art and a natural object but between instances of a single art; yet it illustrates well enough the passage from likeness to symbol, which has been the main concern of this essay.

It is not hard to coin paradoxes concerning the honesty or deceitfulness of representational art: in fact the complexity of the issue invites them. One of the best is that quoted by Plutarch from Gorgias (who is writing of drama): that it is "a deception in which the deceiver is juster than he who does not deceive, and in which he who is deceived is wiser than he who is not."[33] Picasso, in a *bon mot* which is rather too

[33]Plutarch, *Moralia*, "How to Study Poetry," 15D.

precipitate, covers the same ground by calling painting "a lie through which we learn the truth." Such butterflies are obviously not to be broken on the wheel, yet the thing which gives point to both of them is surely that the objective reference in art is an indirection, a necessary pretext by which the "truth" of the human heart is to be displayed. The marriage of spirit and letter in which the primacy of spirit secures the signification of the letter—this is honesty, by the same token that it is revelation, or with due qualifications and precautions, truth. One more quotation will show the artist, not issuing *obiter dicta*, but in the very pain of search for the personal sign of which likeness may become the bearer. It is from the well-known letter in which Van Gogh says, "Tell Serret that *I should be desperate if my figures were correct*, tell him that I do not want them to be academically correct, tell him that I mean if one photographs a digger *he certainly would not dig then.*... Tell him that my great longing is to learn to make those very incorrectnesses, those deviations, remodellings, changes of reality, that they may become, yes, untruth if you like—but more true than the literal truth."[34]

We must still say some things here by way of defence of likeness against charges of sacrilege, presumption, and idolatry. The historic settlement by which the Christian church, alike in East and West, conditionally sanctioned the use of images in worship, shows that in practice such fear can be overcome, just as the long and intense struggle leading to the settlement showed how far from trivial the theoretical issues involved in the making of likenesses are.

While real, old-time iconoclasm is not extinct and still makes sporadic eruptions, it would be generally true today that the charge of idolatry is more likely to be levelled against worship of living beings than worship of likenesses. So true is it that the need of worship is a fixed constituent of human nature that, in the absence of its true object, nearly any substitute, however lamentable, will be accepted. It is not difficult to find the priest or pastor who is literally idolized by his flock, the mistress who is adored by her lover, the despot, alas, who is worshipped by a whole people. Even household pets, by a recrudescence of primitive fetishism and totemism are not infrequently the objects of a misdirected veneration. I do not mean just inordinate affection, though that would be present in all such cases; idolatry, strictly speaking, is the deification of created entities, the confusion of the seen product with its unseen creative source, a superstitious attribution of superhuman powers to what is really only a poor and ordinary fragment of the order of nature.

[34]*The Letters of Vincent van Gogh to His Brother* (London, 1927), II, 522-3.

The menace of idolatry in this sense is nowhere more evident than in the diffused humanism of the present which constantly invites us to overestimate man's powers, his wisdom, or his goodness, and solicits our implicit trust in his ability to take charge of and shape his own destiny. Mankind, in this pervasive superstition of our day, is its own God, and the only deity there is. For a typical expression of such humanistic idolatry in what, to the religious mind, must appear all its grotesque untruth, we need perhaps only quote from Clarence Streit's *Union Now*: "Man has on earth no one but Man to help him, and what a mighty, what a generous, what a kindly and abiding and dependable friend and liberator is Man to Man. Man has already wrought miracles of Man by Man for Man."[35] No doubt this is a rhapsodical utterance intended to enliven the course of a political argument; but that it could be said at all, in the face of the facts of human history and in the very teeth of world catastrophe, is sobering. To what depths of futility and feebleness can the human mind sink?

Artistic idolatry is today something belonging to the same context of fatuous self-worship "of Man by Man." It is evidenced in the very common overestimation of the creativity of the artist and of the power of works of art. This is by no means limited to non-objectivists, or aesthetic Puritans: even a Marxist, like Caudwell in *Illusion and Reality*, is guilty of it when he attributes to poetry the power to tell us "what science cannot tell us, and what religion only feigns to tell us—what we are and why we are, why we hope and suffer and love and die."[36] Whatever can give such a total meaning and sense to life is, by that very fact, a religion; and it is somewhat painful to see this brilliant author attempting to reconcile the illusory "meanings" provided by the poets with the orthodox "Reality" of Marxist dogma. It is another sample of the rivalry, the ancient quarrel between religion and art which is as well established as the necessity of each to the other.

From the time that Plato blamed the poets of Greece for teaching false views of the gods, and a false wisdom obtained by dramatic purgation, by the aesthetic contemplation of suffering, the quarrel in question has gone through nearly every conceivable phase; the party of the artists constantly pushing their claim to possess the key to the mystery of things, and even the power to save; the religious party as a whole constantly striving to enforce the subordination of art as the first condition of that collaboration with art which it needs. Meantime those who may be called religious extremists persist in indignant rejection of

[35]Clarence Streit, *Union Now* (New York, 1949), 197.
[36]Christopher Caudwell, *Illusion and Reality* (London, 1947), 263.

the very notion of such co-operation; whenever art is said to have become the handmaid of the church they rise to insinuate that she is something much less praiseworthy—*meretrix ecclesiae.* Iconoclasm itself is but a special chapter in this wider history of antagonism and mutual dependence.

For it is a fact that religion, stripped of every vestige of art and ritual, would be rendered inarticulate. All attempts to purify worship along these lines have simply demonstrated again the impossibility of success. The Covenanter's dependence on the singing of hymns and on the poetry of the Psalms, like the Quaker's attempt to abolish ritual (i.e. the ceremonial art of the dance) through the ritual maintenance of collective silence and immobility, or the attempt to strip away the architectural associations of ecclesiastical ornament by building in an unadorned auditorium-style—the effect of which is still that worship is dependent upon architectural surroundings but that they have merely become supremely unlovely and graceless—these and many like facts prove that religion and the arts are not to be disjoined. Conversely it is true to say that the arts naturally aspire, especially in their higher reaches, toward religious themes, or a religious function, or even religious status; as we have already noted, this tendency to equate aesthetic and mystical symbolism is a source of friction, and evidence that art may be in fact a powerful rival to religion. Everyone must have noted the truly religious silence with which great music is greeted—"this last enchantment of our kind" as Mr. MacLeish has well called it. And the ecstatic enjoyment of beauty is so easily confused with intense religious experience that even such an experienced saint and artist as Augustine is sometimes uncomfortably uncertain as to which is which: now the beauty of church music seems to him an image or symbol of the beauty of God, apprehensible only by the mind; now it seems a sensuous snare drawing the soul downward; "then I fluctuate to and fro between the peril of pleasure and the experience of wholesome help."[37]

We shall have to return to the whole issue here raised, in discussing the nature of poetry. As it regards our present topic, the defence of likeness in graphic and plastic art, we may conclude that the fears referred to—fear of sacrilege, of presumption, and of idolatry—are, religiously speaking, far from groundless, but that they are not dangers attaching specially or exclusively to the "graven image" or painted likeness. Indeed, though the fact that the arts are so clearly creative products of the human spirit makes them specially liable to idolatrous

[37]St. Augustine *Confessions* X.33.49–50; see also Bevan, *Holy Images,* 122.

overestimation, the danger is not limited in application to the aesthetic field. It results from the wholeness, the total character of religion, and expresses its guardianship over every aspect of life, the ordination (subordination and superordination) of all types of activity and effort to one supreme end of life. Any insubordination, anything properly inordinate—whether it be the claim of morality, of science, or of anything else to usurp the total direction of life—is on this view idolatrous and sacrilegious.

Yet it is worth remarking again and finally that, as far as the art of painting goes, at the present day the rejection, not the acceptance, of likeness is the more likely to be accompanied by such inordinate claims. In acceptance of likeness we may on the whole discern something like humility, a readiness to accept and abide by the limitations of created nature, both in ourselves and in objects. Its rejection may very well manifest an arrogant pretension to transcend these limitations. Whatever we may suppose to be the case with angels and archangels, it is not a normal prerogative of human communication for one subject to be able to reveal himself completely to another without taking the fruitful detour through objective reference and likeness.

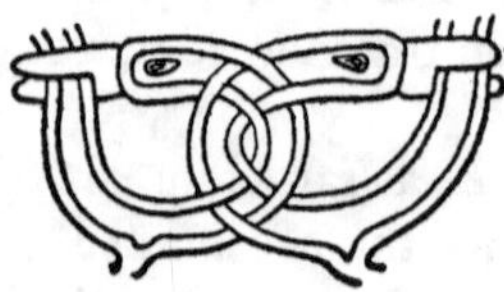

POETRY & TRUTH

THE naïve theory of imitation with which aesthetic speculation begins is capable of extension to the other arts with varying degrees of unsuccess, and at the cost of varying degrees of damage to their practice. The art of the actor is almost entirely mimetic; that of the dancer, while it may be dramatically representational, may also be almost purely formal. Poetry through a maxim like the Horatian *ut pictura poesis* has probably suffered most from the attempt to force the imitationist mould upon a recalcitrant material. To set the poet the task of depicting and recording nature as faithfully as possible is to give the descriptive element an entirely unwarranted emphasis. Any undue stress on description must be corrected by the dictum of Aristotle, that poetry is an imitation (or representation) of action. But even with this correction we have not quite met the case: what requires us to say that the poet seeks poetic and not picturesque effects is the fact that his medium is words, not visible colours and forms. To ask him to paint pictures, even pictures of action, in words is to forget the most elementary fact of all, that poetry is spoken and heard and painting seen. Though the senses are capable of various cross-references and associative connections, it remains fundamentally silly to ask the ear to do the work of the eye or vice versa.

Music is a still harder case for the determined imitationist. No doubt, as Plato said, it can imitate the roaring of bulls and the squeaking of pulleys—or follow the flight of the bumble bee; the question is whether it should. Since direct copying of natural sounds forms such a small fraction of the total body of music, the imitationist is drawn to justify music as a whole on much more acceptable lines—viz., on the ground that it is the various distinctive rhythms of movement and action whose likenesses are captured and enshrined in music, particularly the physiological rhythms which form the bodily basis of the states of emotion and whose establishment through beat and tempo awakens a conscious echo of the appropriate feeling. For instance, in Prokofiev's choral composition "Seven, We are Seven," a savage imprecation set to the words of an Akkadian hymn to the planets, the composer begins with a tempo approximating that of the normal heartbeat and accelerates it with subtle and appropriate accessory devices into the pounding pulse of fear. It is obviously true that certain gross bodily rhythms of this kind easily lend themselves to musical imitation. So, too, does overt movement, from the galloping motion of horses to the delicate monotonous rhythm of knitting needles in Couperin's "The Knitters," with its minute terminal catastrophe and recovery.

Yet such attempts to transfer musical imitation from auditory to kinaesthetic sense-material run at once into the objection that that field is already occupied, aesthetically speaking, by the art of the dance, for the dance expertly and expressively formalizes the various distinctive qualities of movement. Thus, in effect, the imitationist seems to be advising the musician to imitate, not nature, but another art. Or, if it is more accurate, as it may well be, to run music and the dance together in their common rhythmic ground into a single art of "eurythmics," all the difficulties encountered in regard to the transformation of natural shapes into pictorial forms would arise again: deliberate bodily movement, except to the extent that it has already been rhythmically formalized, is merely raw material to be formed, not a pre-existing "nature" or "natural fact" to be imitated.

The same thing has to be said of those involuntary physiological motions and rhythms which underlie conscious states of emotion. Musical "imitation," if it means use of the gross rhythm of heartbeat and breathing, of which we are interoceptively aware, is indeed a restricted and a poor affair. If, on the other hand, reference is intended to all those myriad imperceptible changes, in metabolism, endocrine balance, and muscular tone, which we are conscious of in the form of a confused uneasiness, if at all, the thesis becomes absurd. That the greatest music should have been written and the most delicate discriminations in the musical expression of emotion achieved in ignorance of these recently discovered occult disturbances again demonstrates the musician's independence of nature.

Driven from these positions, the musical imitationist may finally take refuge in another version still: that music is an imitation of the human voice in its variously expressive features of rhythm, pitch, accent, and intonation—abstracting as it were from the words, from what the voice says. This too makes good sense up to a point. We all, in one degree or another, vibrate responsively, like sounding-boards, to the speech of others, registering not only what is said, but, as we put it, how it is said: that is, the immediate expression through these qualities of sound and rhythm of the speaker's mood, sentiment, or state of feeling. Possibly the "voices" of a fugue are not metaphorically so called. Was it not Bach who said that they should sound like the voices of reasonable men engaged in courteous and good-natured discussion? Certainly there are compositions which seem moulded directly on "overheard" speech, i.e., speech without the words and their conceptual meanings. Satie's "Severe Reprimand," for one, goes on and on following the singsong intonations of a monotonous voice of blame running through its list of grievances, and ends with a few chords that form a solemn musical equivalent of those phrases like "It has been very unpleasant for me to have to say all this," "Please don't let it happen again," with which such interviews are wont to end.

In this case there can hardly be any doubt: what we have to do with is not a relation between art and nature, but borrowing by one branch of an art from another. Undeniably the expression and communication of states of feeling through intonation, pitch, and other sonorous qualities of speech is already "song." Every spoken sentence, in so far as attention to how it is said reveals a state of feeling in the speaker, is a song, however poor and rudimentary, and some sort of melodic line restricted to whatever narrow limits is inseparable from spoken utterance. Satie, then, is not imitating nature at all: he is borrowing and transposing to his instrument what is already song, an item from the repertory of vocal music. This may be a perfectly laudable and inventive thing to do, but to point out what it is leaves the musical imitationist without any further visible recourse.

Architecture and the allied arts of furnishing and of formal pattern and arrangement simply cannot be sensibly dealt with in terms of the imitation of nature; the analogies between crypt and cave, nave and forest, ground-plan and the prostrate human body, are too far-fetched for anyone to be seriously taken in by them. Undoubtedly the cruciform Gothic ground-plan is an intentional likeness of the cross, and symbolic as well of the figure borne by it. But all this is by way of consciously symbolic reference; it would be merely ludicrous to try to incorporate architecturally the details of toes, ankle, shin, knee, etc., or of interweaving branch, twig, and leaf, or of stalagmite and stalactite, on the pretext that, since he is imitating nature, the architect would improve his work by greater faithfulness to his model. This attempt would be to confuse architecture with sculpture. Like the corresponding *ut pictura poesis*, it makes no real sense in theory and works nothing but havoc in practice. Nothing could bear more clearly on its face the fact that it is an original, not a copy of anything in nature, than a building. Left to themselves the laws of nature would no more produce a skyscraper or cathedral than a motor-car. These are clearly originals of man's own making, and so are chairs and beds and abstract decorative patterns—though, as we have seen, the imitationist retains a certain toehold in respect to the latter.

Finally, to end this rapid and incomplete review of the arts from the point of view of imitation-theory, an art like that of oratory must present a peculiar difficulty. In so far as it is a form of the actor's art, and imitates in voice or gesture or intonation the states which the orator wishes to induce in his audience, it may pass as a form of imitation. But two significant facts stand in the way of such an interpretation: first, that few, if any, facile mimics have reached any eminence as orators; and second, that it is precisely such imitative, gesticulative speaking which we tend to qualify by the bad term rhetoric, reserving oratory for the true eloquence which laughs at all the small tricks and theatrical artifices of the professional persuader and relies on the force of conviction and the power of reasoning alone. We may even suggest that great oratory is perhaps equalled only by great building in the degree to which it owes nothing to imitation.

Imitationism, anchored as it is and must in some measure remain, to the immediate perception of nature does not provide the most favourable ground for testing the cognitive theory that by beauty we mean truth. We have traced various attempts to interpret graphic and plastic art in this sense, noted the fundamental ambiguity of notions like faithfulness or truth in this art and how it is forced to work within the limitations of likeness, likelihood, and verisimilitude. The examination of poetry to which we now turn gives us the advantage that the very material of the art is conceptual; for all words, as already noted, are abstract concepts, even the most concretely indicative words like *this* or *that* covering all *this*'s and every *that* equally; even proper nouns, John and Mary, are applicable alike to every member of the class of Johns and of Marys. Since truth is a property of propositions which state a certain relationship between abstract terms of this kind, the bearing of truth on art is much more favourably examined in an art like poetry which consists of explicit verbal propositions, than in painting where, if anything at all is affirmed, statement remains virtual.

But we shall be doing more in this essay than merely reopening the problem of meaning and truth all over again in the case of another art. The problem of truth becomes more amenable to treatment where it is actually the truth of propositions which is in question rather than what things in fact "look like" or even the "kind of way" in which they can be presented as looking with plausibility and verisimilitude. By the same token an alternative aesthetic theory will begin to take shape and definition as we proceed to examine the cognitive theory in the context of poetry. This alternative, the affective theory of beauty, has also already appeared, in a preliminary undeveloped way, in what we said about the attractive force of the formal and decorative pole in painting. It is the theory that the specific function of the arts is to develop the life of feeling by the expression which is at once the stimulation and ordering and resultantly the communication of emotion. The exposition of the main points in this definition must await the detailed analysis of the nature of poetic art.

Coal and Diamonds

Poetry is a material of words (concepts) in a particular kind of arrangement or pattern, opposed to which stands the counterpart we call prose. It will be useful to see, to begin with, what we can make of this distinction.

Pattern is difficult to define except by contrast to its absence: it is a wholeness of what, without it, would be fragmentary, unrelated, or chaotic elements. Our starting point should be the attempt to analyse the principal senses or aspects in which speech admits of being patterned. Whether the speech be poetic or prosaic does not yet matter.

The single word, that dictionary abstraction from speech, does, it is true, under the gaze of the etymologist, semanticist, and phoneticist, itself yield distinguishable elements; it is not in isolation quite patternless. But we should be courting trouble if we were to proceed on the assumption that the unit of speech is the single word. We speak, both physiologically and psychologically, in sentences, not in words: in paragraphs when we are specially excited, in phrases when we are very perplexed, but not in words. The sentence, if a somewhat arbitrary unit, is still the most natural one to agree on for working purposes. It is then the structural aspects of sentences we shall analyse, discussing in turn the configuration of sound, of sense, of syntax, of imagery, of practical incentive, and of feeling. If these aspects of pattern are not entirely absent from individual words, if we occasionally fall into the common habit of taking words separately, it is because they may retain, residually and in a derived way, even after they have been stuffed and mounted, some of the wild living qualities they possess in the sentence.

The admonition is simply that we should not think of speech as built up of word-atoms, the same outside a sentence as they are in it. The sentence is the unit of organization, the organism; detached from it, the word-cell lasts for but a moment with a borrowed life, then disintegrates. The organism of the sentence is even audible: a flow of sound going on without real interruption until a breathing point or the end of the sentence is reached—a fact which the written page, this page, with its separated letters and spaced words does its best to disguise. It is also, and more importantly, an organism in logical intention: the meaning of the sentence is a continuous whole which may or may not be got into words; if it is not, it will be necessary to say it all over again in different words, the meaning yet remaining one and the same, and presiding over either choice and arrangement of terms.

Here already are two of the patterns: sound and sense. The first, the flow of sound varying in pitch, accent, intonation, rhythm, and intensity, is a rudimentary musical construction; there is no good reason not to call it the "tune" or "song" of the sentence, abstracting it from meaning, from *what* the voice says. It can be instructively overheard, even where the word-meanings are unheard. Though you do not hear what he is saying, you can vibrate responsively like a sounding-board to the melodic line of the speaker's voice: to amativeness, to reprobation, to whining reproach, to that most important of human accents, the intonation of "reasonableness." M. Jourdain, who was so exercised to discover that without knowing it he always spoke in prose, might have been told with equal truth that he always spoke in untutored song. Of course this music, like the scraps of poetic invention constantly occurring in the small exchange of conversation, belongs to a context so wide and in appearance so undistinguished that we are apt to forget or deny that we are dealing with miniature or rudimentary works of art, not with "nature." Just so we easily forget that without all this more humble leafage, the fine flowers of vocal and later of instrumental music would have nothing to spring out of, perhaps even nothing to nourish them.

The sense of the utterance is a matter of the over-all disposition of concepts modifying and interacting upon one another in ways which are set by the logical rules governing predication.

But not exclusively so; there is also the linguistic twin of logic, grammar, the set of rules governing word-order and word-functioning, the product of a specifically linguistic intelligence from which we may derive another closely allied type of pattern, syntactical form: the pattern by which subject and predicate are located, clauses set in subordination or superordination to one another, verbs inflected to tense and mood and so on. This is not as separable from sense as the sound-pattern is: after all you cannot overhear the grammar without hearing the meaning. Yet you can attend to one while according the other a relative neglect; they are distinguishable. For instance, "This watch is at once ahead of Greenwich mean time and behind it," is a perfectly grammatical statement, but senseless since it contradicts itself in logic. "Were dragon to portables were," on the other hand, does not attain the questionable status of logical absurdity for it is even grammatically senseless.

Fourth: the unit of discourse forms a pattern of associated imagery—auditory, tactile, visual, olfactory, kinaesthetic, images of temperature- or pain-sensations, etc. Here the immense differences in type between one person's associative equipment and another's have produced an unwarranted diffidence about the possibility of poetic communication. Some imagery there will be; and if I, being a visual type, associate with the word "elephant" a large greyish mass, while you, being kinaesthetic, have imagery of lumbering yet intelligent motion, do we have to become mutually suspicious and sceptically dismiss the notion that we have each read the same sentence? Both these are authentic ingredients of the class-concept "elephant"; and as there is a common and public meaning to any sentence, the relatively private imaginative resonances it sets up are in some measure subject to control; the poet, in particular, disposes of special resources to force upon us one set of images rather than another. Perhaps a good sentence imposes nearly as determinate a pattern of images as it does of the conceptual meanings from which, in any case, the images arise. People differ too in the conceptual meaning they give sentences, yet in the overwhelming majority of cases sentences have one actual, public, ascertainable meaning, by reference to which misapprehensions can be corrected. Unless this is so, one really cannot understand the immense amount of communication and dissemination of ideas which apparently goes on all the time.

In the fifth place, words, or the sentences within which words can with some measure of artifice be discriminated, occur in a practical setting. Sound, sense, syntax, and imagery are all involved in what we might dare to call a practical configuration, distinguishable from the other patterns. Someone always wants something from somebody else when they speak, if only an answer, if only the response of being listened to. From here up to the imperative utterance of one who is in command, there is the whole range of verbal inducements and incentives to action: request, entreaty, persuasion, promise, threat. Any sentence has its own total practical shape, its quality as what we might, for want of a more elegant term, call a "slogan."

Finally, the sentence is also a cry. This might seem to be merely a reappearance of our first pattern, melodic line, yet there is a crucial difference. The emotional impact of a sentence, now under consideration, will vary with its tune, but also with its sense, its syntax, its imagery, its incentive; it is a function of all five of them and their distinguishable resultant. For instance, it is because of what the words "Maytime," "horror," "incomplete," conceptually signify that each has its own affective brightness or shading. The affective configuration, then, unlike the melodic line, could not possibly be "overheard": it demands the fullest apprehension of word-meanings and of their logical distribution, attention to the fine points of grammatical order, and readiness to develop to the full the interplay of associated images.

If, thus equipped, we now look at the distinction of prose and poetry, it will be with trepidation, for we seem to have six variables to drive in team. It would not be so bad if poetry were identifiable with one of them; but suppose it lies in the interrelation of them all, their interplay and movement? What if poetry is the way melody and meaning meet and part, sense and emotion chime and clash, imagery and cry anticipate one another, overlap, or overleap, or lap behind each other? Before juggling feats of this kind we might well be reduced to echoing any of those laudatory statements which neither define nor explain: poetry is "the best words in the best order" (though Coleridge gives this bite and meaning by having said that prose is "words in their best order"); "poetry is heightened speech"; or, following Mr. Sassoon, who in turn is following Coleridge in Chapter 22 of the *Biographia Literaria*, we may say that poetry is a kind of liquid, dropped into which the dry pebbles of dictionary-language show their unsuspected, fresh, and delicate colouring. All this will do little to quiet our misgivings; poetry is a *je ne sais quoi* we might as well say, a mystery we must undergo without comprehending how or why; and this is to admit defeat before battle is joined. It may be that there is an inexplicable in poetry as in all art; let us wait till we meet it. But probably the surest way of conjuring it up prematurely would be set out to prove or explain more, so to speak, than the traffic will bear. Mathematical precision and certainty we cannot have but less than that is still worth having. Morality too is refractory to such demonstration, but the man who refused on that ground to try to think out a case of conscience would be acting somewhat subhumanly. Scepticism has too easy a triumph where we suppose that all problems must be capable of the same degree of rational solution, and that the highest. What we can demand is much less than a resolution of the mystery of poetry: let us call it an intelligible exhibition of the nature of poetry. It would be quite useful to have.

For this purpose we shall examine sample attempts to make poetry out of one or other of the six sorts of pattern we noted. Naturally we cannot hope to isolate any quite pure strain; how, for instance, could a logical configuration of words fail to show a syntactical pattern as well? Yet relatively pure cases, especially in contemporary experimental verse, are not hard to find: cases where the author clearly considers one of them to be the essential poetic agency.

For "tune," the following from Gertrude Stein's *Four Saints in Three Acts*[1] may perhaps be allowed to be a fair sample:

All Saints. All Saints At All Saints.

All Saints. Any and all Saints. All Saints. All and all Saints. All Saints, All in All Saints. All Saints. All Saints. All Saints. Saints all in all Saints. All Saints. Settled in all Saints. All Saints. Settled all in all Saints. Saints.

Though certain abortive suggestions of a meaning (in terms of "the communion of saints") may seem to glimmer through this passage, it would be safe to say that it is as nearly meaningless as it is lacking in syntax, imagery, practical intent, and emotional content. What remains is a certain rhythmic and melodic entity on which Miss Stein confidently lays the whole burden of poetic effect. And since tune is an authentic ingredient of poetry, perhaps she may be allowed some thin success; even major poetry, of course with vastly more tact and discretion, employs repetition of sounds and words to hypnotic effect, though Miss Stein's hypnosis is a remote and poor relation. It is based on the fact that if you repeat too often and dwell too long upon a word like "namely," or "sapling," or "trough," you begin to doubt whether it is spelled that way, and finally whether there is such a word at all. The numbness and vertigo of mind thus induced is evidence of word-slaughter: amputated from the organism of meaning, the full life of the sentence, a word is expiring before our eyes. The poet, it is true, must fight prose, for prose usages and prose order menace speech with drabness; but it must be in clean and fair fight—wrestling, not massacre with a machine-gun. The victory, as common sense charges when it says this sort of thing is easy to write, is too one-sided.

[1]"Four Saints in Three Acts," in *Selected Writings of Gertrude Stein* (New York, 1946), 527.

Fairly pure examples of "syntax-poetry," next, are found in surrealism. The following is from the "First All-Vou Chainpoem"[2] (a chainpoem is one in which you write a line and then send it on to the next person on the list; whether, as in other parlour games, you fold the paper over so that the next man cannot see what you have written is not divulged, but I doubt it; what "All-Vou" means is not divulged either).

An umbrella of pencil opens on a street in Tunis
In fine weather as clear as a handkerchief,
And a spectral tube sparkles on a corked chair,
Where cocks upset cutglasses here and there,
And a dark purple leopard roars upward to the crane-stranding sky.

After more of this, it says,

It's wearisome for you to eat a cactus, so
Whip on your head with an averse whip,
And sleep here under this fountain of beams
While an international express breaks from the melon's stripes.

Blessed anonymity! It need hardly have been paraded, for the authors of this poem seem as like one another as the cars off an assembly line, and just as stylish. The piece holds together only by force of grammar; concepts and their adherent images are defiantly disintegrated in contempt of logic and the senses. The practical intent is extrinsic, that is, does not come out of the piece itself, and any other piece of surrealism would convey the same "message" just as well. You have to be told, somewhere else, that this manifests the party platform of a group of intellectuals in revolt against "bourgeois" logic, who find a superior reality in the "insane" worlds of mental patients, drug addicts, and other outcasts from society, and who consequently pursue incoherence and cultivate absurdity as the agencies of a new and higher wisdom, and advocate in practice appropriate forms of disordered activity.

Poetically the most instructive fact about such work, I think, is the chill that creeps out of its feigned madness. Disrupt logic and the configuration of images which logic controls, and you can neither express nor communicate feeling: you short-circuit all the electric currents of speech the moment you plunge it into the over-conductive field of unreason. If this combination of grammar and a faint tune can be called poetry at all, it would be in the highly generous sense in which fifth-hand derivatives of first-rate poems are themselves allowed to be poems.

[2]*New Directions in Prose & Poetry 1940* (Norfolk, Conn., 1940), 372.

And what happens when poetry is composed of images alone, or, since there are no images without prior concepts, as far as possible of images alone? Mr. E. E. Cummings[3] will answer:

r-p-o-p-h-e-s-s-a-g-r
who
a)s w(e loo)k
upnowgath
PPEGORHRASS
eringint(o-
aThe):l
eA
!p:
S a
(r
rIvInG .gRrEaPsPhOs)
to
rea(be)rran(com)gi(e)ngly
,grasshopper;

His aim is to present to the eye, to the ear through the eye (for it can hardly be read aloud) and to the motor sense a series of fugitive images of sound and movement that vividly depict a trivial occurrence, which runs about as follows: a clattering lawn-mower[4] (someone suggests that there is a hopper at the back to catch the grass-cutting) has trapped a grasshopper; at first he is buried under the cuttings in the hopper; but as we look he gathers himself up, and finally disentangled from the grass leaps and lands, perhaps, on the handle of the mower. His presence is recorded four times by different arrangements of the letters of "grasshopper"; first in lower case, with the letters chopped apart by hyphens; we may suppose him to be engaged by the blades of the mower, a slightly anxious moment: will he be killed? Then in capitals; he has escaped; the horrid pun on the grasshopper and the hopper of grass may be read into this jumble of the letters that spell both; it is the jumble of both. Then again, the third time, in alternate lower case and capitals—the whole line presumably being given the visual equivalent of whirring motion and noise by this means, and finally, after the portmanteau arrangement of the phrase "to become rearrangingly," he appears as fully himself again, "grasshopper"; the

[3]E. E. Cummings, *Collected Poems* (New York, 1938), 276.
[4]Michael Roberts in the *Critique of Poetry* (London, 1943) suggests that there is a hopper at the back to catch the grass-cuttings.

story is over. Or our author might prefer us to say with less finality, the story is over;

Judged by its own standards the performance should be called a success, achieved with economy, and with great technical competence in the use of somewhat peculiar means. The jerky, clicking sequences of motion, proper both to the machine and to the machine-like insect, are vividly suggested (why the letter A in "leaps" should be a capital probably only the author knows[5]). To quarrel with the extreme triviality of the matter would be to use standards alien to such imagism; poetic effect is sharpness and liveliness of images simply, and quality of subject-matter is beside the point. Besides, in comparable circumstances, did not Burns write his much-admired poem to a field mouse? This is its twentieth-century counterpart.

Yet Burns used all the resources of pattern; not just images, but those others which are so severely reduced, or even absent here—tune, sense, syntax, exhortation—and the result is moving where this series of hard sharp images is not. I do not know, Mr. Cummings may perhaps consider Burns sentimental. But indeed there is much that is unfeeling and inhuman about the twentieth century; the "wee, sleeket, cowrin, tim'rous beastie" for that reason is entirely likely to outlast this "r-p-o-p-h-e-s-s-a-g-r."

The most instructive feature of this case is the distortion of logic and ordinary syntax, extended to include punctuation and typography. This is surely required, if the story it takes a page to tell is to be compressed into fourteen lines, lavishly interspersed with blank spaces. The question is whether such a triumph of concentration is worth what it must cost in logic and syntax. T. E. Lawrence shrewdly judged that Cummings' verse is "more like Oxo than the normal flesh of poetry. It struck me that in his refusal of phrases with a past there lay as much irritation as power. . . . I suppose . . . that he belongs to some clique which worships reaction more than action."[6] Refusal is the key word here; again it is by fair and open conflict with prose that poetry is won; here, the poet rejects the challenge. But where Miss Stein slaughters with her machine-gun, he employs more refined methods—the rack and wheel, methods of torture. We can admit that prose becomes horribly debased by the ignoble uses to which it is put by advertisers, rhetoricians, hack-writers, and professional talkers of all kinds; yet it is not strength, but puritanic irritability which will set out to punish it

[5]Perhaps because it is angular like a grasshopper's legs, or because it takes a little leap of its own in the middle of the word. W. F. B.

[6]*T. E. Lawrence to His Biographer Robert Graves* (London, 1938), 143.

for this, to wrench, torment, and worry prose to pieces. It is in the nature of prose to be debased, and of poetry to redeem. Puritanism aiming wholly to avoid soiling contacts becomes inhuman. By an admirable proviso of the nature of things, the man who is cruel becomes cruel to himself, the man who tortures torments himself, the man who avoids, whether he avoids ugliness or evil, or even error, ends by avoiding himself. Strength is quite different from refusal and avoidance and negative reaction. It is visible in the "normal flesh" of great poetry. Here prose, debased to whatever point you will, is initially accepted, and ordered to a new and higher intensity, thereby restoring the freshness of what is shop-worn, vitalizing what is in the process of decay, heightening what is flat and drab, cleansing what is foul.

Thus poetry, next, in which the principal agent of poetic effect is meaning will, by definition, be the kind that suffers translation without betrayal. This points directly toward Hebrew poetry such as the Psalms, for neither in the original nor in translation are the Psalms dependent on a certain tune of sounds, or on physical rhythms, or even specially on the associated imagery which clusters so differently around what we fondly take to be the equivalent in one language of a word in another. If they are reputedly as good in French, German, or English as in Hebrew, it is because they are constructed to rhythmic alternance, repetition, and inversion of concepts and only incidentally of sounds and images. Here is Psalm 131 in Miles Coverdale's translation:

> Lord, I am not high-minded: I have no proud looks.
> I do not exercise myself in great matters: which are too high for me;
> But I refrain my soul, and keep it low, like as a child that is weaned from his mother: yea my soul is even as a weaned child.
> O Israel, trust in the Lord: from this time forth forevermore.

On each side of the caesura which marks the mid-point of the line an identical statement balances another. It is differently expressed, but the meanings "rhyme." This beat, this expectation set up in the first two lines with their fourfold assertion of humility is carried on into the first half of the third which, however, bears the additional weight and emphasis of the simile of the mother weaning her child; its balance with the second half, "yea my soul is even as a weaned child," can only be established against its whole asymmetrical weight by implicitly reading into the second half something like the reiteration "I am not high-minded," making a sixth (virtual) repetition of the theme. In the last line "O Israel, trust in the Lord : from this time forth forevermore" two completely new themes abruptly break the pattern. If we symbolized it abstractly, the poem might look like this:

A : A
A : A
Ab : b(A)
C : D

It is to be noted that it is through this established beat, or rhythm of concepts, that the poet makes his meaning good. Expectation will not be cheated by the introduction of totally new material in the last line: underneath, the pattern continues to work and act, so that we understand him to be saying that in time of trouble he and his people are to contain themselves in humility and trust; neither does the baby, suddenly denied his accustomed food, and not understanding why, cease to love and trust the one who deprives him of it.

Such poetry does not require certain numbers of syllables, a scheme of evenly distributed stresses, an artful disposition of appropriate vowel or consonantal sounds. If there can be a poetry of ideas, a grave rhythm of concepts, a stately dance governed by logic, this is it; great weight should be attached to an example which shows that logical configuration, or intellectual structure, with very little or no aid from the other patterns, can issue in deeply moving utterance. To compare it for instance with the passage from *Three Saints in Four Acts*, also ostensibly a religious poem, is to recognize immediately the failure of the principle "Look after the sounds and the sense will look after itself," and the relative success of its counterpart, "Look after the sense and the sounds will look after themselves."

When, next, we look for examples of poetry relying on the cry or effective configuration directly, the first instructive fact is their absence. Not even the boldest experimentalist, to my knowledge,[7] has attempted to compose with exclamatory ejaculations or interjections alone: so far is a string of "hurrahs," "bothers," or "ouches," from forming a poetic texture.

But, secondly, our examination will have confirmed our initial view that the total emotional impact of a poem is a function of all the other configurations at once. It varies essentially as the example of the Psalm has shown, with the sense; but tune, imagery, syntax, even incentive, will modify it, increase or diminish its intensity, or perhaps instantly shift it from the positive pole to the pole of negative affectivity, as with the well-intentioned lines, which turn out to have a directly comical effect:

[7]Professor Finch has drawn attention to the fact that one such attempt has been made by the poet Isou. See Isidore Isou, *Introduction à la nouvelle poésie et à la nouvelle musique* (Paris, 1947). W. F. B.

Oh! What a dreadful night it was,
The night when the boat went down!

If we are to be able to speak of explicit affective configuration, then, nothing less than the full employment of all the resources of speech will suffice, and none of them may usurp the office and intention of the cry; they must be employed in subordination to feeling, if feeling is not to evaporate or be diluted. When George Herbert has to relieve his heart of the pain of grief he does not write,

Oh dear, oh dear, oh dear, oh dear!

nor even, as an archaizing theory of "poetic diction" might prefer,

O woe, woe, woe, woe, woe!

He says,

O what a cunning guest
Is this same grief! Within my heart I made
Closets; and in them many a chest;
And, like a master in my trade,
In those chests, boxes; in each box, a till:
Yet grief knows all, and enters where he will.[8]

He says, of those same griefs,

We are the earth; and they,
Like moles within us, heave, and cast about:
And till they foot and clutch their prey,
They never cool, much less give out.

This is the full-bodied "normal flesh" of poetry, a marvel of health and strength, which scatters everything diseased and debased by its very presence: it puts to confusion the thin ingenuities by which "experimental poetry" seeks to evade the challenge of the poet's task. It is a cry, and the conclusion of our study is the simple one, that poetry is affective utterance. Yet what makes it a cry is the whole denseness of interlacing meaning, syntax, imagery, music, and persuasive intent, all subordinated to the dominating aim, which is to express and convey grief, and in so doing in a measure tame it.

Almost in sight of a definition of poetry, we have again been cheated; we encounter the same baffling complexity as before. So let us settle for something more modest, a working distinction between poetry and prose. And here the remaining type of pattern will be of service, for where it is practical motives that supply the dominant unifying force, there can be no doubt that we are confronted with plain prose.

[8]George Herbert, "Confession."

Ne'er cast a clout
Till May is out,

is prose;

Thirty days hath September,
April, June and November, etc.

is prose; rhymed and rhythmic prose, but obviously unpoetry. These have meaning and syntax, as you would expect where definite rules of action are being laid down: indeed what makes them prose is that the meaning is all that matters. Imagery too is present, but in that significantly suppressed state which is normal to prose. And affectivity is reduced to the vanishing point or beyond.

A still purer case of "pragmatic" configuration would be the famous four-line cypher beginning

Barbara Celarent Darii Ferioque

in which the words have no intrinsic meaning whatever, and only seem to comply with the laws of grammar. All that matters here is the order of the three vowels in each word: they stand for the logical qualities of the propositions in a syllogism while the consonants provide a reference to the rules for logical conversion in the case of each.

We said before that all speech whatever possesses "tune," some sort of melodic and rhythmic form. The ever-present possibility of breaking prose up typographically and presenting it as so-called "free verse" shows that common sense is not to be trusted when it identifies poetry with metrical verse and prose with its absence: it must be in the spirit and intention, the inner difference of attitude between the poet and the prosaist, not in the letter, in the relatively superficial and questionable differences of "tune," that the distinction lies. Our present examples are prose, we shall say, because they exhibit the extraversion, the linear forward-going movement of *oratio prorsa*, speech which is turned forward or ahead; in "Ne'er cast a clout" it is toward a practical issue, in "Barbara Celarent" toward a theoretical one. Poetic utterance, by contrast, follows a looped or helical course; instead of leading straight out into action or knowledge, or both, it is speech turned inward upon feeling, returning upon itself and leading back into itself. Iambic tetrameter, for instance, is an identical entity through the whole course of a poem, possessing the mind by its constant turn and return, serving to bring the beginning on to the end, and the end back into the beginning. We require no more to understand what might otherwise seem peculiar, why unpoetry on occasion seeks verse form: a certain degree of introversion favours memory. Speech which returns upon itself holds together better, and first of all, for purposes of recollection.

But this first degree or level of introversion is all that prose or unpoetic verse can touch; it cannot afford to awaken the deeper levels of imaginative and of affective awareness, for that would break its true movement, its "straightforward" intention to compel words to mean just what is required for knowledge or action, no more and no less. There are syntactical circularities in poetry, too, grammar that works in both directions—double qualifiers, even double tenses and the like—all intolerable to prose. For instance, in Rolfe Humphries' lines,[9]

> Under the ice uncolored earth and stone
> Fuse in the tight contraction of despair,

it is with anti-prosaic, with specifically poetic delight that we perceive the adjective "uncolored" doing double duty—backward for the transparency of ice, forward for the dull hues of frostbound earth and stone.

And doubtless poetic introversion could be shown to extend much further; not only to metre and syntax, but to imagery and to meaning as well, for all are here subordinate to affectivity. The poetic faculty, according to Hans Larsson,[10] is a superior degree of agility; the mind relaxes its hold on a statement, then returns to it; it is at one point, and everywhere; in the present and in the past. This relatively instantaneous ubiquity, as contrasted with the mind's linear progress in prose, may then serve as the primary symptom of the presence of poetry; its absence is the index of prose.

To conclude: the moral of our last set of examples is that the practical—the imperative, hortatory, persuasive, etc.—though it will be present in poetry, must be submerged; where it rises to the top and takes the lead, speech infallibly becomes unpoetic, and so it is probably best that it should be quite deeply submerged.

The moral of the whole section and the working distinction between poetry and prose is this: the relative positions of logical and affective configuration are inverted between the two. In prose, meaning leads; emotion, and image and sound as possible sources of disturbance of meaning, are subdued and depressed to the condition of undertones. In poetry, emotion dominates, and the other factors are undertones, though certainly meaning, the most important of them, lies just below the surface. Poetry as we have presented it is transfigured prose, and it is not the addition of some entirely new ingredient that brings about the transfiguration; rather poetry is a new mixture, a rearrangement

[9]"Belated Valentine," in *Out of the Jewel* (New York, 1942), 25.
[10]*La Logique de la poésie* (Paris, 1919).

of the ingredients shared in common with unpoetic speech. This is a potent kind of formula for the explanation of differences as one discovers in chemistry where the re-configuration of the same carbon atoms makes all the difference between coal and diamonds.

Prose and Poetry

Equipped with what we required, a clue to the internal difference between the spirit of poetry and that of unpoetry, we may proceed to trace a conjectural "history" of the development of human speech. If this history is presented as myth, it will be for the same reasons of essential ignorance as led Plato to present "what may well be so" in a form that does not make an effective claim to be knowledge. The prehistory of speech has naturally left no trace of itself; it is a field of almost pure conjecture in which philologists, even with the most cautious projection of the earliest known facts of language back toward the beginnings, end in general disagreement. Let us blunder in where the scientifically trained linguist almost fears to be seen.

The first human utterance, we may suppose, was affective; let us call it, with the anthropologists, a holophrase—a long rhythmic chant, not a sentence, for as yet there are no words; they, and other things as well, are to issue from this source, by dissociation, and a process of scission. The nearest we come to reproducing it is in the meaningless refrain of poets and song writers, choruses like hey-nonny-nonny-no, or lilliburlero-buller-a-la, repeated at the end of each verse. These cries—both of high spirits, but others could be of fear, of pugnacity, of amorousness, and the like—obviously have their counterparts in the animal world. It is not asking much to suppose that an incipiently intelligent being should begin to talk in this way. Besides we can observe any baby starting with such holophrases, though of course the baby has a tremendous advantage over our prehistoric savage in that there is a language already in existence to which he has merely to shape his efforts at vocalization; he does not have to invent the speech itself.

If we suppose these immediate externalizations of feeling to be largely animal, we should be careful to add that they must have been largely spontaneous and devoid of awareness. To employ a distinction on which much will be found to depend later, it might be said that the primitive holophrase or rambling cry does not so much express *emotion*, as give vent to a diffused semi-conscious *commotion*, for the agitation conveyed in a natural cry, without words, is something radically different from an expression of feeling that becomes clearly aware of itself in and through words.

We have only to suppose that characteristic differences in the objective situation arousing the cry will be reflected in some phonetic peculiarity of the cry itself to find our savages launched on the discovery of prose. After all, the fear aroused by a lion has not just the same shading as that felt in the presence of a tiger; and, to be crudely mythical, the first task of intelligence at work in the shaping of language will have been that of noting variations in the cry of warning, and using them back, or passing them on, to others, so that a certain consensus is established. What is common to the two warning holophrases will tend to disappear while the distinctive part of each will be retained and further diversified, taking on progressively the verbal function of objective signification. Finally, as fossil remains of a living process or as stuffed trophies of intelligence's hunt, the two words "lion" and "tiger" are mounted and displayed in the dictionary. That they are all that is left of the original alarmed cry of warning can no longer be gathered from them; the affective holophrase has evaporated, leaving the purely indicative sign, the conceptual or prose meaning.

That all words descend in this way, by the operation of a dawning intelligence, from the largely undifferentiated, largely animal cry of the savage, can be maintained.

Compare this description with the Romantic over-valuation of the state of nature, primitive man, instinctive speech. For Emerson[11] (and others) the nearer you approach the origins of speech, the more it becomes pure poetry. In that delightful age of "the beginnings" everyone naturally and spontaneously spoke in metaphors, for words were not yet established: their meanings, constantly being enlarged, carried over from one situation or object to another. Then, somehow, presumably through the work of intellect, all this dewy freshness of speech ended; an age of prose succeeded, and the increasingly difficult task of the poet became that of turning the clock back, of recovering the primitive cry beneath the intellectual burden of prose it has come to bear, thereby restoring, as it were, the lost innocence of speech, and the natural metaphorical gift, that of spontaneous transfer of word or phrase to objects which the prose intellect has already named, and for its purposes finally ticketed and docketed.

There are two obvious errors lurking behind this Romantic nostalgia for a lost paradise of poetry. In the first place it assumes that the ancestor of speech, what we have called the holophrase, is already spoken language; but spoken language only emerges *with* prose. The whole

[11]See "Language," in *Nature: Addresses and Lectures, Works*, I (Boston, 1903), 25–35.

process is briefly described by Jespersen, as an evolution "from inseparable irregular conglomerations to freely and regularly combinable short elements."[12] But if the holophrase, the undifferentiated affective refrain, is not yet composed of words, not yet prose, neither is it poetry: it is the ancestor of both and of the song as well, and as such it is not, or is not yet, any of these things. If we are to speak of art here, it will have to be a third or fourth art, different from all the others, the art of language, the art whereby words are invented, and which still ekes out a disreputable existence for the most part in those linguistic slums which we call "slang."[13]

It follows, as has already in part been suggested, that poetry cannot be seriously viewed as a retrospective attempt to undo all the painstaking work of linguistic intellect in order to recapture this primitive cry. The Dadaists of the twenties wrote what they called "poetry" consisting of meaningless syllables, like the da-da enshrined in their chosen title. Alas, they were not aware of the confusion they were making between the art of language and the art of poetry; they were perhaps a million years behind the times, for the language was already in existence, and the attempt to start again from the holophrase was, to say the least, anachronistic.

Secondly, and though we have admitted and indeed insisted that prose is an antagonist to be overcome, the Romantic theory fails to recognize its other aspect as the nourishment and soil of poetry. On the lines laid down in our "mythical" prehistory of speech, there can be no poetry until there is prose. Thus we avoid the highly improbable notion of a kind of linguistic catastrophe by which the primitive metaphoric-poetic age collapses into an age of unrelieved prose.

In other words, our examination of the distinction of prose and poetry is already leading to a result in respect of the next question, that of the place of intellect in poetry. For if it can be maintained that prose is the soil from which poetry blossoms, it is because thought (and prose, which is its mode of utterance) is the agent through which the life of feeling becomes aware of itself, and passes from a mere agitation or commotion to the more human state of emotion. Poetry, though a cry, is a cry transfigured by reason and intelligence. It is affective

[12]Otto Jespersen, *Language: Its Nature, Development and Origin* (London, 1922), 429.

[13]Aptly enough, among the Norwegian derivatives of the old word "sleng," whose second grade he suggests was "slang," Skeat gives one meaning "a little addition, or burthen of a song, in verse and melody"; and he quotes "ettersleng (literally, after-slang), a burthen at the end of a verse of a ballad." H. R. M. See W. W. Skeat, "Slang," in *An Etymological Dictionary of the English Language* (Oxford, 1910).

speech, as the primitive cry was, but at a new and higher level; for the logical discipline of the intellect makes order and clarity and composure possible. Poetry is civilized emotion, intelligent emotion, whereas the holophrase is still a largely animal, a blindly disturbed cry. Let no one lament that a prosaic age has brought poetry to its final agony, that, as Mr. Shapiro movingly says,

> Rime at the ragged edge
> Of civilization weeps among the facts.[14]

The antagonism is real enough; the degradation of language a fact which any sensitive person can estimate for himself, in everything from the abandoned impurities of propaganda to the muscle-bound rigidity of logical positivism—for that kind of cure is almost as discouraging as its disease. Yet we may take heart when we remember that this antagonism has always existed, and how triumphantly it has been overcome. If the poetic possibilities open to Shakespeare really extend beyond those available to Homer (and, though with some misgiving, I should maintain that to be the case), it is in part because of the much more advanced state of prose. There can be no good reason to suppose that such joint forward movement of prose and poetry together has reached its limits, or that the catastrophes of the present age have brought it to an end. Though it is natural to speak of poetry as a delicate bloom, it also possesses a certain resistant vegetable toughness. It is not so easy to kill as people are apt to suppose.

Leaving our myth here, we may now attempt a provisional diagnosis of the internal difference of prose and poetry.

In prose the affective content of words is submerged. It is present; for words, in origin cries, never entirely lose that quality. Further, since their theoretical and practical function (as indicative signs and signals) is inseparable from promise or menace to life, words possess affective resonances which are, as it were, part of their very substance; "massacre," "terror," "famine," "death," are alarming words because what they indicate is dreadful. "Peace," "coolness," "quiet," "breadth," are generally calming words; and so on. But in prose these resonances are deliberately, and by every possible means, reduced to the state of undertones, intended to be overlooked. In its direct forward progress toward knowledge and action, its attempt to make words say exactly what is meant, no more and no less, all emotion is an alien and disturbing intrusion.

Here we should note the other side of the combat; prose, thus de-

[14]Karl Shapiro, *Essay on Rime* (New York, 1945), ll. 1954–5.

fined, is a constant struggle with poetry, an effort—never entirely successful—to fix meanings so that they will be single and unambiguous and will stay put. If a tongue obstinately refuses to be codified to the point where each word has one and only one meaning; if it stubbornly keeps on growing, passing fresh meaning on at one point, withdrawing established meaning from another, and generally infuriating the otherwise passionless logician, academician, purist, or pedant, it is because language is not exclusively the product of a disciplinary intelligence but of the need to give expression to feeling as well; so that the yeast of feeling, however suppressed and ignored by prose, continues to work and ferment, altering meanings, sounds, order, according to its own laws which are not those of logic and may even defy its legislation.

Poetry then is affective speech to which there is a prose meaning, extractable in paraphrase, but a prose meaning which is now the undertone. The relative positions of meaning and emotion have been interchanged; what was dominant in prose is submerged and subservient in poetry; what was suppressed in prose is dominant in poetry.

As to the question of the border line between them, it will obviously be possible for non-metrical prose to be poetic, and metrical verse to be unpoetry. Wherever the affective charge of prose language begins to rise to a certain intensity it is germinating into poetry; and significantly, certain displacements and dislocations of the purely logical and business order, disposition and syntax of the sentence begin to make their appearance. Coleridge, following Wordsworth, illustrates with the 27th verse of Judges 5: "At her feet he bowed, he fell, he lay down; at her feet he bowed, he fell; where he bowed, there he fell down dead."[15] But this, as he realized, was already poetry, the song of Deborah, and a further illustration of that Hebrew poetry of concepts discussed earlier. A more ordinary example may be taken from St. Luke: "When he came nigh to the gate of the city, behold, there was a dead man carried out, the only son of his mother, and she was a widow." "A dead man, a widow's only son" would be a more efficient disposition, more purely prose too in the sense that the order of the text allows a certain pathos to show, while this suppresses it. Here we have in germ the pressure which leads rhythmic, alliterative, syntactical, metrical, and other formal disturbances of prose order in the interests of expression. At an advanced stage, as in this description of a lioness with her young, there can be no real remaining reason to speak of the composition as prose at all: "On perceiving the country-

[15]*Biographia Literaria*, chap. 17.

man, she drew up her feet gently, and squared her mouth, and rounded her eyes, slumberous with content, and they looked, he said, like sea-grottoes, obscurely green, interminably deep, at once awakening fear and stilling and suppressing it."[16]

And for the counterpart on the other side of the border, it is, or should be, a commonplace that perfectly scanning and rhyming lines can be sheer prose. To quote Coleridge again,[17] the prosaic-poetical phrases of conventional greeting—"I wish you a good morning, Sir." "Thank you Sir, and I wish you the same"—do not become poetry by being tortured into the rhythmic form:

To you a morning good, good Sir, I wish
You Sir, I thank: to you the same wish I.

Leaving aside the difficult question of comic expressiveness, in which respect mock-heroic blank verse is highly successful, we should say that such distortion of prose order as this, backed up or made good by nothing in the way of feeling, is a kind of aesthetic monstrosity or contradiction. The metrical and syntactic form would only be justifiable under the pressure of intense feeling, to which the prose (again the theoretical and practical) meaning would serve as an undertone. But the content is such that, on the simplest inspection, we recognize the depressed or lowered status of affective undertone characteristic of prose meaning and prosaic utterance: there is nothing to wax heroic about, nothing fit to heighten. Not that the words are commonplace—it is not a technical question of so-called "poetic diction"—but that they do not proceed from the pressure of feeling toward expression. An aesthetic contradiction, we said it is—or better, since comedy exploits contradiction, a comic ambivalence, whether intentionally funny or not.

Metaphor and Poetry

The subject of metaphor provides a kind of join between our last topic and the next following: in part it is a technical feature serving to distinguish prose from poetry; but it may also be regarded as the distinctive structural feature of poetic intelligence, or of the specifically poetic use of intelligence.

By metaphor, generally, is intended any kind of carry-over of meanings and relations from one situation or object to another: whatever can be described as analogy, simile, comparison, even the pun, is meta-

16The editor has been unable to identify this passage.
17*Biographia Literaria*, chap. 18.

phor, as we use the term. The most characteristic feature of the poet's way of talking is that he speaks of one thing in terms of another. But this is, after all, a prose way of assessing the matter, implying as it does that he could just as well say what he has to say directly in terms of the one thing without dragging in the other. But, poetically speaking, why should we suppose that he is saying in an unnecessarily complicated way what could be said more simply? It would be truer to poetic fact to say that both references are intended: the poet in metaphor is talking of two things at once, and not gratuitously, but for the light which one thing throws on the other, and the other throws back on it. Presumably what is prosaically called "figurative" language is poetically the only proper form of utterance; not a superfluous linguistic luxury, but a strict necessity.

Nor need we be unduly surprised to find that metaphor is our old friend "likeness" back again for discussion, with its retinue of problems, in the new context of the arts of speech. Simile, analogy, figure, image, likeness—all these are synonyms of the basic double reference which, for convenience' sake, we are calling metaphor. We shall be able to effect some economy of exposition by reason of all that has already been said on this subject; but, at the same time, we may hope to substantiate more completely the passage from likeness to symbolic reference then attributed to graphic art. Likeness as metaphor differs specifically from the painted likeness (thus making the maxim *ut pictura poesis* the misleading thing it is), if for no other reason than that both resembling terms are present as aesthetic form in the poem, whereas in the picture one of them is normally absent and even when present should, as we saw, be treated as "natural form" not aesthetic form. Where it is quite proper and natural to speak of a poetic metaphor as a likeness, it would be forced and improper to speak of the portrait as a "metaphor" of the sitter. And it is just this fact—that the whole relation of resemblance, and the two terms compared as well, are within the work of art—that simplifies the issue of symbolism by relegating the indicative sign into the background, and correspondingly bringing forward the symbolic sign. More of this in a moment.

But first the claim that metaphor is a distinctive feature of poetic expression should be examined more closely. A glance back at our examples of undoubted poetry (though the accident of their selection may be responsible for the fact) reveals that they are all metaphorical statements. Even in the dubious case of Mr. Cummings' composition, by an extension we have already allowed, the pun "hopper-grass, grass hopper" is a metaphor serving to bind together the scattered fragments of meaning. Herbert's cunning cabinet-maker, his moles casting about till they can foot their prey; the Psalmist's telling comparison of the troubled soul and the weaned child; the metaphoric account of the lioness' eyes—in each of these we find the characteristic "double talk" of the poet, what Carew calls, though in an unfavourable context, "the juggling feat of two-edged words."[18]

Indeed there is nothing more compelling, more enhancing and enlivening than apt metaphor; a wrong, an essentially prosaic impression of it is given by such abstract descriptions of the form of metaphor as we have just indulged in: the impression that it is merely a case of noting the comparison and likeness of two things. Aristotle, who cannot be accused of unwillingness to find and formulate rules for the sound construction of poems, has to confess that apt metaphors escape his net; it is as an unteachable poetic gift that they appear in the *Poetics*.[19] The pressure of feeling to which we have referred as the force that heightens prose to poetry, the distinctively poetic use of intelligence which we are to examine in the subsequent section, join at this point to bring into being, with mixed spontaneity and travail, the poet's most felicitous, his most characteristic, and possibly central poetic device. All his ideas move and shimmer around the analogy, in surprise at the possibilities of double talk, in delight at the inevitability of the double light thrown backward and forward between the two subjects. Enchanted by the spell of heightened affectivity which the alternating expression itself induces and orders, and rocked as it were on this rhythm, the poet spontaneously begins to speak metrically, in number, rhyme, assonance, and the rest.

The metaphoric idea may be precipitated in many ways. To take an example, consider Ireland, the land which, as Françoise Henry points out,[20] never was conquered by Rome and so escaped the severe logical discipline of the Latin mind, the training in the dialectic of either/or which the other Western nations underwent (the typically Irish joke, the "bull," is still the assertion of two contradictories at once); Ireland with her passionate, unfathomable politics, her insular tenacity to a Celtic tradition reaching far into the pre-Christian past; but Ireland Christian too, in a way that combined both Western and Eastern forms of the faith, and came in conflict more than once in her history with Rome, and made of herself in the age of her glory and the rest of the world's darkness the sole remaining

[18]Thomas Carew, "An Elegy upon the death of the Dean of Paul's, Dr. John Donne."

[19]Aristotle *Poetics* XXII.16–17.

[20]Françoise Henry, *Irish Art in the Early Christian Period* (London, 1940), 15.

spot in the West where the lights of learning, culture, and piety still burned bright. This Ireland; and also, some event in a poet's experience, some isolated, non-calculated, unprudential act, dictated, probably, by affectionate impulse, even perhaps by charity in the Christian sense of the word. The improbable analogy has only to suggest itself—all the impossibility of teaching how to find good metaphor lies in that "only"—and a poem will begin its life and grow; in the end we have Rolfe Humphries' wise, witty, and profound poem, "Scapegrace":

This overt act, a little island
In the great seas of common sense,
Is capable of no defence,
And soft and warm and green, like Ireland,
With politics and solitude
For latitude and longitude.[21]

Yes, but this example, like the others, is a deliberately selected metaphor, and it will be asked: are there not whole poems which contain not a single comparison, simile, likeness, figure, or image? Is there not, in Tillyard's phrase, direct as well as oblique poetry?[22] And still more: are not metaphors of very frequent occurrence in prose? It is in determining the answer to these questions that we are led into the whole problem of the distinctive characteristics of poetic intelligence and poetic meaning.

To start with the last of the questions above, the answer must be the seemingly high-handed one, that where "prose" turns to the loving elaboration of metaphor it has ceased or is ceasing to be prose. It is the same answer we gave before regarding affectively charged language, and because the two cases are the same: intelligence, stimulated by emotion, spontaneously begins to make out likenesses; emotion striving for orderly expression falls inevitably into poetic double talk; so that to pick up an image and become excited about the fitness of the two parts of it to illuminate one another is already to raise affectivity out of its state of suppression as an undertone to prose.

Take, for example, this parable from a thirteenth-century *Fabula Exemplorum*: "A Christian man ought to be like the dog who, entering a room, goes up to everyone in turn and greets them, though they do not respond; and after, if he is driven out with a stick, thinks how he can possibly get back in again, and stays at the door, and when it opens does not hold any resentment, but makes his rounds again, approving of everyone with his tail and his ears, and with a glad face."[23]

[21]In *Out of the Jewel*, 29.
[22]E. M. W. Tillyard, *Poetry Direct and Oblique* (London, 1945).
[23]The editor has been unable to identify this passage.

No doubt, as an example of the preacher's art, we ought to call this true eloquence, oratory, rather than poetry; yet if the view taken here is correct, all the arts of speech—poetry, drama, fiction, oratory—have a common aesthetic quality which lines them up in opposition to unaesthetic utterance, whether we call this unpoetry, the undramatic chronicling of facts, journalism, false rhetoric, or simply "prose." Just as true poetry is certainly eloquent, true oratory may, without forcing the facts at all, be termed poetic; by all the marks which we have been scrutinizing as tests of poetic quality, this little dramatic image of Christian humility and joy deserves to be treated as an example of poetic insight, moving toward rhythmic expression; and showing, especially in the last phrases, the characteristic displacements of the direct or prose order.

Or take Montaigne's answer to the question why, in spite of all the intelligence and expert legal skill embodied in a contract or a will, it is impossible to draw up such a document in a way that will exclude doubt and controversy.

> Why is it that our common tongue, so easy to use in all other cases, becomes obscure or unintelligible in a legal contract or will?. . . It is because the experts in this art . . . have so weighed each syllable, have so picked over each seam, that they become involved in the infinitesimal detail of shapes and partitions so minute that they no longer conform to any rule or prescription, nor permit of clear comprehension. Whatever is divided into a powder becomes confused. Who has not seen children trying to divide a piece of quicksilver into a given number of parts? The more they press and knead it and strive to force it to their law, the more they irritate the freedom-loving and generous metal; it escapes all their skill and goes on breaking up and scattering in fragments beyond counting.
>
> It is the same; for by subdividing subtleties we merely succeed in redoubling doubts; objections are thereby multiplied and diversified, lengthened and dispersed.[24]

Whenever we encounter this peculiar kind of delight and illumination through an image, we are on the verge of poetry. We might *know* more if Montaigne had said directly in *oratio prorsa*, like St. Paul, "the law came that sin might abound"; or that the attempt to work out the last implications of a set of prescriptions and prohibitions simply provides human perversity with a greater range of suggestions how to misbehave; or if he had said, as regards language and its use, that there is a dialectical principle by which the attempt to attain final and complete precision in words is self-defeating. The point he is making is the same we took earlier in discussing the refractoriness of language

[24]Montaigne, *Essays*, III.xiii, "Of Experience."

to pure logic, and the fact that it has laws of structure and development of its own which resist all attempts to force it into the mould of mathematical rigour. It is the point that, when a logical positivist has finished "clarifying" an ordinary statement to the point where no misunderstanding is possible and it means one thing and one thing only, the resulting statement is not even understood by the ordinary intelligent man.

But if these are prose paraphrases of what Montaigne says, this is just because an expression like "the freedom-loving and generous quicksilver of speech" is essentially poetic. It is of the same order as Herbert's lines about the English tongue:

> Lovely enchanting language, sugar-cane,
> Honey of roses.

It is a qualitative analogy whose effect is not primarily instructive (theoretical) or practical, but affective. Yet no doubt it illuminates the two subject-matters to develop their likeness, and with a concentrated light which tends to spread from this focus in all directions. Nothing is more economical, nothing more packed with suggestions to be expanded, than a good metaphor. It is recorded of Buddha that, expounding a difficult point of doctrine to his disciples, he said, "Here I shall draw a comparison; for more than one intelligent man has first understood by a likeness what was being explained to him." The art of illustration, which is the poetic art of analogy and metaphor, is not merely affective: it is an act of intelligence under the guidance and stimulation of feeling. To treat it as a means of instruction merely is not to do it full justice. It is, we shall find, the art of discovery itself; "many an intelligent man has obtained his first insight into a baffling problem in the form of a likeness, or analogy," would be a better reading.

There is of course the purely prose form of analogy, which is ratio, proportion, and the like, i.e. quantitative analogy, one of the major instruments of scientific discovery; but, as was said before, this tool of scientific intellect employs likeness only in the preliminary imaginative stage of search. What science requires is not likenesses, but identities; and the quantitative analogy supplies them. That $a : b :: 3 : 6$ is no metaphor, and does not suggest anything; it gives very precise, exact knowledge—that b is twice a, and that it is some multiple of 6. Analogies between the chemical substances as arranged in the periodic table of elements, the physical analogies between, say, sound and light, are scientifically important only to the extent that they permit of quantitative formulation. Otherwise argument by analogy is highly suspect; no astronomer in his senses will accept the reasoning that because the sun is a star—which means here, is like, resembles the other stars—there must be other planetary systems elsewhere in the universe, or the still feebler argument that because Mars shows traces of vegetation and Venus has a thick blanket of clouds there must be other inhabited planets in the solar system than ours.

Qualitative analogy makes up in range and stimulation what it lacks in rigour. The poet, like the painter, is not in competition with science, nor concerned with adding to our knowledge of nature; like the painter, his references to objective fact are made with a view to giving it symbolic value. Metaphor, for the various reasons discussed, is the most potent device for achieving this end. We could even say that whenever it appears in apt and felicitous form we are already in the presence of poetry, however prosaic the context in which it may be embedded. Of course the qualifications "apt and felicitous" mean that we are to understand the spirit of poetry, not the letter; metaphors do decay into pure formality, descending into clichés at the prose level, like the "helm of the ship of state," "the acid test," "harping on the same string"; these and thousands of others pass from mouth to mouth, sad battered remnants of what were once flashing poetic fragments. Often any sense of their original appropriateness has been obliterated by routine; how would you set out to "make bones about" something, for instance? Yet who is not ready to "make no bones" about something? Fossilization, always a latent menace in prose usage, can attack analogy as well as the single word; prose has many a victory over poetry to its credit.

The question whether there is such a thing as completely direct non-metaphorical poetry would take us too far afield—if we were to attempt the sort of statistical survey it would seem to demand. The reader is merely invited to investigate for himself, bearing in mind the comprehensive definition of metaphor as any kind of analogy here given. Any such survey will, I believe, confirm the impression that in the measure in which poetry is unmistakably direct or non-analogical, it is actually prosaic, or unpoetry masquerading in verse-form.

One illustration is the "Madrigal" from Davison's *Poetical Rhapsody*:

My Love in her attire doth show her wit,
  It doth so well become her:
For every season she hath dressings fit,
  For Winter, Spring, and Summer.

No beauty she doth miss
  When all her robes are on;
But Beauty's self she is,
  When all her robes are gone.

Nothing could be more direct in appearance; yet in fact the poet is affirming—without drawing out in detail—a series of likenesses; he is certainly not stating anything so prosaic as that his love wears summer dresses in summer, and warm clothes and heavy underwear in winter. Wit in attire means dressing in correspondence with the mood of the season or the day, or, since there are after all two lovers, with the mood of their meeting; a perpetual surprise, then, a kind of divination. The slight personification of "Beauty's self" at the end, which could easily escape attention, is the explicit analogy into which the poet is compelled to break, by the accumulation of virtual analogies that precedes it.

Take a further example, James Joyce's version of those epigrammatic attempts to summarize the whole of existence in a single line of poetry; it runs

They lived and laughed and loved and left.

There is no room here for metaphor, and the statement is as bold, as direct, as it could possibly be; nothing but a manifest summary of the normal outline of life, in briefest superficial outline. Yet the repeated assonance, making the statement a fourfold pun, introduces the effect of analogy, as if a ratio were being established between four terms; it is the means by which a latent sense of the unity, compactness, and extreme brevity of a life is conveyed. And the fact that the second of these terms is "laughed," which is pretty well compulsory in the context (there is no synonym of "weep" whatever which would fit the pattern), gives the statement a paradoxical turn: that a creature so ephemeral should love merriment so much is, by this collocation, given as much prominence, is implied to be as mysterious, as the major solemnities of birth, love, and death. Notice, too, for the latent content effected by the sense of analogy, that if "laughed" came third, after "loved," such an order would give the whole statement a less serious, or perhaps an ironic or cynical cast which, as it stands, it does not possess.

Whatever instances of direct, non-metaphorical poetry may be presented, poetry devoid of a single analogy, it would still be true to say that *as poetry* it will be double talk, and in virtue of what we may call the basic metaphor underlying poetry as such: viz., all poetry, while professing to deal with the objective order, is actually concerned with and terminates upon, the order of subjects or selves.

This ambiguity is inherent in all poetry, so that again from the prose point of view poetry has to be described as talking about something else than you are talking about; this is the characteristic usually indicated by calling it "imaginative" speech or writing. The world presented to us by the poet is not the actual world of physical objects, but, in Caudwell's phrase, a "mock-world"; and it is presented not with a view to giving us true and utilizable information about nature, but with an ulterior motive, that of giving indirect access to personal or subjective states, our own and those of others. It is not the physical order as such, but, by a kind of rebound from the facts of nature, it is facts and states of consciousness which poetry illuminates. The examination of this antithesis will force upon us the whole question of the distinctively poetic use of intelligence, and with it the issue of meaning, of symbolism, and of truth in poetry.

Poetic Intelligence : Poetic Sign-Giving

What we have just said amounts to denying that poetry is in competition with science and philosophy as cognitive enterprises, or with those practical disciplines (as, for example, applied science, or economic and industrial organization) which modify the objective world in accordance with knowledge gained. It is neither theoretical nor practical in respect of the objective order.

If this is not recognized, if it is maintained that intelligence is present in poetry with a cognitive or cognitive-practical aim, poetry will necessarily appear to be a poor substitute for science; analogical or imaginative thought will be condemned as a product, not of intelligence, but of day-dreaming and random association of ideas; and poetic expression will be treated as a loose and vague, or lazy and improper way of saying what should be stated with severe exactitude. "Half-a-league, half-a-league, half-a-league onward," grumbled the scientist in the well-worn anecdote; "why can't the fellow say a league and a half and have done with it?" The reply is, of course, that no set distance is intended, but only an auditory impression of thundering hoofs which will reinforce the hearer's image of what it is like to participate in a cavalry charge. The things that science and poetry have to avoid are almost diametrically opposed. The scientist knows that in an experiment nothing is more damaging than to allow his personal feelings and beliefs to interfere with the investigation; it is nature he is interrogating, and nature, as far as possible, must speak out the answer. Let him then recognize that in a poem nothing is more damaging than an actual mathematical calculation, or a scientific preoccupation with physical objectivity; here it is subjectivity that is being questioned, and the heart itself must answer. When Roberval, issuing from the performance of *Phèdre*, remarked, "All very well, but what does it prove?" he was showing as little discrimination as if he had made an irruption upon the stage in order to rescue the heroine from her fate.

Poems, like other works of art, are "unreal" by reference to objective standards. But then they expressly claim to be. Othello or Hamlet are not to be arrested and summoned before any court to stand trial for murder. Even the actors in the play are not really related to one another as they pretend to be: they do not do, they do not even really say to one another the things they pretend to. And so it is only by adopting in advance the attitude which poetry requires us to abandon, the prosaic, the objectivist, or scientific attitude, that the charges of unreality, of subjectivism, of illusionism, of day-dreaming, of unreason, can be piled up against poetry.

But if we take poetry for what it claims to be, and stop trying to force it to aim in the wrong direction, terms like "subjective," or "physically unreal" lose the derogatory sense they have acquired in virtue of the prestige of science and the pressure of scientific method. Where "physical unreality" means "reality for consciousness"; where "subjective" means "characterizing a person or subject," we face a rather different state of affairs. For let us be quite clear about it, "subjective" states are perfectly real facts: trust, fear, loyalty, treachery, sincerity, cynicism, amusement, boredom, humility, arrogance, love, hate, and a thousand others are as "hard" facts as flint, thistle, or a porcupine; though unlike the latter they are not really open to direct empirical scrutiny, exact quantitative treatment, or experimental investigation under laboratory conditions. Furthermore, they yield to no other facts in importance. Our lives are wholly and, in a real sense, primarily embedded from the first in an elaborate setting of such states, our own and those of others, and all this is of such moment to us that the purely physical setting of life is, by contrast, relatively unimportant. Life is lived by subjects, subjectively, in relationships of all kinds to other subjects—and this is the perpetually fascinating, disturbing, disappointing, and rewarding core of our human preoccupations. Of course, the theoretical difficulty of verifying the existence and nature of these important states is increased to the point of empirical impossibility by the fact that many of them are unconscious or only partly conscious states. None the less, even when unconscious, states of subjects are as much "objective" facts as anything could be. It will be less confusing, however, to restrict the term "objective," as is usually done anyhow, to that class of physical facts which does not involve the presence of a conscious intelligence, and the term "subjective" to the order of facts which does. This is a distinction within the real, not a distinction between the real and the unreal.

If this distinction be accepted even provisionally, we can see at once that the accusations addressed to the poet by the scientist will be met by appropriate counter-charges. If "straightforward" or prose intellect dismisses analogical thinking as mere luxuriant fancy, poetic intelligence may retort that it has its own precision and accuracy which would be infallibly lost in a prose rendering. To the charge that poems achieve no truth, that they prove nothing, or even that they show a lamentable irresponsibility in regard to the facts of nature, the poet will rightly reply that his concern lies elsewhere, and retort that the incursions of science into the domain of subjects are marked by the same, or similar, defects: they achieve little or no truth, prove nothing, or show a regrettable blindness to the nature of subjective fact. No doubt it is a theoretical, a scientific error to treat the objects of nature, dancing daffodils, skipping hills, or the stars before dawn ("The sons of the morning shouting together for joy") as if they were animate, conscious beings—in a word, persons. It is true that the poet is habitually impelled to do so, to "humanize nature, infusing the thoughts and passions of man" into nature even where he cannot be said to find them there. But it is also true that to treat persons in the way appropriate to things is an equal theoretical error, and in addition humanly disastrous. Science, with its *parti pris* against indeterminism, against the reality of purpose, and freedom of choice, and against anthropomorphism, only too frequently gives grounds for the poet's charges. Where the object of investigation is *anthropos*, man himself, what could be more proper than to consider him in "man-shaped" fashion, under anthropomorphic categories? Why should we be so sanguine about the results of treating him in terms of his subhuman kinships, in more and more reduced form, i.e., through the categories proper to lemur, rat, amoeba, or mass-particle?

The sentimental animal-lover who interprets his pet's actions all too humanly might be called an unconscious poet who has made the capital poetic error of confusing poetry with objective fact. But, by the same token, the behaviourist who reduces the whole wealth of conscious human experience to the conditioned reflexes which he has studied in the lower animals makes the serious scientific error of confusing objective fact with poetry. His is merely the "tough" obverse of the "soft" attitude underlying the other error. A genuine and sober realism will avoid these hasty elevations and reductions of level, recognizing that the differences between various grades of being are genuine and specific, and not supposing either that a dog must be some kind of inarticulate human being, or that the human being is a sort of specially voluble dog.

Error for error, either of these confusions is both scientifically and poetically misleading. It is a poetic error to confuse poetry with objective fact, as the "soft" or idealizing person does; it is, of course, also an unforgivable scientific blunder, of the kind that justifies the perpetual vigilance against subjectivity which the scientist must display. But on the other hand the "tough," that is, the cynical realism of the other camp is not merely a poetic blunder, but is itself scientifically unsound. Science is concerned with facts, and to approach them in a way which ensures, in advance, that they will either be obliterated or undergo serious distortion, cannot be truly scientific; yet this is precisely what the failure to distinguish objective fact from poetry leads to. An approach to human subjectivity made in terms of severe impersonality, detachment, and dispassionateness infallibly screens out and blocks off the majority of the facts to be ascertained. Whatever is ascertained through the inhuman artificiality of "laboratory conditions" and the relationship of "investigator" to "research material" set up between two persons, will be of universal human relevance only to the degree that some fragments having relevance to the wholeness of subjective or personal existence will filter through. It remains profoundly true that, as Lawrence Hyde says, what is really worth knowing about men and women is learned from them on their own terms, not on those laid down by an investigator. Only what is revealed out of love, to love, he adds, can really illuminate experience.[25] But this, which might be called the secret of "poetic method," or the postulate on which poetic intelligence works, is diametrically opposed to the theory and practice of scientific method.

Let us compare, to illustrate the point, a scientific and a poetic formulation of the experience of disappointment—which would include the sense of loss. In the first we have the order of subjects treated objectively, in the second the order of objects treated subjectively. Professor Clark L. Hull in an article "Mind, Mechanism and Adaptive Behavior" says:

Theorem XI. Organisms capable of acquiring functionally potent anticipatory reactions intimately associated with the reinforcing state of affairs, will manifest a weakened tendency to the consummatory reaction

[25]Lawrence Hyde, *The Learned Knife* (London, 1928), chaps. 3, 4.

if, at the completion of the action sequence, the state of affairs then presented does not permit the occurrence of the complete reaction of which the anticipatory reaction is a constituent part. . . .

Corollary I. Organisms will display disappointment.[26]

We recognize what Lawrence Hyde calls the "devitalized locutions"[27]—the hard, dehumanized metallic terms, the inanimate mechanized constructions characteristic of abnormal preoccupation with the physical environment. Is it any wonder that the poet rejects this objective (objectivized) subject as a monstrosity, untrue to the facts, unreal, if the charge of unreality is being bandied about. The poet will prefer some rhyme like J. C. Mangan's "Double Trouble,"

> I am blinded by thy hair and by thy tears together.
> The dark night and the rain come down on me together.

Here the objects are subjective; the poet is not asserting that as a matter of physical fact the blackness of night has anything to do with a woman's hair, nor the falling rain with her tears; but that to the bereft lover wandering in the dark these palpable signs of absence become reminders, even tokens, of a loving and sorrowful presence. The poet does not begin, as the scientist's profession compels him to do, by eliminating everything private, personal, and subjective from his field of vision as systematically and thoroughly as possible; for in the case of the order of subjects, such a preliminary step destroys or seriously cripples the whole investigation from the outset.

Doubtless a distinction such as this between the order of subjects and that of objects is no sooner drawn than it has to be modified. Obviously there is no coming to awareness of subjects except through experience of those objects we call human bodies and the events and physical movements these bodies undergo or manifest; and it may be added that it is only through such "objective" commerce with bodies and their activities that we become aware of ourselves as subjects. There is probably no direct "contact of minds" which would enable us to dispense with the physical order, through which alone one centre of conscious awareness (or "subject") is able to give signs of its status, or express and communicate them to others. That is indeed precisely why the poet's access to his hearer's subjectivity is never direct, but is mediated by a reference to the mock-reality of imagined objects.

Also it is true that there can be "knowledge" of a physical object only in the consciousness of some subject, and that the objective order

[26]Clark L. Hull, "Mind, Mechanism, and Adaptive Behavior," *Psychological Review*, XLIV (1937), 25–6.
[27]Hyde, *The Learned Knife*, 62.

taken as it is "in itself," or out of any and all correlation to such a subject, is an order by definition "unknown." This is why the scientist's efforts to eliminate everything personal and subjective, and by the rigorous use of scientific method to achieve strictly impersonal and dispassionate statement, can never quite succeed. That is the direction which his science requires him to take, but it remains true that however far he goes on this path, the objective knowledge he has is *his* and is conveyed by *him*; there is no object known except by a subject. In the statistically determined "margin of error" in the taking of observations and measurements he recognizes the presence of an uneliminable residue of subjectivity, and states his result as subject, within certain limits, to revision in either direction; but even this recognition of a "personal" factor is rendered severely impersonal, and is stated as a statistical average which holds for anyone else, as much as for the investigator himself.

It is in another respect, perhaps, that the situation can be more clearly evaluated. If knowledge is necessarily someone's knowledge, its communication is also necessarily someone's act. Whose it is, is scientifically an irrelevance. And yet there is, poetically speaking, no such thing as a purely impersonal subject: it has to be someone—someone with these and these desires, motives, passions, and implications in the general tissue of interacting subjectivities which we call the order of subjects, be his name Faraday or Euler or Newton. To science as such it does not matter, but the point is that it is impossible to speak as objectively as all that. It may be a minimum of insight into the personal make-up of Isaac Newton that we obtain from reading the *Principia*, but still we do obtain some: from the choice and arrangement of ideas and terms, from the way in which the apparatus of thought is displayed and manoeuvred; and—by virtue of the fact noted earlier that the boldest scientific prose contains undertones of sentiment and feeling, repressed as far as possible, but still there—we are able, in some degree and by some reading between the lines, to estimate what sort of person is expressing these thoughts, how the mind of the man Newton works and other such facts in the order of subjects.

We may very well, following Caudwell once more,[28] employ a formula which is the counterpart of that just used. Since objects are knowable only by subjects, we may allow that scientific inquiry demands a mock-subject, or *mock-ego* through whom the investigation and the communication of its results is effected. "Mock" here indicates that any such scraps of information as we may glean about the real

[28]Christopher Caudwell, *Illusion and Reality* (London, 1947), 153.

person of Newton are not material to his work, no part of what he intended to say. It means that as far as he is concerned, the subject making the communication is supposed to be a severely impersonal one, something like a lofty cosmic intelligence which would have a perspective view over all time and space, a subject who is not implicated in all the petty limitations, the confused motivations, the consuming needs and passions of the human situation. If we call this presumptive author of *Principia* a *mock*-person, it is just because no one in fact can be so detached, so indifferent to the whole texture of his existence in relation to others as this; it is only as a pose, or as acting out the role of a disembodied intelligence that such an "impersonal" person can be imagined at all. This imaginary self is just as useful for science as the imaginary real is for poetry. It serves the same sort of function: that of affording access to the order of facts which, so to speak, it subtends.

The theory of knowledge, then, does not invalidate the distinction of two orders but simply qualifies it by reminding us that objects known are necessarily known to subjects, and that subjects in turn are themselves known, whether to themselves or others, through objects. The two orders are not only not detached and severed from one another, but are in intimate interaction, inseparably correlated to the point where neither can be taken as a primary given starting point to which the other is subsequent. The subject which is known through objects is the same as that through which objects are known, and neither sort of discovery can be said to precede the other. However, correlation does not abolish, but rather presupposes, distinction. Though the two orders are not to be severed, neither can they be fused and confused. The distinction of art and science holds good in spite of all the various forms of interaction and mutual influence between them because the order of subjects and the order of objects, which are the termini of their respective preoccupations, are in fact distinct orders, whatever communication or "seepage" there may be from one to the other.

Scientific intellect, it was earlier remarked, by a first, abstractive operation takes the given, the quite ineffable "this" of immediate experience as a sign of some "kind" or class: a flash of lightning, a twinkling star, a lit candle, are all cases of "light." It was, we said, likeness, apprehended imaginatively, that provided this first level of signification; and the specific type of sign involved we agreed to call an indicator. In the scientific elaboration of "kinds," further, the essential instrument of discrimination is mathematics; quotative and quantitative distinctions, based on the investigation of numbers and magnitudes, provide the ultimate criteria, and thus many of the primitive classifications resting on imaginative apprehension of analogies of quality have to be modified or abandoned. Diamonds seem to belong with glass; investigation shows them to belong to the same kind as coal.

At a second and higher level of the use of signs, the concern of science is not just with abstraction and classification. What (depending on the view taken) is called explanatory science, or demonstrative science, or science of correlation and prediction, represents the conversion of indices into symptoms, i.e., a type of sign which in addition to its value as referring to a "kind" is ingredient in a complex of other indices of many "kinds," whose relations have been systematically developed and explored. Botany and zoology, for instance, must first acquire the status of descriptive science, must establish a sound class-structure—an effort which starts from the defective "common-sense" recognition of likenesses of colour, shape, and distribution of parts, and is corrected by substituting the principle of filiation for that of external resemblance. But this in turn requires, and virtually amounts to, the elaboration of a symptomatic complex; the principle of filiation as it works out demands such things as the theoretical account of transformation of one species into another (the theory of biological evolution) or the Mendelian laws of inheritance by which certain characteristics (symptoms) can be known to be dominant or recessive and their distribution in the offspring predicted with statistical accuracy.

Let us suppose that there exists another main branch of the activity of sign-making, or signification—aesthetic (or in the case under discussion, poetic) signification. Here, as noted earlier, it is not so much a case of *taking* something as a sign for something else, as of *giving* a sign of some state of the subject. Whereas scientific signs (indicators and symptoms alike) are impersonal, the expressive or poetic or personal sign is non-scientific, i.e., ultimately neither verifiable by experimental techniques nor mathematically demonstrable. This contrast of impersonal scientific signs and personal non-scientific signs is of course just the equivalent, in terms of the problem of meaning, of that distinction between the order of objects and that of subjects which is under examination. On this second branch of signs there will also be two stages, two operations, one simple and preliminary, the other complex and culminative. Let us call the first type of expressive sign a "signature" and the second a "symbol."

The term "signature" is to be interpreted widely to include even spontaneous, even involuntary, physical reactions like the yawn or blush, which betray a state of fatigue or shame. It would include cries, involuntary gestures such as raising the arm to shield the eyes, frowns, smiles, and all other facial expressions—whatever in fact reveals a state of the subject without making use of likeness to do so. "Signature" is a fairly appropriate name for this sort of sign since the configuration of lines, or rather the trace of the specific motions of hand and fingers, by which a person makes the sign-manual of his identity conforms to this description. It does not function in terms of likeness to the person; it is merely a certain expert gesture by whose trace the person himself and others can be assured of his having been present in certain circumstances.

At once the requisite modifications of the distinction of two types of signs begin to make themselves felt; for if this is all a signature is, it becomes an objective sign, an index, like the signature on the marriage-register. The graphological expert who decides, with a very high degree of probability, whether or not this is the unique trace left by a given individual, whether the signature is genuine or forged, is in fact taking it as an index, to be interpreted by a symptomatic complex, which has been empirically elaborated in the same kind of objective manner as any other scientific theory.

This possibility of taking the sign-manual as an objective indicator, to determine some state of fact in a court of law for instance, is the consequence of the fact that it is through bodies and in the order of objects that subjectivity makes its presence good. Though without the backing of a body of scientific and statistical information (and therefore with the possibility of charlatanism and caprice ever open before him) the graphologist is able from the sign-manual to make shrewd and sometimes startling conjectures as to the character and normal emotional make-up of the subject and even as to his particular state or mood at the time of writing. In so doing he does with signatures something comparable to what the botanist does with indices at the point where the correction of a provisional classification already forces him to anticipate on a system of symptoms. The sign-manual is here already virtually a symbol, as, in the case of the science, the index is already virtually a symptom.

It has been said and should be repeated that such reading of given signs is non-scientific. The critic of handwriting, like the music critic or the literary critic, will certainly possess principles of interpretation which, if formulated, would serve to justify and illuminate his judgments; but anything like the rigorous symptomatic complex of a science is out of the question. He may, like any other of his tribe, be obtuse, irritable, and jaundiced, may be a bad critic or an inspired one;

but even the inspired critic is not a scientist, perhaps for the simple and basic reason that states of human subjects are not open to direct inspection, so that the empirical verification which an index always admits of is precluded in this order.

In explicit, and that is fully developed, symbolic sign-giving the material of the sign-manual is elaborated into a relatively complete subjective context. It is a revelation of internal life, not just in a glimpse, or in latency, or in a conjecture, as has been the case so far, with signatures. Symbols like the wrath of Achilles in Homer, or Dante's love for Beatrice in the *Divine Comedy*, or the fall of Adam in Milton, serve as a kind of flare-light illuminating a whole tormented or grandiose or rudely aspiring inner landscape; nor do they, as tends to be the case with signatures, reveal the secrets of one heart only but those of the heart of man as such, transcending the limitations of the individual subject, without however thereby becoming impersonal in the objectivist sense. Symbols, too, remain in one sense signatures—evidences of a given person's personal style and point of view—while yet as symbols they give access to a realm which should more appropriately be termed intersubjective than subjective.

Further, as was pointed out in the discussion of painting, the passage from signature to symbol is mediated by likeness. The personal significance of any type of sign-manual is latent; it is through a quasi-objective reference, through the mock-world of the poet or painter, through likeness, analogy, metaphor, that it is built up to the point where it becomes explicit. Here is a second point at which the distinction of the order of subjects and that of objects must not be allowed to harden into a dualism. Without the non-scientific, the imaginative and qualitative reference to a world of objects, signatures would remain only dimly significative. Suppose we try to interpret a signature such as a smile, to determine whether it is the bright disarming smile of one who means to get his way, the hesitant smile of one who is not too sure of himself, the ingratiating smile of one bent on some piece of treachery, the smile of genuine availability and affection, or any other one of the thousand different expressions covered by the one poor word "smile." Obviously some reference to objective fact is required for such discrimination; at least it is safer to interpret what is presented not just in terms of facial appearance, but also in the light of what we know about the person's actions, plans, and needs, in terms, that is, of the external facts about him. It is the same requirement that makes the "plot" of a drama or poem a condition of its full expressive and revealing effect. It is the same marriage of expressive pattern and likeness to nature which in the arts of speech gives us poetic symbols, and in graphic art pictorial symbols.

To summarize: there are two kinds of sign, signs *made* or *taken*, and signs *given*: one referring us to objects and the other to the subject himself. In both cases the ultimate referent is ineffable, a *this*, something to which the indicator or the signature *points*, but which cannot be otherwise determined, because to determine it at all is to pass away from its givenness, elaborating the index into a symptom, or the signature into a symbol. However, what makes the first type of sign scientific and the other not, is that the *this* which it indicates is open to direct inspection and verification: it can be checked by the senses of anyone who is interested enough to do so; and so can the symptomatic correlations which are later developed. In the other case only indirect inspection or introspection are possible; the state of consciousness is not a public object and not accessible to the external senses, however truly it may be a fact of internal experience. We are profoundly hidden from one another and even from ourselves, to the point where it is possible for objectivists to deny the very existence of a self, of subjectivity, and of consciousness, the illusion of such an "internal" realm being explained fundamentally as a case of "misplaced objectivity," i.e., some material physiological process mistakenly supposed to possess a character of inaccessibility. For the time being we cannot deal fully with this denial of consciousness but must go on simply to specify the formal nature of the aesthetic symbol, as contrasted with the scientific symptom. The two kinds of sign have been seen to touch at certain points.

A symptomatic complex has a certain unintentional meaning as a sign-manual. To the instructed, a chapter by Newton, Faraday, or Clerk Maxwell may be directly recognized as "in style"; only Newton, or only Faraday, would speak this way, think this way, show this reluctance to exhibit the connections of ideas by which he reached his conclusions, etc. All this, however is without prejudice to the character of mock-subjectivity which infallibly attaches to scientific work by virtue of the methodical elimination of the personal which it requires; it is only at the level of signs-manual that the person of the scientist can be detected and identified; science must strictly avoid the use of symbols, in our sense of that term. Here it should also be noted that it is a really and fully objective inquiry into the world of nature that yields this by-product of "signatures"; in the case of poetry, it is a mock-world of likenesses which enables this subjective sign-material to be heightened till it has symbolic value.

Another aspect in which there can be transference between the two types of sign is in the psychotherapeutic and psychological use. Here signatures of all kinds are interpreted into a symptomatic complex: i.e., they are taken directly as indices. The stutter, for example, is a symptom of repression, of psychic energy blocking itself; or alternating states of depression and excitement present, with more or less intensity, more or less completely, the symptomatic picture of manic-depressive insanity. Here "the" stutter, "the" state of depression or mania are evidently "kinds," scientific concepts; an objective medical approach is taken to the subject, whose symptoms are to occasion some sort of remedial treatment. To make clear the difference between psychology and art in terms of their specific use of signs, it is necessary only to point out that psychology must treat signatures not for eventual symbolic use, but directly for symptomatic purposes: i.e., to view subjects not as subjects, but as objects; hence the inevitable impression of their being at cross-purposes which we illustrated earlier by contrasting the paragraph from Clark Hull and the verse by Mangan.

Objective sign-making has, then, a slight repercussion in terms of signatures, in the order of subjects; and, conversely, the subject can within certain limits and for certain special purposes be treated as an object. We have also pointed out how essential these limitations are, and how severely the subject is impoverished if all that lies beyond these limits is excluded.

Signatures are not of themselves sufficient to function as symbols. A cross-reference to the objective order, carried out in terms of some measure of likeness, is the means of full signification here. The signature is not yet (or it is only virtually) an expressive symbol: signs-manual are the quarry, or at most the blocks extracted from it. Only when embodied in a planned structure where their mutual promises and menaces are systematically organized do they form any edifice. One block attacks another by the crushing action of its weight; or by shouldering it off through lateral thrust; or it supports another through its cohesion and self-contained hardness. So it is in the poem where, though the "materials" in some measure decide what kind of end-product you may expect, everything still depends on the use made of these materials. The poem is a real *transformation*, a leap across from the virtual forms implicit in a material of signatures to the single and total form which radically alters the characteristics the materials have in themselves. Poetry can achieve this only through the use of indicators, through concepts and ideas, and through logic. Indeed this is just what mediates the transformation, the transition from cry to poem, from signature to symbol.

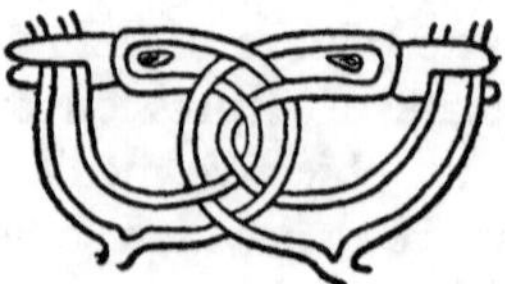

MYTH & INTELLIGENCE

NO doubt in the most sweepingly general sense of the term, intelligence is always one and the same thing, whether employed by poet, scientist, or anyone else. It is the art of setting limits and boundaries and thereby articulating a certain total field; it is the art of differentiating and integrating. But if we restrict the use of the term to this most abstract general level, much that is specifically intelligent will have been excluded—all the distinctive and specific features of integration and differentiation as they are pursued in the various fields of scientific, political, moral, aesthetic, and religious experience. Failure sufficiently to recognize these specific features means in effect that a single one of them, the scientific use of intelligence, has been regarded as the norm for all the others, which are thereupon taken either as inadequate first approximations toward science, or else as erroneous and meaningless substitutes for it. On this view, whatever is not already science must aspire to become science; there is but one goal for all thought, and intelligence is effectively present only where this goal is sought and achieved.

This monistic "scientism" must be challenged if we reflect at all upon the ends mankind pursues in the various fields mentioned. Is there not, for instance, a political form or use of intelligence, whose purpose is to order the collective life justly, rather than to procure knowledge? No doubt knowledge is needed to succeed in this purpose, as in others; but the fact remains that the statesman aims at something more and other than a cognitive goal and that he may display greater or less intelligence in its pursuit. So too in religion intelligence is in the service of worship, not of knowledge; in the shaping of language it is in the service not of knowledge but of communication; and in the arts, in the service not of knowledge but of expression.

This contention may well be brought under detailed consideration in regard to one field which must always seem refractory, if not preposterous, to the scientific mind—the field of myth.

This case has the advantage of presenting us with a primitive type of religious life, in which the distinctive features of that mode of experience are present in unreflective or immediate form and are the more manifest for the fact that primitive myth and the higher religions are so closely distinct—as distinct, perhaps, as bud and flower. Relevance of this case to the main topic of the two preceding essays is secured by the fact that it is from within the context of myth that all the arts originally arose and that their attachment to this source has been much more prolonged than in the somewhat parallel cases of moral and legal systems, political organization, technologies, even the sciences themselves—all of which, as we shall see, have this same mother and nurse, all of which grew up in the same household and in close relationship to the arts, though leaving the family home somewhat earlier. It is indeed doubtful whether the tie that unites mythical thought to poetry and the other arts has been or ever really can be severed.

A preliminary definition of myth is needed here, one which will put us, from the beginning, within and not outside the field under study. There is a rich variety of ways of defining it as something other than myth, of making it respectable by reducing it to something else. From the time of the Sophists rationalistic interpretation of myth has attempted to find some simple dietetic, hygienic, prudential, or scientific truth disguised in allegorical or fictional trappings, but has succeeded only in demonstrating its own futility. The intensity and tenacity of a people's belief in its myths is, to begin with, quite inexplicable on the supposition that they are merely dressed-up scientific or ethical truths. Besides, such interpretations are able at best to cope with details at the periphery: the core of the myth remains not just irrational, but unrationalizable; and the result of such an approach is that the essentially "mythical" becomes synonymous with the "objectively null and void," with error as such. Plato, as is well known, protested against the rationalism of the Sophists and asserted the autonomy of mythical thinking. Myth for him was not something needing interpretation so much as itself an instrument of interpretation, having its own rights and attaining its own peculiar objectivity which is other than and supplementary to that of philosophical inquiry. He is quite right that a point of view which begins by destroying what is characteristic of and peculiar to myth-making will not serve; and myth in fact does, characteristically and peculiarly, deny just that separation of symbol from what is signified which rationalistic interpretation must make.

Myth has its own logic, or if you like, illogic, by which different things are the same thing, by which the symbol does not represent but *is* the thing symbolized. Myth cannot proceed very far, nor can it be grasped in its inner unity of form if you rob it, as rationalism does, of this idea of "trans-substantiation."

In our own time, largely through the labours of anthropologists, we have given up the attempt to find such plain sensible meanings behind all myths: we accept them as irrational and explain them, with the French sociological school as "collective representations" of primitive mentality, with Freud as manifestations of sexual complexes, with the Marxists as reflections of stages of economic production and as instruments by which to enforce or prolong class-dominance, and in an amusing variety of other mutually exclusive ways. In fact, we are inclined to listen to anybody who does not ask us to make the attempt we are seriously making here, to measure myth by its own measures and postulates, as we would art or speech.

The sociological and the psychological reductions of myth call for brief examination. For the sociological schools, the objective reality which it is felt myth must express to account for its persistence and power is simply the reality of the social structure as deduced from the being of society itself. But the point of view which makes myth entirely derivative, a mere sign of pre-existing social relationships, involves a radical misinterpretation: religious-mythical ideas are not mere desiccated deposits made every so often by the independently proceeding stream of social life, not mere by-products, but living and dynamic factors. Tribal, totemic, patriarchal, or other social form is not an ultimate given, as Durkheim presupposes, but a variable which is conditioned to such an extent by mythical belief that we can justifiably speak of the primacy of religion or myth over society. As Schelling insisted, it is a people which is determined by its mythology, not the mythology by the people. Its myths, he said, *are* its destiny. What he meant, I imagine, was that myth is a shaping force, not a shaped product as the Durkheim school assumes, not something deliberately and arbitrarily chosen as a mere sign to reflect pre-existing realities which appear thus in disguise. A people does not select its myths in this fashion any more than it chooses its language. Its language is an instrument by which social forms, knowledge, and practice are shaped, not merely a reflection of these things as supposed to exist somehow independently of verbal formulation and embodiment.

As regards the other most popular reduction of myth, the psychological, I can only say this, that it points to a truth which need not be the whole truth—that mythical thought is something taking place in human consciousness and is therefore subject to whatever laws may finally be ascertained to hold in that realm. It is, for instance, a commonplace of religious experience that we come to God through our awareness of other people, or, paraphrasing this in more philosophical terms, we come to a realization of a personal infinite through awareness of finite personality. Hence psychology, both individual and social, will certainly be relevant to this experience. But its relevance still leaves entirely open the question how the experience itself is to be interpreted: whether, that is, the processes immanent in consciousness are to be regarded as nothing more than immanent, or, as the mythical consciousness always reports, revelations of a reality transcending that consciousness.

What is meant may be seen directly if we proceed to the promised definition. We might say that myth is any sort of belief in the supernatural, but since that term too has come in our age to be a synonym of the purely fanciful or fictitious, we must start lower down, from a point where the distinction of nature and super-nature may seem to be purely psychological. Myth is any belief which involves the distinction in human feeling between the sacred and the profane, between that which is overwhelmingly attractive or repulsive on the one hand, and that which is just ordinary on the other. These are the basic categories of mythical or religious experience, in terms of which the world is mythically articulated—in a bewildering variety of ways, it is true, but nevertheless intelligibly in a sense because of the constancy of the ground-plan of articulation itself. What is holy may be nearly anything—bacilli or daily bread, prostitution or celibacy, stocks and bonds or poverty, capitalist imperialism or the cause of the proletariat; but for every man that has ever lived something is necessarily holy. Each of us is likewise bound to lump together, as the primitive does, those things which do not possess *mana* or sacredness—all that is usual or ordinary, those things which can safely be treated without precautions and without respect. These categories are so solidly grounded in experience, so compulsory for the human being as such, that it may be argued that there is only one way in which primitive myth can be disposed of, and that is by transforming it, as the higher religions do, through reflection, into less inadequate forms than those in which it first appears. Religion is not myth but the result of overcoming myth, in the only way in which this can be effectively done, by a more adequate, more subtle and refined, more comprehensive articulation of the world in accordance with the same two basic categories.

Naïve mythical consciousness takes this ground-principle objectively: for it the distinction between the sacred and the profane provides an authentic basis for progressive discovery and elaboration of the real. Psychological sophistication consists in challenging the external reference of such a distinction through showing it to be subjectively grounded. Of course it *is* subjectively grounded; but setting aside for once all the rival psychological reductions, we should not exclude the possibility that mythological consciousness may be right in asserting that it is *also* a revelation, a valid means of approaching and attacking the real, and not merely a reflection of the subject beyond itself into the objective realm. There is certainly no chance of finding out whether myth has any real significance unless we do consider this possibility; just as there is no finding out the significance of art if we determinedly take up a position outside it, from which all aesthetic judgments are seen as the self-deceptions of the highbrow or as fantasies of wish-fulfilment. Thus in each realm, art, speech, myth, and even logical thought, an initial act of faith is required, by which you put yourself within the field, instead of cutting yourself off from it, and this means admitting that in each there reigns its own specific and peculiar type of necessity.

No man can evade the necessity whereby as a human being he is in some sense a religious being. Whether we call this standard feature of the human make-up the need for worship or the need to distinguish the holy from the profane matters little: the point is that this need cannot be escaped by any expedient so simple as staying away from church. To do so, to reject the more highly developed forms of religious life, is automatically to relapse into some form or other of primitive myth. At its crudest, for example, the attitude of a highly civilized person to dirt and germs may reveal all the characteristics of the mythical outlook: the loathing and horror aroused by filth are still forms of that awe which goes out to anything terribly special, and the precautions taken in dealing with it, the ritual of ablutions, garglings, disinfections and so on, may easily reach the proportions of the most oppressive of primitive cults. Many a spotless modern house is a temple of this cult; for many a housewife an unending preoccupation with dirt and germs has come to be so truly "mythological" as to absorb all life and action into this one channel. Myth, I repeat, does not mean unreality of the object—here dirt and germs—but a special quasi-religious attitude toward the object, real or fancied.

I need not speak of sex, money, and the cult of violence. Each produces awe, arouses an irresistible attraction and terror, demands an elaborate set of special precautions or a ritual from millions of devotees; each exacts from its worshippers the total subordination of all ordinary activities and objects to the one supremely exciting and terrifying thing. In addition to these survivals of early myth—the temple of Venus, the temple of Mercury, god of commerce and the stock-market, the temple of Mars, god of violence—there are of course many other rivals to religion, the temple of the Muses for instance: did not MacLeish, remembering the enthralled silence of the thronged concert-hall, call music the "last enchantment of our kind"? All of which points up the fact that it is impossible to regard all things as uniformly "ordinary," and that what a person or a people worships is perhaps the most important fact about them, since what is at issue is nothing less than the total direction of their life and action.

Of course, the affinity between religion and myth, the fact that myths give rise to and pass over into religions, no more invalidates the latter than that common sense has to precede and prepare for science invalidates science. No doubt the types of sign employed by intelligence in these two fields are quite different, common sense and science dealing in what we have called indices and symptoms, myth (like the arts) in signatures and symbols. The question of direct verification of these latter signs in sense-experience does not therefore arise. Yet the parallelism between the cases is sufficiently close to be instructive in spite of these differences, and the fact that symbols, in our sense, do not stand for any sensibly verifiable object does not mean that they are arbitrary or devoid of a certain compulsory quality.

To illustrate this from what I called a moment ago the worship of Mercury, i.e., the mythical evaluation of money and profit, a $100 bill is of course a token of something quite intangible, that public confidence in the soundness of government and the economic system which is the last ground of people's willingness to exchange goods for currency. That is why, though the bill is objectively a symptom, verifiable by experience, of the variety of goods which it will purchase, this fact depends on and is derived from a more fundamental fact in the order of subjects. Destroy that confidence and the "verification through purchase" will no longer work. The bill may in a prolonged inflation end by being worth no more than the paper it is printed on.

Why then do we behave in such a special way toward money? Why is it impossible to pass a $100 bill lying in the gutter with the casual indifference of one who registers the fact that something is "only a symbol"? Clearly because, though it is a symbol, it is not only, not merely, a sign, but an embodiment, an effectively working and compelling embodiment of what it stands for. Again, if we point out that the devotee of Mercury is giving money a mythical evaluation, this is to imply that he is making a grave mistake, certainly, but a mistake which, like others of its kind, conceals a core of truth. Money *is* a momentous thing, not to be treated as ordinary or commonplace: the subjective fact of confidence to which the economist traces its value is something which translates the lives and labours, the very life-blood of our fellow men, and calls thereby for respect.

To pass from the mythological atmosphere of the higher mysteries of finance, where the possession of the adored object is the single goal of longing, to the context of a higher religion like Christianity is to find the symbolic worth of money justly and penetratingly evaluated. "Gold," said Mère Angélique, "is an image of love." Love is a much stronger term than confidence; and it can be applied to money only in a religion advanced to the point where the truly holy has been identified as a creative spirit of love transcending the universe in which it dwells. By this statement the error of the myth is unveiled: it is to mistake the image for the reality, and, as the sacrifice of children in burnt-offerings to the golden idol Moloch so vividly shows, the image of love so mistaken turns to hatred and cruelty. By this statement, too, the core of truth in the myth is displayed. The value of money is a by-product of something infinitely more valuable than itself, of those relations of affection, trust, and willingness to give freely (and to receive freely too) without which neither society nor human life itself would long continue; and beyond this again it points to a "principle of love" in the nature of things—only that it is persons, never principles, that arouse and give love.

In stressing the survival of mythical thinking in contemporary life and its refinement and development in the higher religions, we should not lose sight of its immense historical significance as the womb from which are born the arts, sciences, and techniques. It would be a mistake—and a dangerous one, as the Nazis showed—to advocate any return to primitive mythical thinking, but it would be equally a mistake to regard it as hopelessly defective and fit only to be dismissed. Already in its intimate structure it is virtually intelligent. Clement of Alexandria's view that the whole of pre-Christian history was a *praeparatio evangelica*, a development leading up to and preparing men for the revelation of the Christian gospel, and that the heathen Greeks had as essential a role in the preparation as the Jews, may be extended in the context of our argument to apply to the secular sphere as well. It is impossible to believe in Christianity if its Jewish, pagan, and primitive antecedents are dismissed as an entirely gratuitous tissue of fictions; it is, on the contrary, precisely the valid element in myth which survives on and is, in Clement's phrase, baptized by the Church. Myth is similarly the matrix of secular developments.

Let us take first the mythical categories as the agents of mathematical knowledge. Spatial, temporal, and numerical relations do not originally constitute a body of secular knowledge which is then arbitrarily seized on by a priesthood and given mystical symbolic significance. Rather, just as astrology is the parent of astronomy and alchemy of chemistry, so the knowledge of space and time and number arises first within and as part and parcel of the holy. This point is so central that I repeat: myth does not take over ready-made distinctions, but serves to discover and fix the original distinctions themselves. The basic, the original limitations are the inner ones which man places upon himself when confronted with the holy, and these he progressively applies outside himself, to places, times, numbers, till all reality and happening is woven into a fine network of mythical relationships.

For example, in places as far apart as Egypt, Mexico, China, and Rome, we find a four-fold sacral articulation in space determined by the equatorial east-west line of the sun, known to the Romans as *decumanus*, and the north-south line, known as *cardo*, along which the sun deviates from the equator to create the four seasons. These cardinal points are not indifferent quantitative or purely dimensional directions, but each is the magic "home" of a miscellany of sacred things and actions. As we shall see later, each is for the Chinese the home of one of the four elements, of a sacred animal, of a human organ, of one of the professions. This religious system of co-ordinates dominates Roman theology, and flows over into law and politics. The "temple" (from Greek *temnein*, to cut) is made sacred by being oriented in accordance with these co-ordinates: i.e., what is holy or supernatural and what confers holiness or *mana* upon an object is the act of setting definite limits. The cosmic limits, *decumanus* and *cardo*, show heaven itself to be the great cut or temple, and the earthly temple obtains mythical identity with the heavenly through this basic act of "cutting"; what is left, the *ager publicus*, is secular or profane. When a legal document is signed with "John Smith + his mark," this relic of primitive Roman magic indicates the sacred act of appropriation by which the cosmic order as a whole is invoked to support any fixing and delimitation of boundaries. It is my point that out of this originative act of "templing" and necessarily presupposing it arises the pure con*templ*ation of spatial relations trimmed of their mythical qualities (though the affiliations of the word "contemplation" suggest that a certain awe attaches to this kind of act, which is very holy, very special and extraordinary); that the Roman priest is the direct ancestor of a line which ends with Descartes and his purely secular co-ordinates. Out of mythical orientation to cosmos arose by degrees an orientation in pure thought which became geometry, astronomy, natural science.

Time-discriminations proceed toward elaboration under the same aegis, for it is no accident that *tempus* and *templum* have the same root. Here we begin with what has been called the "primitive phase-feeling," an often astonishingly fine and precise sensitiveness to periodicities which appears long before primitive man has learned to count or measure. This sense is guided by mythical thought and by the ritual observance which precedes that thought—for here too *im Aufgang war die That.* The holy as it appears in time, in happenings, is ritual action, which is consequently to be regarded as absolutely prior to and the ultimate source of that conscious mythical speculation which in turn gives rise to the other modes of experience and intelligence. Passage from one phase to another, from one season to another, from one phase of life to another, demands the most careful rites of initiation or transition. The lines of cleavage introduced by ritual times and holy days have, like the primitive distinctions in space, no neutral character but are charged with qualities, are like-unlike, corresponding or opposite, friendly or hostile to one another. Since the actual sowing and harvesting, etc., depend on engaging the friendly and thwarting the inimical forces, and since this can only be accomplished by the correct rites in the correct order, the sacred compulsion to pursue and elaborate time-discriminations with increasing rigour and the burden of evaluating time as a whole are mythically self-evident. The providential time-framework then is the parent without which astronomical time could not have been born.

The same sort of considerations apply to number, which arises always as a means of giving religious meaning to the world, of articulating it in mythical form. The history of mathematics from Pythagoras to Galileo, if we had time to consider it, would be found to exhibit the disengagement of a purely secularized science of quantity from a mythical and mystical view of number, and it would be possible to show in Galileo's case that the original motive was still at work.

All that has been argued here on these three heads might be summarized by referring to the awe and respect with which early Greek philosophy, arising as it did in close association with Greek mathematics, regarded *peras*, the limit or form, as opposed to the *aperion*, the unlimited and formless. Naïvely—or perhaps not so naïvely—the Greek philosophers proceeded to identify any kind of value with *peras* and disvalue with the *aperion*. When I say that there is something left of myth after the birth of the sciences, I mean for one thing that the most civilized man is bound to feel the same reverence as the Greek or the primitive before the power of discriminating and setting limits. It is true that the primitive feels that it is the embodied limitations which are to be revered, whereas the civilized man feels respect for the intelligence as a human power; but this is only the result of clearer sight and does not affect the underlying identity of belief as between primitive and civilized.

Perhaps I may strengthen this point by a reference to language. Words, as themselves instruments of definition and limitation and classification, possess to a marked degree the mythical properties of *mana* or sacredness: to the primitive there is in the mythical identification of object and work, name and person, a trans-substantiation which is more than a relation of symbol and symbolized. Possession of the name is possession of the person or thing, so that in Africa a child's real name, being too dangerous to leave around, is written by the priest on a leaf which is then burned, and the child is then given another name, not really his. I imagine that to some degree we all realize in the case of our own given names and surnames how deeply rooted in personal feeling is this curious religious shyness; but what is important is to notice with how slight a shift this magic power of words over things can be validated and the mythical feeling for the holiness of words justified and shared by the most civilized person. Here again of course it is true that we have clearer sight, that what we respect is more the inner than the outer, not words so much as the power which forges, fashions, and employs them; but for us as for the primitive it must be true that words confer power over things. Without the conquest of signs which we call language, there could have been no such conquest of things as man has achieved. Destroy all that men now dead have put into words, and the best-endowed scientific genius will be reduced to repeating the painful beginnings of science.

The primitive's awe before his own creation of language is perfectly justified; so, properly interpreted, is his sense of its uncanny power. The magic of language is not direct as he imagines, submitting things immediately to his wishes, but is an instrumental magic, indirectly submitting the real to his will by first serving as a tool for grasping, sorting, and articulating it. Nevertheless, speech still gives evidence of something more-than-natural in man, meaning at the least that we are compelled to recognize a breach of continuity between ourselves and the rest of organic and physical nature, whatever degree of continuity we may otherwise posit; and rational thought based on language is strange and wonderful, even terrifying in its potentiality, an agency of transformation almost unlimited whether for good or evil.

From the original matrix of ritual action come also the arts and techniques. At first art and technique form an inseparable whole under the predominant idea of magic, or the acquisition and utilization of *mana*. The buffalo dance is not play, but as integral a part of the real hunt as the bows and arrows. But long after they have developed from this common root the arts and techniques still retain their magic qualities. The handling of weapons and of implements like the plough is still surrounded with ritual precautions long after their mechanically causal use is recognized. This is a point for Marxists: they like to point out how technological changes work spiritual effects, transforming man's ideas and beliefs; but here is a case of the opposite, a case where the spiritual function of the implements does not develop out of their mechanical functioning, but determines and conditions that mechanical functioning. Techniques and implements are developed primarily for giving religious significance to things and only secondarily for mastering them; the mastery is a by-product which gradually usurps the leading role. It may seem fantastic to suggest that in this technological context also primitive myth retains a validity of its own other than the value of the processes, inventions, etc., to which it gives rise, but I would maintain this to be the case. Rite for rite, the sacred ritual of the plough or of the threshing floor is definitely a sounder way of ordering experience and thus more intelligent than the mechanized formal movements of the factory hand on the production line. The basic revolutionary idea of the dignity of labour is a protest against such secularization or degradation of action to the mere obtaining of results, at the cost of all spiritual significance. And it is an idea which makes no sense apart from a mythical evaluation of human life: if man is not more-than-natural, his labour is no more sacred than that of the ox or the waterfall.

This last point should be developed at greater length. One of the signal achievements of myth is in giving rise to the fundamental ideas of individual personality and of society which determine the lines that history, political theory, law, and morals shall take. We have already said that it is mythology which makes the tribe, that mythical beliefs and rituals are conditions of any social structure and actual formative agents of that structure, so that it would be a mistake to reduce myth to sociology, to make what is conditioned prior to what conditions it.

Now we must add that not only the original collective or community feeling, but the process of detachment of individual self-feeling from it, is the work of mythical thought. This process is primitively led, mediated, and conditioned by myth as surely as, at a more complicated and evolved level, the emergence of Renaissance individualism from the relative collectivism of medieval thought and feeling was determined by changes in religious belief.

In the childhood of the race, as of any member of it, there is nothing that deserves to be called self-awareness. The idea of the self gradually develops out of what may be termed a neutral consciousness. This neutral consciousness should not be confused with direct consciousness of others, since the "other" is a correlate of the "self" and you cannot have either term when one of them is lacking. The development of a child's vocabulary in an egoistic direction is significant here. I speak under correction and from limited observation, but I seem to detect that the child in speaking of itself first uses the possessive pronoun *mine*, i.e., finds itself first in the things it appropriates; advances from that to the accusative *me* when it sees itself as at the receiving end of actions and attentions; and only much later, by a final effort of abstraction, arrives at *I* when it has realized its isolation and placed its centre of gravity within a region inaccessible to others, instead of outside itself in the group.

This paradigm is necessary to guide us in assessing myth. The main reason that the old-fashioned animistic accounts of myth have been abandoned, for instance, is that it is ludicrous to suppose that the savage interprets forests and clouds by analogy with himself when he has not yet managed to distinguish himself from what is outside him. The myth function is not an attempt to interpret the objective in subjective terms, as animistic theories suppose, but is rather the activity by which the inner and the outer worlds are originally differentiated and their limits drawn. *Anima* or the soul is the end, not the beginning, of a long process of mythical reflection. The beginning is, like the child's awareness in which neither the self nor the other is actually distinguished, neutral: there is only the sense of the holy, of *mana*, which is neither stuff nor force but is indifferent to such distinctions, being possessed by anything alive or dead and magically transmissible to anything else.

The next moment in the child's dawning consciousness is one in which the accent is on the others, where its consciousness is a collective consciousness. It is much more sensible to suppose that the child disengages himself from an awareness which is primarily awareness of others, than to suppose that he starts with self-awareness and projects this into hypothetical constructions which he then calls "other people." Such direct awareness of others, in which individual consciousness is still submerged in group consciousness, of course characterizes the primitive too. The deep mythical sense of the unity of all life which reappears in sophisticated form with Samuel Butler and Bergson has already led to such primitive manifestations as totemism and theriomorphism. (Incidentally, how is theriomorphism—the creation of animal gods—to fit in with the rationalistic view that man creates God in his own image?)

At this stage, when magic connections between man and animal rule, when there may be a mythical identity between the tribe and any member of the totem species, there is the same mythical indifference between the whole and the part of the tribe, between the individual and society. The sin of one falls on all, and for an individual to be banished from the tribe is for him to lose God. But as mythical reflection proceeds and the god takes on personal form (often through the mediating concept of the tribal hero) this indifference begins to disappear. Or in other words, as *mana* loses its neutral character, as reflection reads it back from all sorts of performances, actions, rites, objects, and persons into a spiritual and individual source, individual self-feeling begins to arise out of the collective life-feeling. We are not concerned here to trace the further transformation of the idea of God, but it would seem that every step in that development initiates a corresponding transformation in the concept of the self, that the amazing plurality of selves which characterizes Egyptian and Mesopotamian and Indian thought—never fewer than three and usually as many as seven or eight—is a correlate of polytheism and does not disappear until monotheism becomes predominant as with Socrates and Plato, and that it always does disappear with monotheism. I realize that changes in the conception of the Deity may also be attributed to increasing philosophical or psychological insight. When two things are such as to reflect one another, it is always possible to give an account of either in terms of the other; but it seems to me that the purely anthropomorphic account of religious development does less than justice to the originative fertility of mythical thought. It is like that dry rationalism which makes our awareness of other centres of consciousness a projection by logical inference of our own consciousness. I would prefer to say frankly and even outrageously that it is the successive forms which a man gives to the idea of God which first determine the discovery of the subjective and then condition the progressive grasping of this inner nature of the self.

Let me illustrate by referring to a deepening series of transformations of one of the fundamental religious categories, that of sacrifice. In the earliest stage, the undifferentiated or neutral stage of *mana* and magic action, there is hardly a trace of this self-limitation, or at least it is present in a hardly recognizable form which is fundamentally materialistic. Such ascetic self-control as exists is not renunciation at all, being determined by the belief that strength is increased by limitation, that *mana* may be stored up to the point where it will control material things like herds and enemies by superior magical force. It is true that the idea of compelling the gods by meeting them with their own captured force lives on and is even found today in some grosser forms of Christianity, and it is also true that limitation does increase strength; but this should not be confused with sacrifice. The idea of sacrifice has generally evolved, as personal deities emerge, along with the idea of an exchange: the god and the worshipper have reciprocal needs, and if you give him what he wants, he will see that you get what you want. This too obviously survives, and to a great many people religion is a sort of celestial book-keeping. But the progressive interiorization which arises and develops with monotheism brings a still further transformation of this concept; the only valuable religious offering, it is now seen, is the inner state of the worshipper himself, and this must be a real gift. He must now renounce or sacrifice himself really and gratuitously, surrender the whole claim to be the natural centre of things, really give up the ego which, in the previous forms of sacrifice, hoped to win by force or persuasion all that it wanted for itself. Doubtless the man who loses his life will find it, and so the most primitive pattern survives; but it is completely transformed, for doubtless also if he tries to give up his life for the sake of the reward, as a bargain, there is no real sacrifice, nothing given and so nothing found.

I need hardly conclude this branch of the topic with the usual little moral that mythical reflection still has validity in civilized society. If religion is not merely in historical fact the organ of progressive self-knowledge but the likely source of all future integration of the self on higher levels, then these ideas are really among the most momentous that the mind of man has reached. I may also add that in every realm in which self-feeling or community-feeling or the painful tension between them is involved, the categories of mythical thought are essentially involved too. These realms, in spite of repeated assaults by Hobbes, Bentham, Marx, and others, have resisted satisfactory and complete secularization, and I should say that they always will, for the simple reason—to take the socially simplest case, that of you and me—that your reality as a consciousness with which I come in contact through the material agency of external and visible or audible signals is and must be a function of faith: I cannot prove, what I am certain of, that you are there, and you cannot prove it to me if I am resolved not to make the necessary act of faith. Your presence to me, not as something merely to be physically registered, but as an actual contact of two minds through signals, is a mythical presence, and so is my presence to you. That I am also a myth to myself and you to yourself is a further point I have been trying to suggest, acceptance of which would remove the last obstacle to a real entry into the region of mythical and religious belief. Thus the point that myth cannot be dismissed from the "sciences of man," from the "moral sciences," from "*Geisteswissenschaften*," has been made as well as I can make it.

As it will certainly be objected that I have been making heavy draughts on other departments and crediting them to myth, I might supplement the earlier definition with a description of the principles of mythical thought, or specifically distinguish *mythos* from *logos*. There is a definite conflict between them. Myth does not distinguish part from whole; it identifies symbol and object symbolized, name or picture and thing, dramatic representation and real action, thing and meaning, wish and fulfilment, dream and actuality: your shadow, your name, your picture, your image in another's dream, a lock of your hair—all of you is in any one of these. Consequently, since the part works as the whole, mythical causation pervades everything, there is nothing accidental, *post hoc* is regularly taken for *propter hoc*, and the finest details of individual existence and happening are explained through magic correspondences, harmonies, sympathies. Whereas scientific thought, as Aristotle pointed out, reaches knowledge which is always knowledge of the universal and never of the particular and unique instance as such, myth is always interested in the particular and unique. Whereas scientific reason or *logos* is analytic, distinguishing part and whole, substance and quality, *post hoc* and *propter hoc*, *mythos* is indifferent to analysis, remaining always in a given representation as a whole. Whereas *logos* finds the ultimately satisfactory type of explanation in causal determinism, *mythos* finds it in purpose. Mythical synthesis is thus basically different from logical synthesis.

But surely it will be objected that this distinction takes away with one hand all that has been given with the other. We have been asked to view mythical reflection with sympathy and respect, and now it is exhibited as the essence of unreason. We appear to have reverted to the position of enlightened distrust of myth: the various basic forms of culture may have been shown as springing from a source in mythical consciousness, but it is quite another matter to engage in any mythical reflection now, in the twentieth century.

I should reply that far from being no longer possible it is still inevitable, and that the attempt to avoid this inevitability leads to the position so clearly and admirably and disastrously worked out by Auguste Comte. Knowledge, Comte said, necessarily began with a theological stage when the world was first a world of *mana*, of mythical powers and forces, demons and gods. These were then gradually attenuated and depersonalized into the abstract forces of metaphysics and metaphysic-ridden science—forces of gravity, heat, electricity, and the like. In a third, positive stage, reason finally comes of age, true enlightenment at last banishes even these ghosts of the early gods and confines itself to the discovery of laws, of precise quantitative correlations between empirical facts; reason triumphs when it finally renounces the attempt to explain and settles down to collect and correlate facts with a view simply to use. Myth, for Comte, is valuable indeed as a sort of hotbed of unreason from which reason had to spring and without which it could never have flowered; but it is valuable only as a stimulating error which is eliminated in the end, completely transcended because now known to be objectively null and void.

The revenge of myth was not long in coming. When Comte came on to the last and highest science, sociology, which by his own act was to issue from the metaphysical to the positive stage, when he had as he thought discovered the essential uniformities and correlations between observed social happenings and was about to apply them scientifically to determine the first completely rational form of society and political organization, he paused. What I still need, he said in effect, is to engage people's feelings and loyalties. It is true that these are the observed uniformities; but it will not be enough to set them down in the form of a scientific text-book of sociological principles. People must be made to be haunted with a sense of what they owe to society before these laws can really serve to reconstruct society. The upshot was a fantastic myth, the "religion of humanity," on whose weak spot the French with witty insight put their finger when they said, "une religion sans Dieu—Monde, quelle religion!" Mankind in fact may have an unduly exaggerated idea of its own significance and importance, but it has sense enough to know intuitively that it is so far from being good and great, or perfect, or divine, that it does not make sense to ask it to worship itself. The only thing which slightly obscured the utter absurdity of positive religion was that it borrowed all the ancient rites and usages of the Catholic faith, robbing them of all their traditional meaning, and thereby produced a caricature of a living faith, its essentially low-grade character as a myth being partly concealed, as I say, by the forms it borrowed.

The case of Comte is enormously instructive. It explains why it should be the age of enlightenment itself, the eighteenth century, that was the parent of "enthusiasm," camp meetings, and other revivalist phenomena, and of Swedenborg and the beginnings of spiritism. It speaks a direst warning to our age in which astrology, fortune-telling, emperor and fuehrer worship and all kinds of similar aberrations are flourishing—aberrations which we do not take seriously until we find that they have captured the mind of a supposedly civilized state. We should realize in regard to the religious structuring of experience, that it is impossible to go back on the most highly developed and intelligent refinement without relapsing into something counter to intelligence. To abandon Christianity for a belief in a master-race is not to dispose of religion but to ensure a luxurious crop of low-grade or primitive myths which flourish like weeds when intelligent effort is relaxed. In Germany the Aryan myths flourished in this way, and the symbol of the celestial axis, the pattern made by the Dipper about the Pole Star in the four seasons, became the symbol of relapse into destructive and aggressive tribalism. The cross arms of the Swastika made it a pin-wheel, as indeed is the Dipper—except for the fact that instead of revolving clockwise around the centre, this pin-wheel moves from left to right. Now this symbol probably did not consciously influence events, yet it remains a fact that the order of Nazi attack in the War, from Poland, through Denmark and Norway, to Holland, Belgium, and France, the attack through Italy on the north coast of Africa followed by the invasion of Yugoslavia and ending in Russia constituted one complete turn of the pin-wheel in the required direction. There the matter may be left for reflection. I am unable to believe that there is no connection at all between these two phenomena.

The case of Comte also teaches us not to be surprised when we find instances of typically mythical ways of thought in contemporary doctrines which lay claim to be instances of sober intellection. For example, there is the dialectial union of opposites in Marxism, where in regard to necessity-freedom, theory-practice, absolute-relative, etc., we are exhorted in definitely theological terms not to lose sight of the unity in the difference or the difference in the unity. I confess that I find this to be intellectually neither more easy nor more difficult to accept than the dogma of the union of the two natures, divine and human, in the person of Christ; it seems to me the same kind of thought. I say nothing of Freudian theory, where the primitive view of the plurality of selves is resurrected, where the burden of guilt is assumed, by transference, by a living human saviour, and where a primitive idea like demonic possession is not very skilfully concealed. A thorough examination of present-day economic theory, political theory, or psychology would reveal that it is not only the primitive mind which tends to take *post hoc* as *propter hoc* and the part as equivalent to the whole.

From our examination of *mythos*, the possibility of aberrations is perfectly apparent. Faith is not reason, and the kind of thought it produces, while subject to criticism and control by intelligence, is not intellectual thought. But I repeat that the presence of aberrations does not show that a given function of the human mind either can be or should be eliminated. The aesthetic function is similarly menaced, or the speech function, or the moral, economic, or legal functions; but we do not expect that a man can or should cease to be an artist, speaker, moral agent, worker, or law-maker. The function of intellection itself is no exception to this rule: crazy and monstrous conclusions are continually being drawn in strict logic, and for that matter on experimental grounds, in the name of reason; but we are not entitled, because of its aberrations, to suppose that man either can or should discard the scientific intellect.

I have asked you to think of mythical thought as a powerfully fertile historical force from which as from a common matrix all that we value most has been derived. But such an admission, as the case of Comte clearly shows, cannot be made with impunity. The force of myth remains and works within every civilization, however far advanced, and it has rights which cannot safely be ignored. It is only reasonable to recognize this force and ally oneself with it. The amazingly tenacious resistance which mythical and religious thought and forms offer to the ravages of time does not argue that they are essentially conservative, static, retrospective things. Precisely because of their relatively high resistance to change they are the sources of the most permanent and enduring transformations, whereas more plastic and variable functions produce changes that are themselves ephemeral—as for example changes in taste, where *plus ça change plus c'est la même chose.*

If the past is a reliable guide, to take one point only of those we have touched on, I should expect the progressive fixing of limits in new and more adequate ways between subjective and objective to be determined in the first instance from the side of religious experience; for here is involved a progressive discovery—not something that we start from, but that we aim at; and no one can honestly say we have yet arrived at more than a transitional and provisional view of the lines of demarcation. What novelties lie in store I can, of course, no more predict than the primitive in totemic society could have predicted the emergence of individual self-feeling; but I am sure we are mistaken if we suppose that everything that can happen has happened; and I am also certain that the main fruitful source of lasting innovations is the one we have been examining.

The Chinese Mythical Ground-Plan

Intelligence, as displayed in myth, is a matter of the skill with which the categories of the sacred and the profane are employed to the ordering of experience. It may be that the case for a special "mythological" function of intelligence, parallel and quite closely related to poetic intelligence, can best be supported by examining some of the large-scale patterns of articulation—let us call them ground-plans—along which the ordering of the holy and secular takes place.

These are quite various, like the general laws of structure underlying the different languages or families of languages in the world. One language will proceed by inflecting noun and verb endings, another by varying the position of the word in the sentence and using prepositions and conjunctions freely, to achieve the same effect. In one, all nouns must be masculine, feminine, or neuter; in another, such as Algonkin, the line of cleavage is between living and inanimate; in a third, such as South Andaman, the genera of nouns vary in terms of the parts of the body, so that there are head-nouns, chest-nouns, and belly-nouns. Similarly in mythology, the ground-plan or structural basis along which the holy is articulated and distributed varies greatly from place to place. Though it is always the same task with which the mythological intelligence is occupied, there is an apparently inexhaustible capriciousness about the way in which this task is executed.

One such ground-plan will be described here rather fully, to confirm the analysis of mythological thought just given and to suggest parallels with the intelligent use of symbols in poetry. This is the ground-plan of the four quarters, with the cross-line joining them, such as is found on any weather-vane. It plays either a predominant or a prominent role in the mythologies of nations culturally as remote from one another as Rome, China, Egypt, and pre-Columbian Central America.

Its basis is probably some version of sun-worship, a widespread and natural phenomenon among men once they realize the complete dependence of all organic life on the never-ending river of light and warmth flowing from the sun. Whether as in Egypt the sun itself is regarded as the greatest of the gods, or whether as in China no such explicitly theological interpretation is made, the earth is always presented as depending on the vivifying and fructifying energy that descends from the heavens. The Chinese in fact make a five-fold distinction, adding the Centre to East, South, West, and North; and they speak of a perpendicular line of descent from Heaven to this Centre, a kind of axis of the whole system, the primary line of action of Yang, the active and life-giving male principle, upon Yin, the passive and life-bearing female principle.

"One round of Yin and one round of Yang equals the Tao." With this statement from the *Hsi-Ts'u* we are introduced to the unnameable, undifferentiable "beginning of heaven and earth," the principle from which all names and all things come to be. The Way, or Tao, the unchanging law of happening and change, works through a dialectical process whereby all its creations are continually being turned inside out and changed into their opposite; and it is through the alternation and opposition of Yin-force and Yang-force that such complete reversal is effected.

The basic symbolism is compelling. Around the motionless inert land on which he stands, man sees the heavens sweep daily; and the changes on the surface of the land—growth, decay, wind, flood, drought—depend so obviously on the state of the heavens that it is most natural for him to find the source of all change in the movements of the heavens, and all resistance to change in the passivity of the earth. The tiller who lays the surface of the soil open to the fertilizing action of light and moisture cannot miss the force of the compelling symbol: his very act becomes sacred, and he himself a second edition of Heaven, an intermediary between Heaven and Earth, even making a trinity with Earth and Heaven.

As the sun moves north to the winter solstice, darkness, moisture, and cold increase; toward the southern end of its journey, in summer, it is the Yang qualities of light, dryness, and warmth that wax, while the other, the Yin qualities, wane. Thus it is not Heaven but the sun which is purely male: the sun is Yang-in-Yang and sets the predominant note of the heavens, though, in subordination to it, there is the female moon, Yin-in-Yang, whose presence, especially in the winter time, causes a dimming of the Yang force. Similarly with Earth. She is herself purely female and yielding—Yin-in-Yin; but since she has her own active phase in summer, there is also a Yang-in-Yin, Yang contained in subordination to Yin, balancing the lunar Yang-restricting-Yin.

Accordingly, across the main north-south co-ordinate of the "great Yin" and "great Yang," which determines the alternation of winter and summer, we must draw the other co-ordinate, the line of the sun's daily course, with which the two remaining directions, east and west, and the two remaining seasons, spring and autumn, are bound up, and to which respectively the qualifications "little Yin" (Yin-in-Yang) and "little Yang" (Yang-in-Yin) are assigned. Dawn and sunset are not seasons, but their analogies with spring and autumn are obvious. The winter of day is midnight, its summer high noon, and the other two divisions which terminate the sun's most obvious trajectory mark the point where the increase of Yang overcomes Yin (though Yin is still present in a waning state), and the point where Yin is in the ascendant (though Yang is still active).

This account of the origination of the ground-plan of the four quarters (conjectural though it remains at certain points) is required to account for its full symbolic force. The formation of a pattern that combines the two distinct motions of the sun, bound up as these are with quite different units of time—the year and the day—is clearly a considerable and difficult feat. It involves the disentangling of the two crossing linear constituents of the pattern from a visual material which would much more naturally be described as a spiral path. A first-rate effort of abstraction upon this material is required to integrate two such discrepant time-intervals, for if the solstices easily provide the north and south termini of one branch of the cross, the east and west boundaries fall into place in the pattern only twice a year, at the vernal and autumnal equinoxes when day and night are of the same length, and all the intervening instances of this daily repeated line have to be disregarded in favour of the single instances where dawn can be thought of as the beginning of spring and sunset the beginning of autumn.

It is open to anyone to object that the widespread use of the ideograph of cross-in-round to symbolize the sun, even by quite primitive tribes, makes unnecessary any such sophisticated and reflective origin as we have been tracing in China. It may even be pointed out that this is more a pictograph than an ideograph—a direct copy of the pattern given off by the sun when glimpsed as the human eye can only glimpse it, through half-closed lids. The four-fold streamers of irradiated light and the circular disc are given directly to perception, and so the cross-in-round is no abstract intellectual construction.

This alternative explanation, though clearly unverifiable, is not lacking in plausibility. But I am not sure that it matters greatly which view is accepted. If we have here a coincidence, it is a peculiarly happy one that has encouraged the development of such a momentous system of interpretation around this schema. From this focal point of discrimination and articulation, order spreads and floods out over everything as liberally and pervasively as sunshine itself, making the whole world luminous.

For example, the moment the four seasons are assigned to the four quarters, the cycle of vegetation and that of animal and human life are at once integrated into the scheme. The shoot (Yang-in-Yin, spring), the stalk (the great Yang, Yang-in-Yang, summer), the harvested grain (Yin-in-Yang, autumn), and the fallow land and buried seed (the great Yin, Yin-in-Yin, winter)—all go to illustrate the statement, "one round of Yin and one round of Yang equals the Tao." That the same pattern is reflected in the normal outline of human life could not escape notice. From the springtime of conception and childhood, through the summer of adolescence, the autumn of maturity, to the winter of old age and death, the cosmic Tao is repeated in miniature.

Again, to continue the process by which the Tao gives rise to Yin and Yang and they engender the four seasons and the four seasons "form the multitude of things," these notions taken together make possible a theory of the elements whereby the "ten thousand things" in the world are composed of a very few basic types of matter in differently proportioned mixture.

In Western mythology these elements are, of course, four in number—*air* (of spring), *fire* (of summer), *earth* (of autumn), and *water* (of winter). This distribution is bound into place by the view that air is moist and warm, fire dry and warm, earth dry and cold, water moist and cold, so that the "home" of each element is in the appropriate "quarter." In China the list of elements differs, and there is a total of five. They are distributed as follows: *wood* to the East and spring, *fire* to the South and summer, *water* to the West and autumn, *metal* to the North and winter, *earth* to the Centre; and since this mid-point of the cross, as already noted, is the point of the vertical axis leading from Heaven to Earth, it belongs to no season in particular, but to them all. Tung Chung-shu says that Earth is the main agent of Heaven, and that since its intrinsic power is on a bountiful scale, its controlling influence cannot be limited to one season only. Metal, wood, water, and fire, each has its own office, but these are ineffectual unless based on earth.[1]

Only air, of the Western elements, it will be noted, is absent from the Chinese list. Inclusion of what, to the Western mind, seem obviously composite bodies, like metal and wood, is to be explained through the influence of the Yin-Yang theory. Wood is the little Yin, when in a Yang season the cold and dampness of winter still persist but a new warmth and dryness and activity are making for growth; clearly wood is intended more as a symbolic element than as a physical constituent of mixtures. Metal, too, pliable and yielding and passive, is a symbol: it is the little Yang, liquifiable under the action of pure Yang or fire, but a portent of winter in that what might have been molten in great heat is actually in a congealed or "frozen" state. In China, as elsewhere, the peculiar qualities of the crystalline state may have served to suggest the effects of cooling upon a previously molten material. In any case, however we try to establish the improbable affinity between metal and harvest time, the essence of Yin and Yang with its cyclic alternation of flourishing and declining is held to be manifest in the elements. Thus in the *Tse-hua-tse* we read: "In the North, Yin reaches its maximum and brings forth cold, but cold produces water; in the South, Yang reaches its maximum and brings forth heat, but heat produces fire. In the East, Yang is in motion and emits, bringing forth wind, but wind produces wood; in the West, Yin is at rest and absorbs, bringing forth dryness, but dryness produces metal."[2] The cycle of the elements is sometimes called the "five wanderers" and sometimes the "five robbers," because each lives at the expense of the one before and each flourishes in turn.

It will be noted, again as in Western mythology, that this distribution of the elements carries with it a distribution of qualities as well. In the West, these qualities are the four groups obtained by combining cold, warm, moist, and dry, in pairs. To East and air belong the warm-moist, to South and fire the warm-dry, to West and earth the cold-dry, and to North and water the cold-moist. This more flexible and mythologically more adequate scheme of qualities, which would have fitted the Yin-Yang theory precisely, does not seem to have occurred to the Chinese: in the quotation given it is cold, wind, heat, and dryness that are used. Perhaps the absence of air from the list of elements and

[1]Fung Yu-lan, *The Spirit of Chinese Philosophy* (London, 1947), 120; slightly rephrased.

[2]Otto Franke, "Der kosmische Gedanke in Philosophie und Staat der Chinesen," *Vorträge der Bibliothek Warburg*, V (1925–6), 19; translation by H. R. M.

the presence of wind in the list of qualities indicates a certain inability of the Chinese myth-making intelligence to see through the metaphors such as spirit-breath, essence-effluvium, or in Chinese itself *chi* (universal)-vapour, by which the human mind has employed its experience of the most tenuous kinds of matter to symbolize that which, like thought or idea or consciousness, does not belong in the material order at all.

In West and East alike, this framework of quarters, seasons, elements, is clothed with all sorts of other qualities. For instance, the four humours of the human body in Galen's medicine fall readily into place: blood to the East (since it is warm and moist), gall to the South, bile to the West, and phlegm (the cold-moist humour) to the North. Bound up with this is the ingenious theory of the mixture of humours to form "temperaments," which is another and more strictly physiological way of referring to the tempering of the elements by one another in four mixtures, in each of which one of the humours or elements predominates and gives the body and the personality its "complexion." Blood is dominant in the sanguine type, gall or yellow bile in the choleric, black bile in the melancholy, and phlegm in the phlegmatic. Since the Western theory too is one of cyclic transformation, there is even a sense in which, whatever his complexion, the four ages of a man's life will manifest this temperamental cycle. Doubtless a sanguine person will always be sanguine, or predominantly so; in childhood and youth, however, he will be especially so; in maturity, relatively choleric; in later life, relatively melancholy; and in old age, relatively phlegmatic. The temperamentally phlegmatic man will be doubly phlegmatic in old age, and so on with the others.

In the Chinese version there is no trace of this theory of temperaments, though it would have accorded well with the Yin-Yang theory. There is, to be sure, a quite elaborate five-fold classification of the limbs, the features of the face, the viscera, the bodily fluids, in accordance with the general notion of man's correspondence with Heaven and Earth, and no doubt this served as a basis for medical practice; but it seems to lack the combination of flexibility and accuracy of application that mark the Western variant.

The five flavours fit the Chinese scheme much better:

The nature of water is to moisten and descend; of fire, to burn and ascend; of wood, to be crooked and straight; of metal, to yield and to be modified; of earth, to provide for sowing and reaping. That which moistens and descends produces salt [obviously the ocean provides the basis for this statement, with its implied localization of the taste of salt to winter, and the North]; that which burns and ascends becomes bitter [maybe the smell of smoke or the taste of ashes serves to assign bitterness to summer]; that which is crooked and straight becomes sour [perhaps the widespread fact of fermentation in vegetable matter provides this link between sources, the East, and spring]; that which yields and is modified becomes acrid [the taste of a metal such as steel thus belongs to autumn]; sowing and reaping produce sweetness [sweetness belongs to Earth and the Centre].[3]

The five colours fall into place with the five tastes. Earth is yellow and at the Centre; wood, the shoots and verdure of spring, is green; fire, at the South, is of course red; metal, in the West, is white—this probably in reference to the gleam of reflected light from polished metal surfaces and mirrors; and water, presumably winter water, is black. This last, apparently arbitrary, attribution may be better understood if, asking as the Chinese must have asked, what colour water is, we answer by saying that it is every colour, since it reflects the images or, when disturbed, the lines of its surroundings. The *Huai-man-tzu*, without actually going so far as to identify black with the absence of all colour, makes the receptive Yin-force of water the ground for affirming its darkness. It is the obverse of fire, which is externally and visibly bright, being an emission of Yang fluid, whereas "darkness is that which absorbs fluid, and therefore water is bright internally," though in appearance black.[4] The missing primary colour, blue, is probably not included for the same reason that air is not one of the five elements, namely (to ignore the suggestion previously put forward) because it belongs to Heaven, not to Earth. There may be an additional linguistic reason in the use of the same word in Chinese for both blue and green.

It would be possible to amplify this list of "correspondences" much further: thus to each quarter belongs one of the cultivable grains, one of the viscera, one of the features, one of the professions. Creatures fall into five classes, according to their integument—the scaly, the feathered, the naked, the hairy, and the shell-covered. Their arrangement is accounted for by Kuan Yin-tsis as an amplification of the rising and falling aspects of Yang and Yin, which are opposites also in respect of lightness and heaviness. "That which rises," he says, "is fire; that which descends, water. That which would like to rise, but cannot, is wood; and that which would like to descend, but cannot, is metal."[5] That is to say, water can sink into the earth, but metal can only fall to its surface. Omitting the naked creatures whose locus is the Centre, this means that fish and other scaly creatures belong to the East and

[3]Fung Yu-lan, *A History of Chinese Philosophy* (London, 1937), 163; interpolations by H. R. M.
[4]*Ibid*.. 397.
[5]Anton Forke, *The World-Conception of the Chinese* (London, 1925), 264–5.

to the element wood, since they would like to rise but cannot; feathered creatures, as the lightest and most active, belong to the South and the realm of fire; hairy beasts belong to the West and the element metal, since they would like to descend but cannot; and shell-covered creatures, as the heaviest and most lethargic, belong to the North and the realm of water.

Finally, the feelings of Heaven, according to Tung Chung-shu, are evident in the cycle of the four quarters. To the growing warmth of spring corresponds love; to the heat of summer, joy; to the clearness of autumn (apparently the first stage of winter cold) corresponds the anger or "seriousness" of Heaven; and to the cold of winter, grief, for this is when the heavens mourn, and conceal and enclose their produce in the earth. To Earth as pure Yin in contrast to the Yang of Heaven belongs desire.

Schematization of the sort just described permeates and powerfully influences the whole of Chinese life, collective and individual alike. In the political sphere the whole system of order above is transferred directly to the earth beneath. In their celestial setting the cardinal points are named in terms of appropriate constellations—the Green Dragon (East), the Scarlet Bird (South), the White Tiger (West), and the Black Turtle (North). But the celestial mid-point is provided not by the sun but by the night sky: it is the pole-star which is the centre of the axis of the heavens' revolution and the dwelling place of its Ruler. The handle of the Dipper, turning annually and clockwise about the star, points in each season to that one of the four quarters in which Yang is present. The Dipper's diagrammatic symbol is the swastika.

Below, a human ruler is its counterpart. The Emperor of the Middle Kingdom, Son of Heaven, is by divine right a kind of pole-star around which all human affairs revolve; and the consequent claim to universal dominion was a constant feature of the Chinese Imperial system.

The geography of the earth faithfully reflects the celestial pattern. There are, for instance, nine continents, separated from one another by seas and disposed about the central continent (China) in the configuration of a central square surrounded by eight others, one for each major point of the compass.[6] This is the same scheme that we encounter in the feudal "well-field" system of land division: eight equal squares of land, each supporting a family, disposed about a central square which is collectively cultivated for the feudal lord. We shall meet it again in the Chinese town-plan.

[6]Fung, *History*, 160–1.

The Middle ("Celestial") Kingdom itself, as the receiving end of the Heaven-Earth axis from the pole-star, was conceived as surrounded by either four or eight vassal states, arranged in concentric squares.[7] Internally, too, the Celestial Kingdom repeats the same pattern, for there are nine provinces, or component states, the seat of the Emperor being in the middle province. And government itself is accordingly organized. The Ministry of Heaven, that of administration and civil service, carries out the government of the component states of the Kingdom and helps the Ruler to keep them in equilibrium; the Ministry of Earth, that of education, keeps these states peaceable and cultured; the Ministry of Spring regulates religious affairs, its main task being to preserve the rites; the Ministry of Summer is the war ministry; the Ministry of Autumn is that of Justice; and the Ministry of Winter has charge of public works and the supervision of commerce and industry. The parallels with what has preceded are too multiple and complex to draw out in detail. Some, indeed, seem arbitrary: is it not a quite fortuitous connection between justice and the metal instruments whereby it is executed that gives the Ministry of the West its name and place?

Yet it would be hard to over-emphasize the significance of the scheme as a whole, both as expressing and as shaping the basic characteristics of Chinese culture, and serving thereby to explain the millennial stability of the Chinese state. To think of the main Yin-Yang axis as that which leads from the heavens to the centre, and of the four directions, each with its distinctive mixture of Yin and Yang, as ordered cyclically about this axis, is to establish the following hierarchy: Emperor, civil servant, scholar, priest, warrior, judge, industrialist. That this should be precisely the order of evaluation of men's public functions is surely central to any understanding of the traditional Chinese outlook, indeed of the course of Chinese history; and it is part and parcel of the Yin-Yang system.

The counterparts of the two primary forces, in the realm of man's collective life, are music (which is considered to be Yang) and *li*, ceremonial and sacrificial rites (considered as Yin). "Music makes for common union," says the *Li Chi*. "The *li* make for difference and distinction. . . . Where music prevails, we find a weak coalescence; where *li* prevail, a tendency to separation." Thus only under joint stimulation from both can unity as well as differentiation be realized. Growth in spring and maturing in summer resemble the Yang aspect of virtue, the quality of "human-heartedness." The Yin counterpart of this

[7]Franke, 25–6.

human-heartedness is "righteousness," which harvesting in autumn and storing in winter resemble. Human-heartedness is akin to music, righteousness to *li*. The natures and endowments of things are not the same; this being so, the *li* represent the distinctions of Heaven and Earth. The Yin and the Yang act upon one another: "They are drummed on by thunder, excited by wind and rain, moved by the four seasons, warmed by the sun and moon, and all the processes of change and growth vigorously proceed. This being so, music represents the harmony of Heaven and Earth." "Music appeared in the Great Beginning . . . and the *li* took their place on the completion of things. What manifests itself without ceasing is Heaven. What manifests itself without stirring is Earth. Movement and quiescence sum up all between Heaven and Earth. And so the Sages would simply speak about *li* and music."[8]

The same Confucian document that we have been following presents the *li* as regulating desire which without ceremonial quickly leads to disorder, and music as bearing on emotion and hence on the deepest springs of action. Ceremonial, we might paraphrase, is a dampening influence, and ensures stability. To be able to stand firmly is to "subdue one's self and recover the ritual disposition."[9] Music, on the other hand, stirs and energizes, correcting the apathetic passivity which ceremonial by itself would induce. It is a curious corollary to this view that raving madness results from the entire Yang being concentrated in the upper part of the body, and the entire Yin in the lower part.[10] Crudely, in terms of the microcosm of man's body, this presentation expresses the requirements of that well-being which *li* and music together secure in state and individual alike, namely, the harmonious cyclical interplay of Yin and Yang, of receptivity and aggressiveness, withdrawal and expansion, yielding and initiative, combining the movement of closing and contracting with that of opening and dilation.

The enlightened ruler "conforms to Heaven by giving without taking." Han Fei-tzu and Taoists such as Chuang-tzu draw this conclusion from the analogy of Emperor and pole-star: neither acts, but each functions through non-activity. To quote the first writer: "Affairs lie in the four quarters. . . . What is important is in the centre. The Sage holds what is important, and the four quarters come to imitate him. He awaits them in a state of 'emptiness' . . ., and they all work by themselves."[11] The same implied parallel with the pole-star's immobility leads Chuang-tzu to conclude as follows: "Therefore rulers of

[8]Fung, *History*, 343–4. [9]Lun Yu, Book XII, quoted by Fung, *Spirit*, 21.
[10]Forke, *World-Conception of the Chinese*, 199. [11]Fung, *History*, 330.

old, although their knowledge spread throughout the universe, did not themselves think. Although their eloquence beautified all things, they did not themselves speak. Although their abilities exhausted all things within the limits of the seas, they did not themselves act."[12]

In the circumstances set by this theory of the universe the function of the sovereign is thus one of maintaining the *li*, the regulation of becoming conduct and of the various types of collective activity. More especially, since with the cycle of Yin and Yang the most essential and delicate matters are always those of timing, the Emperor is in charge of times, dates, and the fixing of seasons. Franke remarks that nothing confirmed the impregnation of the ruler of the Middle Kingdom with heavenly powers so clearly as the stately ceremonies in which the new calendar for the year was communicated from the throne first to the ministers and then through emissaries to outlying parts of the Kingdom where also it was received with rejoicing and festivities.[13] The adoption of this calendar by a conquered people signified their integration into the community of the civilized; the use of any other calendar was a serious act of rebellion.

The ideal of uniting government with the process of exchange between Heaven and Earth and the procession of the four seasons through the action of Yin and Yang is set forth in the "Grand Norm." According to the view we have already mentioned, man, in the person of the king or sage, forms a trinity with Heaven and Earth or mediates the will of Heaven to Earth. The Inner Sage, while not in fact an Outer King, can be almost his equivalent, and the union of the two in the same person has always been the supreme ideal for man, in the mind of Chinese thinkers. Thus Hung Fan asserts: "Gravity (of the sovereign) will be followed by seasonable rain; his regularity will be followed by seasonable sunshine; his intelligence by seasonable heat; his deliberation by seasonable cold; and his wisdom by seasonable wind. . . . The madness (of the sovereign) will be followed by steady rain; his insolence by steady sunshine; his idleness by steady heat; his haste by steady cold; and his ignorance by steady winds."[14]

For the sovereign's adjustment of collective action to times and seasons, we may quote from Kuan-tse. Five administrative measures are proper to the winter months, and there are of course similar regulations for the other three seasons. "The first is providing for orphans and destitute persons and succouring the old; the second is conforming to the Yin, preparing the sacrifices for the spirits, bestowing titles and emoluments, and conferring ranks; the third is verifying accounts and

[12] *Ibid.*, 332. [13] Franke, 36. [14] Fung, *History*, 164.

not exploiting the treasures of mountains and rivers; the fourth is rewarding those who seize runaway criminals and arrest robbers and thieves; the fifth is prohibiting the moving about of the people, stopping their wanderings and preventing their settling in other parts of the empire." Or again, in terms of irregular, ominous signs in the heavens, "at an eclipse of the sun, a wise Emperor improves rewards; at an eclipse of the moon, he improves punishments; when a comet becomes visible, he improves harmony; when wind (*i.e.* storm-cloud) and sun fight together [by far the most frequent of these "meteors" in the old sense of the word], he improves production."[15]

Beneath the arbitrary quality of all this we can easily discern the curious mythological coherence provided by the ground-plan. For instance, the apparently random collection of administrative measures for winter prove on examination to belong together through the properties of enclosure, completion, and storing-up, which are three of the outstanding signs of the Yin-force.

Again, and still remaining in the context of collective social life, the Chinese have this system of belief to thank, quite as much as their persistently rudimentary methods of production, for the fact that in spite of an enormous population, they did not develop the cancer of metropolitan growth until the industrial invasion of the West forced some measure of it upon them. E. A. Gutkind, in his *Revolution of Environment*, takes account of the extent to which the mythology we have outlined played a really effective role, along with economic and social factors, in leading to a result which can only be called a triumph. Belief in the Tao as the eternal law of the cosmos to which man must adapt himself, and the linking of the Tao with space in such a way that the forces of magic oppose any change in the existing space-relations, secure, he explains, the abnegation of science and technique as a system of thinking and inhibit the industrialization of the economic structure. "The system of magical dependence was, as it were, the substitute for scientific knowledge and, at the same time, the buffer which absorbed the dynamic of the subconscious forces of man"; in other words, it prevented their transformation of inventions into instruments of aggression against Nature.[16]

Gutkind goes on to say that the balance of Yin and Yang effected by the Tao allows a conception of the universe in which thinking occupies a very high rank, but a kind of thinking markedly different from that which permits the European exploitation of cosmic forces

[15]Forke, *World-Conception of the Chinese*, 256–8.
[16]E. A. Gutkind, *Revolution of Environment* (London, 1946), 199–200.

by rational technique. The Chinese, with his sense of reality as distinguished from the European sense of possibility, shares the attitude of a woman, especially of a wife and mother, in "her awareness of Nature's growing and passing away and her acceptance of the natural order." While this attitude prevailed, no industrial state could grow up on Chinese soil, and "no urbanisation could develop to debase the rural population into a mere appendix of the towns."[17]

In fact, the Chinese town is and has immemorially been a statically conceived construction built from the exterior inward, the walls being erected first and intended to outlast nearly all the buildings within. The walls, the gates, the altar, and the temple trees give the town its religious consecration and constitute so to speak its "cathedral," within which—not grouped around and outside it—the inhabitants dwell. "From the very beginning, the town was conceived as one coherent whole and as a single entity."[18]

Needless to say, the walls and gates were oriented to the four quarters, and the two main streets, running north-south and east-west, were normally joined in that cross which serves so widely to designate the earth. However, in China, as for instance in the character for "field," this earth-sign is a cross placed not in a circle but in a square; and for the same reason the ideal town-plan will be a square, namely, because the Chinese regard the Tao of Earth as square and that of Heaven as round. This is why, in the microcosm, the squareness of man's feet imitates Earth, the roundness of his head, Heaven. Roundness goes with mobility, squareness with stability. The palace will be in the centre of the town, surrounded by its own square wall, a town within the town; and each of the four quarters will have its own peculiarities and very often will repeat within itself this encasing of the town-plan, in the same manner that the Chinese puzzle encloses one within another identical but ever more diminutive examples of the same shape. Naturally, such towns could be, and were, enlarged—as the city of Peiping, for example, was enlarged on five occasions; but this was invariably done by the same method, that of setting up the sacred boundary, the wall with its gates, first, and enlarging the town inward from these preordained limits. Obviously this method excludes unrestricted expansion in advance.

The *Shu King* reports how the founder of a city, attired in special robes, with his sword at his side, inspects the proposed site. "To ascertain the points of the compass, he studies the shadows. He examines the declivities in sun and shade, the Yang and Yin of the country, to

[17]*Ibid.*, 292–3. [18]*Ibid.*, 295.

know how the chief constituencies of the world are divided." He also will take account of the direction of the running water. It is of these and the other geomantic practices presupposed in the founding of the town that Gutkind tellingly remarks that they reveal "the extraordinary flair of the Chinese for adapting their works to their surroundings. Magic thus becomes a very effective agent in town planning. It helps to harmonise the rational layout with the environment in a perfect way."[19]

We have claimed that our "myth" effectively shapes political life to the special forms appropriate to the genius of the Chinese people and indeed serves in a quite indubitable way to determine their destiny and the course of their story. This implies a similarly powerful working of myth in the lives and thought of the individuals themselves, who alone are the ultimate bearers of that destiny and subjects of that story. It is clear that what we have sketched is a fairly comprehensive attempt to understand the world, though not in the way of scientific or even of philosophical understanding. The categories employed remain decisively mythical: the ground-lines of the scheme, whatever objective references they may be capable of bearing, are stamped with the distinctive sign of the "holy." But though the scheme is thus not to be regarded as an abortive first sketch of science, or as a moral-technological undergirding for practical matters, it does not follow that a mythological synthesis such as this is divorced from understanding and action. In its own distinctive way it includes both.

The mythological cosmic picture presented by the Yin-Yang theory is that of the marriage of Heaven and Earth. The passage quoted earlier, "one round of Yin and one round of Yang equals the Tao," continues explicitly: "The passionate union of Yin and Yang, the coupling of husband and wife, is the eternal rule of the universe. If Heaven and Earth did not mingle, whence would all things receive life?"[20]

It would be a mistake to treat this as the product of a commonplace sort of rationalization, as a banal projection upon the cosmos of the human sexual act, yielding merely a series of rather stupid and far-fetched analogies. Such a literalist approach to the myth would ignore what the Chinese recognize, the mysterious, the awe-inspiring or holy quality of the cosmic Tao, "unnameable, beyond shapes and features." As the *Hsi-Ts'u* says, "the inexplorable nature of the Yin and the Yang is what is called mysterious." And again, "the man who comprehends the Tao of transformation, comprehends what the mysterious does."[21]

[19]*Ibid.*, 306–7; Gutkind gives the quotation from the *Shu King* on pp. 294–5.
[20]Forke, *World-Conception of the Chinese*, 68. [21]Fung, *Spirit*, 92.

Instead of a reduction of the cosmic order to an inadequate analogy with human sexuality, what issues from this conception is rather a recognition of the high mystery accumulated behind and manifesting itself in a partial and restricted form in the relation of male and female.

As the picture affects the individual's outlook and hence his actions, it is a myth which presents the world as man's home. The peculiarities of the Chinese attitude toward evil, toward activity, and toward harmony can be used to illustrate this point. Generally, it may be stated thus: that the child, growing out of the world of paternal and maternal protection, finds himself not in an alien and hostile surrounding, but in a new relation of childhood to a universal, living, parental couple, who have all men and all things in their care. That he is thus spared a severe psychological shock and wound, goes without saying. He is reborn, one might say, as naturally as he was born in the first instance.

It is, however, a condition of this rebirth that evil, pain, disturbance, misfortune, and the like be regarded as essential to the cosmic order; and in fact they are Yin. The more obvious physical contrasts of male and female include above-below, rising-falling, emitting-transforming, hard-soft (Heaven being of a substance so hard that Earth by comparison is most yielding), full-empty, light-heavy, moving-quiescent, dry-moist, expanding-contracting; but there are also the less physical and more psychological contrasts of active-passive, advancing-retreating, assertive-docile, initiatory-completive, and, as the primary couple summer-winter illustrates, the contrast on the one hand of manifestation and form and bringing to act, and on the other of concealment, matter, enclosure, and storing-up. But beyond these again, and symbolized in the pair light-dark (and in modified form, as between sun and moon, illuminating-illuminated), there is a set of moral oppositions: generous-selfish (the moral equivalent of opening-closing), benevolence-justice (warmth-coolness in the moral realm), vivifying-lethal (moving-quiet in a somewhat forced analogy), creation-destruction, and order-confusion.

Two observations seem called for in this connection. First, Yin and Yang cannot as such be identified with woman and man, who are among the "ten thousand things" produced by their interaction, each containing components of both forces, so that any human being will be relatively Yin or Yang according to circumstances or behaviour. Though a certain misogyny may seem to be implicit in the identification of darkness, cold, and earthiness with the female principle, misanthropy would be as good a term, since Yin is present in all mankind. Secondly, it would be misleading to present negatives like ugliness, vice, destructiveness, confusion, egoism, ignorance, and death as objects of strenuous avoidance, for in terms of the symbols just used, dark, cold, and earth have a necessary share in the process of fructification.

The West with its long tradition of dualism, often Manichaean in character, understands the symbols light and darkness instantly in a completely antithetical fashion, as a war to the death between good and evil, Heaven and Hell. It requires a serious effort of readjustment to envisage light and dark in Chinese fashion as a married couple who, though separate and opposite, yet have a common will. The negative, desolating aspects of Yin—winter, grief, poverty, ignominy, death, and the like—are simply corollaries of that extremity of docility, enclosure, withdrawal, and storing which the cycle of fertility requires. It is not the basically absurd notion of a "marriage of Heaven and Hell" with which we are presented, but that of the "marriage of Heaven and Earth." Most of what is conventionally regarded as evil is thereby reassessed as a condition of the achievement of a good which also transcends such conventional goods as pleasure, utility, comfort, health, reputation.

By the tenth century B.C. the essential Yin-Yang theory seems firmly established; from then on, with whatever variations, Chinese speculation proceeds within this framework. This is true of the two main currents, the Confucian and Mohist, which seek in compromise the mean between the extremes of Yin and Yang, and Lao-tze's Taoism, which attempts to unite them in a mystical dialectical union where the Sage is the man who has learned to pursue two opposite courses at once. In illustration of the latter current we may quote typical paradoxes from the *Tao Te King*: "The Way to lightness seems as if dark. The Way that goes forward seems to go back. The Way that is level seems as if it were uneven. The Power that is loftiest looks like an abyss. What is sheerest white looks dark. The Power that is most sufficing looks inadequate. The Power that stands firmest looks flimsy. What is in its natural, pure state, looks faded. The great square [i.e., the square of the earth itself, indefinitely wide] has no corners. . . . What is most full seems empty, yet its use is inexhaustible; . . . . the greatest skill seems like clumsiness; the greatest eloquence seems like stuttering."[22]

"He who knows the male, yet cleaves to the female, becomes like a ravine for the world. . . . He who knows the white, yet cleaves to the black, becomes the standard by which all things are tested. . . . He who knows glory, yet clings to ignominy, becomes like a valley for the world."[23] This aphorism illustrates the extent to which any misogyny

[22]Fung, *History*, 184–5; slightly modified. [23]*Ibid.*, 185.

in the Chinese view is only apparent, and it confirms Gutkind's previously mentioned emphasis on the attitude of wife and mother toward life and Nature as distinguishing the Chinese outlook. The Taoist Sage is one in whom the Yin-pole is heavily charged, for it is through Yin that Yang obtains completion. An "intuitive" non-knowing (not to be confused with blank ignorance) and an expert non-activity (not to be confused with mere inaction) are his chief characteristics. He "rests in the revolving of nature" at the empty centre, the axle, of that axis of revolution which is the Tao itself. One with this Way of the Universe, he transcends all such distinctions as that of construction and destruction. "Clouds change and become rain. With regard to the rain, then, it may be said to have been constructed; with regard to the clouds, they may be said to have been destroyed. Each of these expressions, construction and destruction, is made from one angle of vision. From a limited point of view this is so; but from the point of view of the Tao, there is neither construction nor destruction, but interpenetration and oneness."[24]

The quiescence, tranquillity, and nescience of the Sage are thus the truest forms of activity, engagement, and knowledge. Acting with the very spontaneity of the Tao with which he is united, the Sage becomes the third member of the trinity of Earth, Heaven, and Man. The Sage or True Man "has a spiritual power which is in accord with Heaven and Earth, sheds a light like that of the sun and moon, proceeds in such orderly fashion as the four seasons; in his mastery of the good and bad issues he is like the manes and the gods. When he acts before Heaven, Heaven does not go counter to him; when he acts after Heaven, he serves the timeliness of Heaven's acts."[25]

Finally, to convey the Chinese recognition of the power of the Sage, we may quote the statement of Chuang-tse: "I know only that one must let the world live and grow; but I do not know that the world must still be put in order. Only by doing nothing does one provide quietness for the development of the true nature of man. Even if such a man conceals his innermost soul and does not direct his energies towards things that are outside himself . . . it is yet as if lightning and thunder emanate from him. How could the thought of putting the world in order occur to such a man?"[26]

The influence of this "myth of the Sage" has not been confined to scholars but has deeply affected and shaped the thought and action of the Chinese people generally. It is a typically superficial Western mis-

[24]Fung, *Spirit*, 68. [25]*Ibid.*, 101.
[26]Gutkind, *Revolution of Environment*, 191.

take to write it off as "blind fatalism." The Sage, we have seen, knows when to strike, when to "anticipate Heaven," as well as when to follow; and Heaven does not fail him. Our own crass and violent conception of activity, a compound of the ideal of record-breaking and the practice of a technological rape of Nature, is such as to blind us to the accuracy and solidity with which the Yin-Yang myth permits the integration of the rhythms of life into the encompassing rhythms of the cosmic process. It is much easier, as well as more flattering to ourselves, to call it fatalism than to admit its superior wisdom.

It may be that the difference between East and West lies in the fact that, for the Chinese, symbols are in the foreground, leading into the "backdrop" of perceived reality, whereas in the West the foreground is the perceived world, which disappears into a construction of abstract symbols; in consequence the Western mind challenges the reality of the perceived world, which is one way of saying that it aims to revise that world.[27] I should prefer to retain the distinction of the two main branches of signs made in an earlier essay and suggest that the Western mind dissolves the perceptual world into a tissue of scientific symptoms. Thus it has instituted that restlessly dynamic relation to the world which amounts to a programme of incessant and accelerating revolution. If it would never have occurred to the Chinese to set out to split the atom, for instance, this is because thought in their culture has been generally and traditionally symbolic, in the sense of the word previously defined. The expressive symbolism of Yin and Yang, serving as a buffer to absorb the dynamic of the subconscious forces of man, leads thought and action into the given world of Nature with a creative gracefulness, an effortless adaptation to periodicity, rhythm, and timing, the upshot of which is to leave man at one with Nature, rather than glaringly at odds and at cross-purposes with her.

[27]This is Gutkind's view.

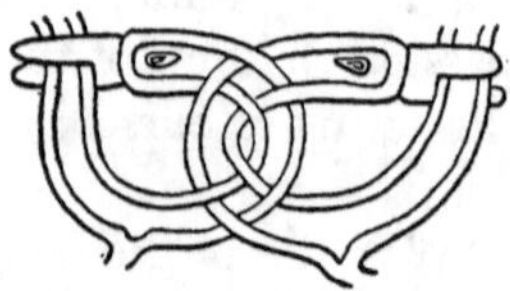

TIME LOST & REGAINED

MR. ELIOT is very exact in his language. When he calls his latest book of poems *Four Quartets* that is what he means. Now a quartet in music requires four instruments sounding together; in poetry, of course, only one line of sound at a time can be voiced. If these are called quartets, and not four solos, then, it means that they are not to be taken as four separate poems; as thought and memory may, they are to be held together in the mind in wholeness. But then you should have one quartet resulting: one instrument to each poem—say first and second violin, viola, 'cello, each successively playing its part unaccompanied, but collected in the mind. If it is four quartets and not four solos or one quartet, the conclusion, which is alarming, is that as you read each in turn, "Burnt Norton," "East Coker," "The Dry Salvages," and "Little Gidding," the three that you are not reading must be sounding in your mind at the same time, and sounding very nearly fully, to a unique and different result in each. A complexity faces us which calls for an almost unbearable effort of concentration: these poems could not be read as quartets on the first reading; on the fifth, perhaps they might for the first time be so read.

What will be attempted here is entirely by way of a commentary on the *Quartets*, so viewed. I shall try to fix a rough, simple, surely over-simplified structure, a kind of loom on which the complexities of exchange between the poems may be woven by yourselves, at your leisure.

Let us lay out the four poems first side by side and look at their titles. Burnt Norton is a country house in the Cotswolds with which, it seems, Eliot had no special ties or acquaintance. It is there simply for its garden, which typifies Eden, the beginning; and the beginning is of course the place to start. The last quartet, "Little Gidding," ends by returning to it, "And the children in the apple-tree . . . heard, half-heard . . . Between two waves of the sea."

The predominant element in "Burnt Norton" is air; though it is mentioned only twice by name as "vibrant air" and "faded air," the poem is full of crossing eyebeams, bird-calls, laughter, a cloud shadow, a shaft of sunlight, footfalls, a draughty church, echoes, the wind over London's gloomy hills; after all you do not have to be talking about air all the time to achieve an aerial quality. Each of the other quartets has its element too. And it confirms what was said about a quartet as such that the first section of the first has a passage showing the coming together and association of all four elements, while the last quartet, in verses on the death of air, earth, fire, and water, shows them dissolving into dissociation.

Since the first passage is an almost explicit reference to creation, we may begin with it. At the centre of the garden, indeed at the centre of a kind of formal, circularly disposed box-tree labyrinth or maze, we reach a dry, that is air-filled pool.

> Dry the pool, dry concrete, brown edged,
> And the pool was filled with water out of sunlight,
> And the lotos rose, quietly, quietly,
> The surface glittered out of heart of light,
> And they were behind us, reflected in the pool.
> Then a cloud passed, and the pool was empty.

The mysterious "they" may be our first parents, or what is nearly the same thing, angelic beings: we are told only that

> There they were, dignified, invisible,
> Moving without pressure, over the dead leaves. . . .

Concrete is earth; the pool water; sunlight, glitter, heart of light are fire; the cloud passing and the empty pool are air; the lotos, that is the water-lily, rooted in mud, growing through water, reaching to air with its leaves and blossoming, yellow or white, with a flower which is sunlike and often serves as a symbol of the sun, the lotos then, wrought out of the mixture of all four, is the mysterious appearance of life in time, shown in a glimpse of creation itself, at the heart of the maze, in the garden.

East Coker is the village from which Eliot's own ancestors left for America. We are still dealing with origins, but narrowed, now, to the Eliot family. Its element is earth, though, as in the other quartets, the other elements make courteously subordinate appearances to remind us that other instruments than the one we are attending to are sounding also. There is dust, the dust of crumbled or crumbling houses; the turning of wood to ash and of ash to earth; an earth which is already "Bone of man and beast, cornstalk and leaf"; the rather gnome-like figures of dancing peasant forbears in the midsummer darkness, who withdraw at dawn into the dark under the hill—all show that earth dominates the poem. So does the clumping rhythm of "feet rising and falling" in the dance

Rustically solemn or in rustic laughter
Lifting heavy feet in clumsy shoes,
Earth feet, loam feet, lifted in country mirth
Mirth of those long since under earth
Nourishing the corn.

"The Dry Salvages" ("presumably *les trois sauvages*," three dangerous rocks off the coast of Massachusetts) is filled with reverberations of the ocean. Its element is water.

The sea howl
And the sea yelp, are different voices
Often together heard: the whine in the rigging,
The menace and caress of wave that breaks on water,
The distant rote in the granite teeth,
And the wailing warning from the approaching headland
Are all sea voices, and the heaving groaner
Rounded homewards, and the seagull:
And under the oppression of the silent fog
The tolling bell. . . .

There is also that "strong brown god" the river—the Mississippi, near which Eliot spent his childhood; the "sullen, untamed and intractable" river,

with its cargo of dead negroes, cows and chicken coops,
The bitter apple and the bite in the apple.

In this poem we narrow the matter of origins and ancestry still further, to the child, father to the man; Eliot's own past existence on this continent. Perhaps because the father to the man is now so dead and gone, the leading theme of this quartet is death, throughout.

With "Little Gidding" we return, as the poet did, to England, and finally reach a "present" as of, say, 1942; a highly detailed and vivid moment when the ageing poet, caught in the catastrophic events of our time, wanders, as air-raid warden in a bombing raid, among the seven gloomy hills of London.

In the uncertain hour before the morning
Near the ending of interminable night
At the recurrent end of the unending

After the dark dove with the flickering tongue
    Had passed below the horizon of his homing
    While the dead leaves still rattled on like tin
Over the asphalt where no other sound was
    Between three districts whence the smoke arose. . . .

No more distinguished from this London scene than was St. Louis from Boston in the previous poem, we are also shown Little Gidding itself, the quiet village where in the seventeenth century Nicholas Ferrar attempted to institute a new model of Christian living: something between life in the world, since the basis of the community was the Ferrar family of about thirty persons, and the monastic life, since they lived in strict observance of a religious rule, which however did not require celibacy.

In this last quartet fire predominates: the flaming glow of sunlight on ice-covered trees; tracer-bullets—the flickering tongue of the dark dove—the fires started by bombs: pentecostal fire, purgatorial, refining fire, the fire of sin, the fire of love, and finally the tongues of flame in-folded into a crowned knot of fire, "and the fire and the rose are one." This symbol fulfils in the rose what the lotos of "Burnt Norton" promised: it is a symbol of the incandescent absorption of time into eternity, and ends the last quartet.

By a series of progressive narrowings and sharpenings of focus, Eliot presents us with four inseparable sets of reflections on the mystery of time. The opening section of each quartet deals with one aspect of succession; the second sections concern time at a given moment; the third sections concern the "meantime," the duration of intervals, or call it time between; this is followed in the fourth section by a brief religious lyric, invocation, prayer, or hymn as you choose, addressed, in the order of the quartets, to God the Father, to the Son, to our Lady, and to the Holy Spirit. Appropriately upon this invocation each quartet concludes with a fifth section presenting an aspect of eternity-through-time, the permeation by the timeless of moment, interval and succession alike. Each quartet deals with these subjects in a manner roughly appropriate to its dominant theme, viz. in "Burnt Norton" to the theme of birth time, in "East Coker" to that of generation, in "The Dry Salvages" to the time of death and in "Little Gidding" to the future life.

For the reader's convenience a tabulated presentation of these points is given. We shall deal with the topics listed reading from left to right (the four first sections followed by the four second sections, etc.) instead of in the more usual (Chinese) fashion reading each poem vertically through from top to bottom. In this way we will have more chance of achieving what the title *Quartets* requires, viz., a collation of four meanings brought to bear simultaneously, in turn, on the theme of succession (the passage of time), the moment (time now), duration (the time between), and eternity-through-time.

But first a word to situate the main issues about time raised in the text. Time moves on, we say, advances, into the future, as an arrow into space away from us. But if so, we at once encounter another arrow coming in the opposite direction, toward us. For we also say the time draws near, approaches, and call the future *coming* time; this is a movement from futurity through presence into the past; it may be the real direction of flow, that of the river itself, against which our oars carry us up-stream, through the constant effort which is living.

It is possible to become so obsessed with this metaphor of the boat propelled against the current, that you can apprehend your inhalations as the swing of the oars momentarily above the surface, ahead into the current; and your next following exhalations as the sweep of the same oars, now immersed, in the direction of the current but at a greater velocity, so that their pressure drives the boat effectively up-stream. When, momentarily, we rest on our oars, or row slowly: when, as happens each night, the rhythm of our breathing slackens, the effort being partly suspended, we slip back, following the direction of oblivion, abdication, unconsciousness; with daybreak we resume the oars, and the task of forward motion once more; when at last the boat cracks and sinks, it and we are carried relentlessly into a past ever more remote and dark. The miracle of moving against the stream into the future is over; the future, into which we project persistence, reversibility, intelligibility, and predictability, in a word all the "preferential" values of truth and goodness which it is our effort to attain, abruptly ceases; we become, for the other rowers, simply one of the objects carried away by the stream, *past* them i.e. no longer joined with them in the up-stream course which is not so much the movement of time as our counter movement *against* it. The past is the "backward abysm" into which we project breakage, loss, dissolution, failure, and error. Time, no doubt, holds all things together, as the treacherous water-surface does the boats; but it also internally gnaws, wears, and disintegrates them by its noiseless friction—keel, hull, lungs, heart alike. It is endurance or lasting, as well as passage and disintegration, persistence as well as succession. Or say, with "East Coker," that it is *rhythm* that unifies these opposites, for rhythm is both the lasting of change and a change of the lasting. It is still true that we require two opposite

Burnt Norton	East Coker	The Dry Salvages	Little Gidding
Place: Eden Time: "in the beginning" Theme: birth Element: air	Place: Home of forbears Time: of seasons Theme: generation Element: earth	Place: St. Louis, Boston Time: the end of time Theme: death Element: water	Place: Little Gidding, London Time: Now (1942) and forever Theme: future life Element: fire
I: Time as succession, passage			
The time-arrow to the future immobilized by reason	Rhythm as instinctive union of change and permanence	The time-arrow moving into the past immobilized by passion	"Still" time resolves the opposite movements through devotion
II: Time at a "given" moment			
The *now* of the body and that of consciousness	The *now* of experience, and that of humility	The *now* of death: living backward	The *now* of union and revelation: re-enactment as rehearsal
III: "Meantime," interval or duration			
The interval of lost time, and that of emptied time	Duration as waiting: emptiness-plenitude	The interval of dying, voluntary or involuntary	Historical duration redeemed in Love
IV: Invocation			
Invocation of the Father: "Let Thy light shine upon us"	of the Son: "Heal us of our diseases"	of our Lady: "Be with us in the hour of death"	of the Holy Spirit: "Inflame us with celestial fire"
V: The Timeless through Time			
The always-now	The timeless pattern in change	Time redeemed in detachment and attachment	The "condition of complete simplicity"

directions, and that one, that of lasting, persistence, and endurance, as all three words reveal, is the forward direction of effort; the other, the direction of passage, attrition, interruption of continuity, is that of lapse and abandonment—"abdicative" Souriau justly terms it, where the first is actively "preferential."[1] Whatever may be the facts about physical time, this is how the problem it sets must be stated in and for consciousness: either keep rowing or drift back; and in the end we drift back anyway.

The destructive effect of this tension upon consciousness of the present is one recurrent theme of the *Quartets*. It is no solution to seek the immediacy of instinctive life, mindless of past and future alike; to be mindless is precisely to abdicate or drift back; the best that could be said for this remedy is what Part II of "East Coker" asserts: the ripeness of experience, the sureness of instinct provide only a "receipt for deceit"—the imposition of outworn patterns from the past upon new and unpredictable contingencies. The wisdom of experience is a compound of inertia and fear. Such an "instinctive" present, then, is still retrogressive, if less perceptibly so than in the case of complete abdication.

If the present cracks and disintegrates, it is because it has not sufficient weight and authenticity of its own to overcome the tension between these components, the preferential and abdicative. No doubt time is not pure irrationality, as those who drift backward, seeking oblivion in the false eternity of passion, suppose. If it were, it might not be such a fatal thing, perhaps, to abandon oneself to the stream, setting out "In Search of Time Past," i.e. of some previous present. But then neither is time pure intelligible order; to assume that it is, is to advance prematurely upon the future, and to court another kind of disaster, where the present is lost in the illusory eternity of the laws of nature and reason. The rationalized time of cinematics clearly shows what happens when this course is taken; its components are an endless straight line, and an evanescent point too small to be determined, the instant, which moves uniformly along it. This so-called present instant, gone before you could possibly find it, is the very symbol of absence, not of presence; and what is left, the continuous straight line, is all given at once; it represents that spurious rational eternity in terms of which it is thought that change has been explained, when it has really been explained away, showing that nothing has happened—the "eternity" referred to by Eddington, when he says that to predict the visibility of an eclipse in Cornwall on August 11, 1999, amounts to pre-

[1]Michel Souriau, *Le Temps* (Paris, 1937).

dicting that on that date gravitation will still be gravitation, and two and two will still be four.

The temptation to follow one of these arrows or the other is very great; and to follow either is to destroy the present; to live, in reason, in the future, or in passion in the past; on either alternative, time is arrested, assuming an illusory fixity whether it be that of irrational immobilization upon the past, or that of purely intelligible order from which the fact of change has been excluded.

Developing Souriau's suggestion, we might say that the "natural," i.e. vital, instinctive, solution is just to keep on vacillating briefly between the two; this is perhaps the core of our conscious experience of time—rhythmic alternance at different but mutually adjusted rates, those of systole and diastole, inhalation and exhalation, waking and sleeping, etc., between the preferential and the abdicative. But it is no true solution to emulate in this way the animal equanimity that arises from mere absence of foresight and aftersight: these things are our privilege, as well as our torment, and to suppress them in the name of living in the moment is neither to be really rid of them, nor to regain the lost present.

So far natural, or fallen humanity. If there is a fourth possibility, if time can be redeemed, it will not be through man's own aspirations and efforts to evade passage, which are necessarily abortive; it will be through the entry into time, at the moment, of a genuinely external consciousness other than his own; liberation from past and future alike (which is quite different from mindlessness about them) is

> something given
> And taken, in a lifetime's death in love,
> Ardour and selflessness and self-surrender.

This is the other main topic of the *Quartets*: the *given* moment of contact with the divine eternity; its *taking*, its expansion through submission to the will and love of God, till it covers not just the whole lifetime, but a past and future extending beyond those terminal points; not dissipating the now into past and future, but drawing past and future both into the now, where they are transformed in meaning and in act; the collaborative action, then, of man with God, under God, which allows the Apostle to speak of this redemption as a task, in the imperative: "Redeem the time."

And what of the image of the boats bearing up-stream? Images have a way of playing false, as this one already, no doubt, has done; I think redeemed time has however once before, at the close of *The Waste Land*, been presented by Eliot in something very like this image. In the three-fold invocation of the Deity on the last page of that poem, in the section where I take him to refer to the controlling action of the Holy Spirit "in whose will is our peace," he says:

the boat responded
Gaily, to the hand expert with sail and oar
The sea was calm, your heart would have responded
Gaily, when invited, beating obedient
To controlling hands.

The context is of course different—the sea, not the river, of time; and the point is rather different: to establish a parallel between the sailor managing the boat and the Spirit directing the sailor, in gaiety and peace whichever term of comparison you take; not in arid repressiveness, but according to that "law of liberty" which transcends the law. Shall we forcibly extract the sail from this passage and insert it in our image of the river? It would almost do. A steady, a gentle wind, a force external to the muscles and joints of the rower, but capable of being inserted into his predicament by one who raises the sail with which his boat is after all equipped, should he see fit to use it; a force in no sense bound within the banks of the river, nor subject to its direction of flow; a force from that omnipresent ocean of air that touches all the successive points of the moving stream at once—with such an enlargement, our image of time is at once transformed. The navigator is not freed from time, for that is to be only when his body is committed to the stream and his conscious soul leaves it. He is freed from the future and the past; carried up the broad river by the sail, not without tacking, not without recourse to the oars, for the spirit blows where is listeth; but yet liberated from past and future alike, from backward-turning nostalgia and remorse as from anticipatory impatience and anxiety, from the tyranny of the "abdicative" and that of the "preferential" alike.

"Burnt Norton" opens[2] with the linear time of scientific determinism, really a supplementary dimension of space, any point in which is the equivalent of any other. "All time is unredeemable" on this view, freedom an illusion, "what might have been" a merely theoretical possibility: for science there never is and never has been a real alternative; which is a consequence of its attempt to immobilize change into a purely intelligible order, all of it simultaneously apprehensible to reason.

The contrary belief that alternatives are more than theoretical pre-

[2]Cf. William Blissett, "The Argument of T. S. Eliot's *Four Quartets*," *University of Toronto Quarterly*, XV (1946).

cipitates us at once into the garden, into the most momentous of all cases of "what might have been," if man had not fallen, that is, not chosen to lose contact with his origins, chosen to centre his will upon himself instead of on God.

A thrush—an air-bird if the awkward phrase may be overlooked, for the petrel of "East Coker" and the gull of "The Dry Salvages" are water-birds, and the dove of "Little Gidding," like all birds with irridescent colouring, is a fire-bird—a thrush leads us into the garden.

> Quick said the bird, find them, find them,
> Round the corner. Through the first gate,
> Into our first world, shall we follow
> The deception of the thrush! Into our first world.
> There they were, dignified, invisible,
> Moving without pressure, over the dead leaves. . . .

When the vision of the lotos in the pool at the heart of the maze dissolves, the bird again cries

> Go, said the bird, for the leaves were full of children,
> Hidden excitedly, containing laughter.
> Go, go, go, said the bird: human kind
> Cannot bear very much reality.

With choice, with the reality of alternatives restored, succession too is restored. The illusion of a rational, eternally fixed, unredeemable course of things begins to fade, and the predicament of passage resumes its true, its almost unbearable prominence; the section closes with a dull and flat repetition of the view of succession with which it began, the one that is intended to mask the predicament, by making time seem unredeemable.

What are these disparate themes, the myth of Eden, and the severely scientific notion of succession, the Newtonian "independent variable," doing together here? Let me put it this way. Of the various accounts of the disorder caused by our first parents' choice, several of which are given in Genesis, and all of which are ways of saying that man chose himself instead of God as his centre, one is to say that they yielded to inordinate curiosity. Perhaps the poet intends that the "independent variable," still an essential instrument for satisfying man's curiosity about nature, prolongs, extends, and continues to express that wrong choice. Or put it this way: anything which encourages us to continue to make ourselves the centre leads us further away from the true centre; curiosity is the path that only leads away from Eden, and even curiosity about Eden leads us still farther away from it. Or this way: our temporal experience is just what it is because of the abdicative component in our nature; not just abdication of the effort of reason, but oblivion of our true centre; the continued victory in us of curiosity over devotion, or the fact that we have made, and continue to make, the wrong choices.

"East Coker" presents succession in a different manner: not the inhuman simultaneous straight line of geometry with its ever-just-absent present, but the reassuring time of the calendar where days have some thickness, and weeks more, and where every sort of period duly makes its return; the sequence of seasons, then, a seasonable time, because rhythmic, one in which recurrent pattern confers a duration upon the successive, and a successiveness upon duration, so that

> there is a time for building
> And a time for living and for generation
> And a time for the wind to break the loosened pane. . . .

The quartet itself accordingly revolves once upon itself, between the words "In my beginning is my end," with which it opens, and "In my end is my beginning," with which the last section closes.

The scene, as befits an earth-poem, is dark, "dark in the afternoon"; later, still darker at the summer midnight. It is placed in a field near "the deep lane" whose deepness is again spoken of and reinforced:

> the deep lane insists on the direction
> Into the village. . . .

It is deep, it insists, for it is the impress of the immemorial rhythm of traffic to and from East Coker.

The midnight spectacle is that of the rhythmic ancestral dance of generation, to the sound of

> the music
> Of the weak pipe and the little drum. . . .

See them dancing around the bonfire—and appropriately, the poet begins to introduce antiquated phraseology from the *Gouvernour* of Thomas Elyot, his forbear—

> see them dancing around the bonfire
> The association of man and woman
> In daunsinge, signifying matrimonie—
> A dignified and commodious sacrament.
> Two and two, necessarye coniunction,
> Holding eche other by the hand or the arm
> Whiche betokeneth concorde . . . :
> Keeping time,
> Keeping the rhythm in their dancing

As in their living in the living seasons
The time of the seasons and the constellations
The time of milking and the time of harvest
The time of the coupling of man and woman
And that of beasts.

"Keeping" is very nearly the key word to this section, and gives a strong new meaning to succession. For if time can be *kept* it is not the perpetual evanescence of a point too small to be seized along a line which is actually all there at once. Though to say that time can be kept is not, or not yet, to say that it can be redeemed.

The conclusion of Part V shows the old, moving on, as they should, in exploration

Through the dark cold and the empty desolation,
The wave cry, the wind cry, the vast waters
Of the petrel and the porpoise. In my end is my beginning.

This not only joins "East Coker" with its own beginning, but announces the theme of "The Dry Salvages," namely, time "in my end," death, and the retrospective view of succession from the point where it stops; a difficult vantage point, rarely taken, though presumably to be taken at least once by each of us. It is the view of time's flow which, we said, might best correspond with the facts, a movement from future into past.

The images for time used here—river, ocean, and ground swell—are not abstract and linear as in "Burnt Norton," but dense and massive; not social and seasonable as in "East Coker," but menacing and alien. We are shown a "time not our time": that of the implacable rager, destroyer, preserver only of wreckage, wastage, corpses, bones and abiding agony in man's heart—the brown god Death, who is at once river and ocean.

"The river is within us, the sea is all about us"; difficult images to combine, but evidently pointing to the immobilization of this flow that occurs with any abandonment to it. In this sense, though there seems to be a river, the "sea's lips," the "sea's jaws," the "sea's throat" are always where we are, and always waiting for us.

The tolling bell
Measures time not our time, rung by the unhurried
Ground swell, a time
Older than the time of chronometers, older
Than time counted by anxious worried women
Lying awake, calculating the future,
Trying to unweave, unwind, unravel

And piece together the past and the future,
Between midnight and dawn, when the past is all deception,
The future futureless, before the morning watch
When time stops and time is never ending;
And the ground swell, that is and was from the beginning,
Clangs
The bell.

This ground swell may have a sort of rhythm, like the seasonable time of "East Coker," but is not truly successive; it has no more direction or flow than the ocean itself. There is a simultaneity of death all about us. Death and destruction are always now, just as the ocean is always there. If the river is within us, the ocean all about us, there only *seems* to be a river, a flow, and a direction; there *is* nothing but the directionless ground swell and the clanging bell; shall we say that succession thus viewed is swallowed up in the apparent eternity of the pattern of death, horror of which drives men back, in passion not in reason, in the attempt to recapture, perpetuate, and eternalize an earlier past,

to ring the bell backward . . .
To summon the spectre of a Rose,

as "Little Gidding" says. If so, the perspective is a dangerous one to take: a sure way of lapsing into the arms of that very horror which precipitates the flight.

"Now and in England": after the time of birth, of coupling, of death, "Little Gidding," the most explicitly religious of the *Quartets*, presents succession redeemed; still time, though—and "still" time, in that sense of stillness of which the last section of "Burnt Norton" speaks:

as a Chinese jar still
Moves perpetually in its stillness.

Time, through devotion and prayer, becomes the vehicle of the timeless, without ceasing to manifest succession. The church at Little Gidding had been a sort of fountainhead from which the whole life of the community derived nourishment; even those activities such as the cultivation of the soil and bookbinding by which it supported itself emanated from this centre and were held in the closest relationship to it. Perpetual prayer was maintained there, the night being divided into watches. It is a place which, therefore, is always the same, whoever you are, whenever you visit it, and for whatever reason.

If you came this way,
Taking any route, starting from anywhere,
At any time or at any season,

It would always be the same: you would have to put off
Sense and notion. You are not here to verify,
Instruct yourself, or inform curiosity
Or carry report. You are here to kneel
Where prayer has been valid. And prayer is more
Than an order of words, the conscious occupation
Of the praying mind, or the sound of the voice praying.
And what the dead had no speech for, when living,
They can tell you, being dead: the communication
Of the dead is tongued with fire beyond the language of
the living.
Here, the intersection of the timeless moment
Is England and nowhere. Never and always.

If the dead in such a holy place communicate as burningly as this with the living at prayer, succession is not quite what we naturally suppose it to be, the endless disappearance of the present into nothingness.

To emphasize the paradoxical nature of this "still" time, the scene is set in "midwinter spring," a season of its own, not provided for in the cycle, "not in time's covenant," "not in the scheme of generation,"

Suspended in time, between pole and tropic,
When the short day is brightest, with frost and fire,
The brief sun flames the ice, . . .
A glare that is blindness in the early afternoon.
And glow more intense than blaze of branch, or brazier,
Stirs the dumb spirit: no wind, but pentecostal fire
In the dark time of the year. Between melting and freezing
The soul's sap quivers.

If winter-spring is achieved by the brief union of the sun's blaze and a certain degree of cold—not too great, for the scene becomes "sodden towards sundown"—where, the poet wonders, is the midwinter-summer, "the unimaginable Zero summer," in which the highest pitch of frost and fire are one, the opposition, of timelessness and succession, quite overcome?

And now the *moment*. The second section of each quartet opens with a lyric passage before going on to this theme. In "Burnt Norton," this lyric presents the body as a kind of microcosm recapitulating in

The dance along the artery
The circulation of the lymph

the whole past of organic life. This passage establishes in terms of interlocking physical, biological, and physiological rhythms what he is about to call

the enchainment of past and future
Woven in the weakness of the changing body. . . .

Then abruptly we find ourselves

> At the still point of the turning world. Neither flesh nor fleshless;
> Neither from nor towards; at the still point, there the dance is,
> But neither arrest nor movement. And do not call it fixity,
> Where past and future are gathered. Neither movement from
> nor towards,
> Neither ascent nor decline. Except for the point, the still point,
> There would be no dance, and there is only the dance.

Freed, we cannot say for how long, for that would be to place it in time, freed, however, from inner compulsion and outer compulsion, from action, that is, and passion, from living ahead or living backward, the moment, the now, becomes fully actual, gathering past and future into itself. True, such a *now* is not right out of time; otherwise it would be an unbearable ecstasy (or horror).

> . . . the enchainment of past and future
> Woven in the weakness of the changing body,
> Protects mankind from heaven and damnation
> Which flesh cannot endure.

This enchainment, however, is at the instinctive or biological level, that of the organic darkness within us, of unconscious memory; in the sense of this enchainment, then,

> Time past and time future
> Allow but a little consciousness.
> To be conscious is not to be in time
> But only in time can the moment in the rose-garden. . . .
> Be remembered; involved with past and future.
> Only through time time is conquered.

The moment of rapt consciousness already points to, though it is not yet, the redemption of time. It already reveals that, if time is to be conquered, it will be *through* the moment, and through involving and implicating it with past and future. It is to be redeemed, as well, then, through the humble agency of "the weakness of the changing body."

Part II of "East Coker," the poem of season and rhythm, starts with another cosmic lyric in which the ageing world is depicted as moving towards chaos and

> that destructive fire
> Which burns before the ice-cap reigns,

and a new cosmic cycle begins. There follows an examination of another sort of *now*, the ripe moment of serene autumnal age and rich experience. This, we have already seen, is declared a fraud. It is not the dance "at the still point of the turning world." It is routine, caution (and therefore fear), "deliberate hebetude"; abdicative, we said, though not so conspicuously that instinct, experience, and ripeness are without their advocates. But, in reality,

> the pattern is new in every moment
> And every moment is a new and shocking
> Valuation of all we have been.

There is no security as the ripe but not yet rotting wish us to believe,

> In the middle, not only in the middle of the way
> But all the way, in a dark wood, in a bramble,
> On the edge of a grimpen, where is no secure foothold,
> And menaced by monsters, fancy lights,
> Risking enchantment.

Only humility is wise, not instinct, not experience, ripeness, or age; only humility, which is endless, can restore us to our present, to the moment, or *now*, when we cease to be afraid of fear

> of possession,
> Of belonging to another, or to others, or to God.

Part II of "The Dry Salvages" starts with a rather longer lyric on death and that omnipresent dying, wasting, fading, passing away signified by the calamitous annunciation of the clanging sea-bell. There is *no end* to decay; withering flowers never come to a point where they stop withering. Endless, apparently eternal, seems to be the unchanging law of decay and death.

Yet if in reality death has been swallowed up in life, this triumph originated at the moment when one, a woman, prayed: "Lord, be it unto me according to Thy will." There is no end to it other than this moment. No end of it, says Eliot:

> There is no end of it, the voiceless wailing,
> No end to the withering of withered flowers,
> To the movement of pain that is painless and motionless,
> To the drift of the sea and the drifting wreckage,
> The bone's prayer to Death its God. Only the hardly,
> barely prayable
> Prayer of the one Annunciation.

The prayer of bone, the only thing in us to last and outlast the flowing centuries, is a prayer to Death, its God. So is the whole abdicative direction, with its fixation upon the omnipresence, omnipotence, and endlessness of death. Prayer to Death is only to be countered by prayer to The Living God.

After this important lyric passage, the poet turns to re-examine the meaning of the moment. There is further comment on what the previous quartet required: that the moment should be implicated and involved with past and future; here, as befits the "backward" perspective of the poem, it is the past, and specially the relation of the present to earlier "moments," whether of ecstasy or agony, that is taken under consideration. For moments of agony too are permanent, "with such permanence as time has," especially the agony of others, for our own becomes

covered by the currents of action,
But the torment of others remains an experience
Unqualified, unworn by subsequent attrition.
People change, and smile: but the agony abides.

The agony is like the Dry Salvages themselves, "ragged rock in the restless waters,"

On a halcyon day it is merely a monument,
In navigable weather it is always a seamark
To lay a course by: but in the sombre season
Or the sudden fury, is what it always was.

Whether in happiness or agony the "moment" always carries with it a sudden illumination of the meaning of the past; it reforms, takes on a new pattern; ceases to be just a chronicle or sequence of events, not even a development; for that view of the past is a partial truth that encourages you to disown, rather than to redeem it. The task of age, which "Little Gidding" will call "re-enactment," is not that of repudiating the past, but that of restoring, even reviving it in the present *as* present, with its significance; it could be called the task of making the past one's own. And not just

the experience of one life only
But of many generations—not forgetting
Something that is probably quite ineffable:
The backward look behind the assurance
Of recorded history, the backward half-look
Over the shoulder,

the half-look we took in the garden of Burnt Norton. This is not the abdicative attempt to perpetuate and eternalize a past, whereby our present is emptied of all significance. On the contrary, it is the drawing of the past into the present, in-folding it into the illuminated *now*, in an understanding which goes beyond happiness and agony alike.

"Little Gidding," Part II, begins with the lyric on the dissolution and "death" of earth, air, fire, and water, a fitting apocalyptic prelude to the sharply detailed moment of the air-raid scene that follows. Here the theme is the future—the poet's future—old age and the possibility of redeeming it afforded by the illumination of this moment, and as is proper, he adopts the first person.

> Between three districts whence the smoke arose
> I met one walking, loitering and hurried
> As if blown towards me like the metal leaves
> Before the urban dawn wind unresisting.

In this moment of vision, the past has really come alive. There is no hindrance any longer to passage of

> the spirit unappeased and peregrine
> Between two worlds become much like each other,

and the familiar compound ghost, both intimate and unidentifiable, whose brown baked features would primarily seem to be those of Dante, but not in such a way as to exclude Milton, Crashaw, and other dead men too, draws the poet out of his ordinary routine self, momentarily and partially into that other world, so that the two are

> In concord at this intersection time
> Of meeting nowhere, no before and after,

and they can speak to each other.

> . . . I assumed a double part, and cried
> And heard another's voice cry: 'What! are *you* here?'
> Although we were not.

The poet, aware that he was still himself but also partly someone else, "And he a face still forming" finds that the words of salutation sufficed "To compel the recognition they preceded"; for with any actual invasion of eternity into time strange things happen to succession; the recognition precedes and causes the cry, yet follows and is produced by it.

The visionary figure turns the moment prophetically away from aftersight to foresight, to incorporate this moment with the coming remainder of the poet's life, i.e. his old age (and age has been the concern of this section in the two preceding quartets). It is indeed a communication "tongued with fire beyond the language of the living" that we overhear.

> 'Let me disclose the gifts reserved for age
> To set a crown upon your lifetime's effort.
> First, the cold friction of expiring sense
> Without enchantment, offering no promise

But bitter tastelessness of shadow fruit
As body and soul begin to fall asunder.
Second, the conscious impotence of rage
At human folly, and the laceration
Of laughter at what ceases to amuse.
And last, the rending pain of re-enactment
Of all that you have done, and been; the shame
Of motives late revealed, and the awareness
Of things ill done and done to others' harm
Which once you took for exercise of virtue.
Then fools' approval stings, and honour stains.
From wrong to wrong the exasperated spirit
Proceeds, unless restored by that refining fire
Where you must move in measure, like a dancer.'
The day was breaking. In the disfigured street
He left me, with a kind of valediction,
And faded on the blowing of the horn.

The meaning of the future, like that of the past, is only to be found when it is drawn, in-folded, into the dedicated moment; the moment of humility, surrender, prayer, and the penitential fire where you must move in measure, like the dancer at the still point of the turning world. Consciousness, like the organism, has its law of return; its beginning turns up at its end, and age *necessarily* goes through the movement of re-enactment; a meaningless repetition which merely exasperates consciousness and leads it from wrong to wrong, except on this one redeeming condition; but, on this condition, re-enactment is both revival and rehearsal: both past and future are gathered into it and given their meaning.

Part III of "Burnt Norton" is as far from Eden as you can fall—into the London underground, a wasteland,

Time before and time after
In a dim light: neither daylight . . .
Nor darkness . . .
Neither plenitude nor vacancy. Only a flicker
Over the strained time-ridden faces
Distracted from distraction by distraction. . . .

The life of the underground is the epitome of *lost* time, time made up entirely of intervals between departure and arrival. Apathy, indifference, distraction, mark it. It is not, however, a truly empty life, any more than it is truly filled; it is filled with empty day-dreams, with appetites, and does not know the meaning of either filled eagerness or empty deprivation. Call this interval the interval of appetency, or of indifference, or of disaffection, or of the Fall.

In contrast, either of the ways of fullness or emptying, the mystic's positive or negative path, the way of the affirmation of images of the divine or that of their denial, is salutary and realistic; both ways, moreover, agree,

> not in movement
> But abstention from movement; while the world moves
> In appetency, on its metalled ways
> Of time past and time future.

Appetency, which is self-will, fatally implies loss of the present, life lived either in past or in future, or more probably on both rails at once, life moving, no, not moving, but *being* moved along senselessly, with no real present and therefore no effective duration.

Part III of "East Coker" starts with this unreal duration again. Here the train in the tube has stopped between stations,

> And the conversation rises and slowly fades into silence
> And you see behind every face the mental emptiness deepen
> Leaving only the growing terror of nothing to think about,

for life lived in times that are no longer or not yet ours has no meaning. Then, in the tradition of Western mysticism (which takes on the whole, the negative way), and almost in the exact words of St. John of the Cross, Eliot presents the remedy of true emptying, ignorance, deprivation, and dispossession.

> In order to arrive at what you are not
> You must go through the way in which you are not.

This is that real *waiting* of which man alone of all creatures is capable: not distracted from distraction by distraction, but waiting with a patience indistinguishable from humility, a patience which redeems the interval, as humility redeemed the moment; for "the faith and the love and the hope are all in the waiting." Such true emptiness becomes, or is the same as, fullness:

> I said to my soul, be still, and let the dark come upon you
> Which shall be the darkness of God. . . .
> So the darkness shall be the light, and the stillness the dancing. . . .
> The laughter in the garden, echoed ecstasy
> Not lost, but requiring, pointing to the agony
> Of death and birth.

Part III of "The Dry Salvages" also has its interval,

> When the train starts, and the passengers are settled
> To fruit, periodicals and business letters
> (And those who saw them off have left the platform)

Their faces relax from grief into relief,
To the sleepy rhythm of a hundred hours.

Death, the theme of this whole quartet, is here handed out in small change, not in a lump sum. The travellers never arrive at the terminus because they are not the same people that left the station: dying and being reborn in each instant of change, they have, we said, no effective duration: they themselves do not endure, to have one. They need not, watching the rails slide together behind them, think "the past is finished" for there is no true past to a being who is never the same for two moments together; nor, watching the ocean furrow widen behind the liner, need they think "the future is before us" (for someone else will arrive at the docks). Here, in this interval "between the hither and the farther shore," then, consider only this one truth:

'on whatever sphere of being
The mind of a man may be intent
At the time of death'—that is the one action
(And the time of death is every moment)
Which shall fructify in the lives of others.

This "time of death" is something other than the constant expiry and renewal, vacillation between the abdicative and the preferential we called it, which fills the interval of disaffection with meaningless change; for it is not involuntary, and through it the interval becomes the interval of waiting. The ecstasy of the garden, lost in the Fall, yet "Not lost, but requiring, pointing to the agony Of death and birth," requires that you should go through the way in which you *are not*, the way of death to self-will, in order to arrive at what you are not. To make each moment such a death, keeping the mind intent on that sphere of being which is appropriate to dying, is both to empty the interval and to fill it—to empty it of self and fill it with God; and to produce true fruit in the lives of others. Though, since self-will takes the noblest, most treacherous disguises, precisely in the desire to be of help to others, and then perhaps hurts and harms them most, we are warned

And do not think of the fruit of action.
Fare forward.

This, travellers, is your real destination: always here, always now, always with the same requirement. The redeemed interval, in which every moment is such an emptying and filling, is the interval of true waiting.

Part III of "Little Gidding" gives a very explicit statement of the issues involved in the "meantime," now expanded into the duration of a lifetime, or even the historical period, the seventeenth century of Little Gidding, or our own.

> There are three conditions which often look alike
> Yet differ completely, flourish in the same hedgerow:
> Attachment to self and to things and to persons, detachment
> From self and from things and from persons; and, growing
>   between them, indifference

which, however easily mistaken for either (and especially perhaps for detachment), yet differs radically from both; it is a dead thing between two lives, or more ambiguously, a nettle neither dead nor living, between two blossoms. True attachment, true detachment, moreover, play into one another. Love, any love, love of country for example,

> Begins as attachment to our own field of action
> And comes to find that action of little importance
> Though never indifferent.

To "redeem the time," on the public, national scale of history, as on the scale of individual existence, is to overcome indifference, the product of appetency and disaffection, with love, in its twin manifestations of attachment and detachment—"not less of love but expanding Of love beyond desire." Such redeemed time is freedom: liberation from the past, from the sin of old factions and the routine of old national policies; more important, or just as important, it is liberation from the future too. Eliot does not specify in what respects, but we might conjecture that they would include impatient regimentation in the name of a better world, and anxious destructiveness in the name of the fact that the world is no better than it is.

At any rate the nation in which love is expanded beyond desire is alone free, alive, and sound. Mr. Blissett, in the paper noted above, takes it that the antagonists in seventeenth-century England, Charles, Strafford, Laud, Milton, and others, to whom the poem may glancingly refer, and who are declared to be "United in the strife which divided them," are here being considered in terms of the history of the Church of England. He is surely right and it is this love of that church, expanded beyond the desires which brought them into conflict, which secures that they collaborate, victors and victims alike, in a common end which none of them could foresee, a renewed and transfigured pattern of history. Yet Eliot would not make one compartment of ecclesiastical history and another of political or social history. The "expanding of love beyond desire" here is, in principle, applicable to every aspect of the seventeenth century, overflowing inevitably upon even the most bitter "secular" disputes. Now

These men, and those who opposed them
And those whom they opposed
Accept the constitution of silence
And are folded in a single party.

The section concludes accordingly, in the words of the Lady Julian of Norwich, with an expression of that Christian hope for history which requires us to *own* the past, and does not, like an unrealistic belief in inevitable progress, invite us to *disown* it:

And all shall be well and
All manner of thing shall be well
By the purification of the motive
In the ground of our beseeching.

Upon these third sections ensue the four lyrical invocations, each peculiarly appropriate to the character and content of its quartet.

That Part IV of "Burnt Norton" is an address to God the Father may seem to follow only by indirection from the fact that the three other places are so explicitly filled, and from the other fact that this quartet is preoccupied with creation and the Garden of Eden, and with time as the sequence of man's fall. Yet the concluding lines,

After the kingfisher's wing
Has answered light to light, and is silent, the light is still
At the still point of the turning world,

are capable of bearing such an interpretation; and the tone of the whole is not unlike that of some such supplication as "Let thy light shine upon us."

There can be no doubt concerning the Good Friday lyric of "East Coker." It begins with the passion and crucifixion of Love, and ends with his sacramental presence in the Eucharist. The "wounded surgeon" of the first stanza—that is Love himself, nailed to his cross—

The wounded surgeon plies the steel
That questions the distempered part;
Beneath the bleeding hands we feel
The sharp compassion of the healer's art
Resolving the enigma of the fever chart.

The terrifying surgical metaphor is continued in two stanzas which I take to refer to the church; there follows an obvious reference to the sacrament of penance, still cast in terms of our essential illness:

The chill ascends from feet to knees,
The fever sings in mental wires.
If to be warmed, then I must freeze
And quake in frigid purgatorial fires
Of which the flame is roses, and the smoke is briars.

The last stanza speaks of the Presence with the same sort of violence and directness. Here is the only medicine, the only true sustenance for us in our incurable illness:

The dripping blood our only drink,
The bloody flesh our only food:
In spite of which we like to think
That we are sound, substantial flesh and blood—
Again, in spite of that,

i.e. in spite of our inability to discriminate between the substantial and the insubstantial,

we call this Friday good.

"The Dry Salvages" has a prayer to the "Lady, whose shrine stands on the promontory," on the lines of the traditional theme, "pray for us now, and at the hour of our death." She is called, in Dante's words, "Figlia del tuo figlio"—daughter of thy son, i.e. of him through whom all things, including the Virgin Mary herself, were made. Thus again, through paradox, there is displayed the mysterious disturbance of the order of succession that takes place when any exchange is set up between the timeless and time.

"Little Gidding," having just shown how Love turns even discord to its own end, securing that

all shall be well and
All manner of thing shall be well

invokes the Spirit of Love in two stanzas on fire, the opposite fires of sin and of love; both are fire, yet they cannot be confused:

The dove descending breaks the air
With flame of incandescent terror
Of which the tongues declare
The one discharge from sin and error.
The only hope, or else despair
Lies in the choice of pyre or pyre—
To be redeemed from fire by fire.

Who then devised the torment? Love.
Love is the unfamiliar Name
Behind the hands that wove
The intolerable shirt of flame

Which human power cannot remove.
    We only live, only suspire
    Consumed by either fire or fire.

As is natural after such directly religious poems as these, the concluding section of each quartet goes on to deal with time redeemed, eternity-through-time, or call it boldly "Christian time." Eternity, though radically timeless, once, in the fullness of time, became Incarnate, and entered the temporal order.

"Burnt Norton" tries to formulate, in the poetic notion of "still time," what theology wrestles with as the "union of two natures," the divine and human in one Person.

Not the stillness of the violin, while the note lasts,
Not that only, but the co-existence,
Or say that the end precedes the beginning,
And the end and the beginning were always there. . . .

In a temporal, i.e. successive, order, it is only a pattern of motion that can be *always now*. Its detail will be movement, which involves desire, even temptation—and this is what makes it *now*; but the pattern embodied in the detail is set by timeless, unmoving Love—and that makes it *always* now.

These are lightly touched-in features of the traditional view of Incarnation. For example, when Love was in the desert, he was

        most attacked by voices of temptation,
The crying shadow in the funeral dance,
The loud lament of the disconsolate chimera.

Yet, though transitory,

Caught in the form of limitation
Between un-being and being,

he was in the beginning and *is always*. This is the true significance of those quick glimpses of heaven, still mediated by the same Love, to which the last lines of "Burnt Norton" recur:

Sudden in a shaft of sunlight
Even while the dust moves
There rises the hidden laughter
Of children in the foliage
Quick now, here, now, always—
Ridiculous the waste sad time
Stretching before and after.

It might be observed that the strong name, Love, occurs in the last section of each quartet; once along with "the Word," once also with "Incarnation." Except in "Little Gidding," which is almost the vertical counterpart of the line of meaning we are following horizontally, and except for one appearance in Part III of "East Coker," where "the faith and the love and the hope are all in the waiting" this name is not used anywhere else. "Little Gidding" expressly calls it "the unfamiliar Name."

In the last section of "East Coker" the Christian interval, time-being, or duration, is presented, at first casually and informally as the years between the two wars, and in terms of the poet's life in those years—a series of wholly new starts leading to different and fresh kinds of failure; on the whole, though,

> perhaps neither gain nor loss.
> For us, there is only the trying. The rest is not our business.

The pattern of Love, it develops, while it may be glimpsed in the moment, requires much more than that:

> Not the intense moment
> Isolated, with no before and after,
> But a lifetime burning in every moment
> And not the lifetime of one man only. . . .

For it is a complex pattern, including other lives than our own, and the lives of the dead as well as those of the living; its designer and animator is Love; and, so long as we continue to explore, to be

> still and still moving
> Into another intensity
> For a further union, a deeper communion,

it continues to alter; it becomes stranger, the longer we live.

Thus the redemption of time in Love is a spreading of the incandescence of the Christian moment to cover a whole duration, a lifetime, even an age: for

> Love is most nearly itself
> When here and now cease to matter.

In the corresponding section of "The Dry Salvages" Eliot manages his theme more expertly and states his meaning more clearly than perhaps anywhere else. The three "conditions" are vividly contrasted; they are, first, the burning lifetime-in-Love of the saint; then the lives of "most of us"

> Who are only undefeated
> Because we have gone on trying;

and thirdly, the condition of the appetitive, which is that of indifference. As to the first, the "negative way," he says

to apprehend
The point of intersection of the timeless
With time, is an occupation for the saint—
No occupation either, but something given
And taken, in a lifetime's death in love,
Ardour and selflessness and self-surrender.

The saint's life is the "condition of detachment," the identity of frost and fire, the unimaginable zero summer of "Little Gidding," the life redeemed from fire by fire. The saint is one for whom it is always now, never any other time; for whom in the waiting, darkness has become light, the stillness the dancing, who moves in measure in that refining fire; the one who, "still and still moving Into another intensity," finds his true destination in a now which is always the moment of death and so brings fruit to the lives of others. He is the one, then, with whom this book is centrally preoccupied throughout.

The second condition, which we called the affirmative way, is the way of the affirmation of God's image in his creatures. It is the condition of genuine "Attachment to self and to things and to persons." It is permissible to point out, without prejudice to the fact that self-will is the cause and essence of man's fall, that there *is* a genuine attachment to self. As another poet has said, self-love too, "is either sacred or profane," and the gospel, if you read it with perspicacity, commands us to be as good to ourselves as to others. "Burnt Norton" says that the two ways are the same, at least in contrast to appetency. But the affirmative way is the more usual (in spite of its dangers, matched by possibly equal dangers on the other); it is that of most of us, "Who are only undefeated Because we have gone on trying"; though not many of us are aware that God's image is to be found in the men and women around us, that it is this image we love, that this is a "way" at all, or that we are taking it.

For most of us, there is only the unattended
Moment, the moment in and out of time, . . .
a shaft of sunlight,
The wild thyme unseen, or the winter lightning
Or the waterfall, or music heard so deeply
That it is not heard at all, but you are the music
While the music lasts. These are only hints and guesses,
Hints followed by guesses; and the rest
Is prayer, observance, discipline, thought and action.
The hint half-guessed, the gift half understood, is Incarnation.

Here, then is the alternative: it is between the loss of time and its redemption. Either a man takes one of the "two ways," or he lapses into the lost state of indifference, appetency, disaffection, and curiosity. Despite the misleading resemblances between the disaffected and the saint—for the phrase "death-in-life" is applicable to either—there is the whole distance of abdication and preference between them; for the dead-alive on the alternative of appetency, are the walking dead who have survived themselves, and no longer contain any principle of vitality; the death-in-life of the devoted is a perpetual refusal and surrender of self-will, and resultantly a supreme vitality and efficacy in action beside which all other manifestations of energy and power, however impressive at first sight, prove pallid. If we give this vitality its traditional name, eternal life in Love, it is to make clear how decisively the concluding sections of the quartets shift the locus of that distinction of abdicative and preferential with which we began. As we began with it, it was something like a distinction between inattentiveness and attention to the act of living; which led, we found, in the direction of oblivion, toward passion; and in the direction of attentiveness toward reason and morality. Now, with the rower's oars supplemented and in part replaced by a sail, the up-stream motion of our "race against time" is given a new significance. It is not intelligence and truth, not even morality and goodness, which redeem the time and regain the present for us: the truly preferential lies in a point outside the natural order, in the will of God; morality, science, art are to be preferred not in themselves, but in the measure that they can be willed by him; pursued not for our glorification but for his glory. They are conditionally, not unconditionally preferential, and this is the condition.

This fifth section of "The Dry Salvages" also depicts the "lost" state, with remorseless clarity, in terms of its coefficient of curiosity; to

> Describe the horoscope, haruspicate or scry,
> Observe disease in signatures, evoke
> Biography from the wrinkles of the palm
> And tragedy from fingers; release omens
> By sortilege, or tea leaves, riddle the inevitable
> With playing cards, fiddle with pentagrams
> Or barbituric acids, or dissect
> The recurrent image into pre-conscious terrors—

these are the familiar drugs of those with an absent present, who are driven in curiosity to search past and future

> To explore the womb, or tomb, or dreams:

the womb if they live backward in passion in a past that is no longer alive; the tomb if they live ahead, in reason in a future not yet real;

dreams if they try to grasp a present which dissolves at a touch into its intrinsic nothingness. It is the previous diagnosis over again, but very sharply stated.

Driven by demonic powers, those in this condition have in them no proper source of movement: they are acted through rather than act. Those in either detachment or attachment are, through Incarnation, freed both from past and from future: freed from the womb and the tomb and so most certainly from dreams; they alone can act; for here, completely in the case of the saint, intermittently in the case of most of us

> the impossible union
> Of spheres of existence is actual,
> Here the past and future
> Are conquered, and reconciled, ...
> And right action is freedom
> From past and future also.

The concluding section of the last quartet is by way of a coda to the whole work, in whichever order its parts are read. It allows the poem to end musically in a series of echoes—"What we call the beginning is often the end"—"the end is where we start from"—"History is now and England"—"With the drawing of this Love and voice of this Calling"—which draw together the various established meanings without making any essential addition. At its very close we find ourselves, however, back in the garden of Burnt Norton; a new description of Christian time is added ("a condition of complete simplicity") and the book ends with the magnificent symbol of the burning rose—the product of foresight carried to its ultimate pitch in the effort to envisage the consummation of time and creation, as the lotos of "Burnt Norton" was the product of an extreme effort of aftersight directed upon their origination:

> the children in the apple-tree
> Not known, because not looked for
> But heard, half-heard, in the stillness
> Between two waves of the sea.
> Quick now, here, now, always—
> A condition of complete simplicity
> (Costing not less than everything)
> And all shall be well and
> All manner of thing shall be well
> When the tongues of flame are in-folded
> Into the crowned knot of fire
> And the fire and the rose are one.

Since we started with the difficulty placed upon the reader by the perplexing title, *Four Quartets*, we might end with the far greater difficulty, the impossibility, implied in their writing. "Burnt Norton" was written in 1935. What are we to say: that it was written as a solo, became a duet in 1940 with "East Coker," a trio in 1941 with "The Dry Salvages," and at last a quartet in 1942 with the writing of "Little Gidding"? If so, it never really was a quartet. How could it become a quartet if it were not written as one to begin with? It must remain, as it was written, a solo, the only one in the book; "East Coker" will be its only duet, "The Dry Salvages" its only trio, and "Little Gidding" alone a quartet. Let us say, as is reasonable, that a certain scheme and disposition of five sections was laid down in 1935, and that from the first this framework called for supplementation by three other poems, and that in view of the ways in which the main themes were to be presented in these subsequent developments of the pattern, "Burnt Norton" from the first took account of its own not yet actually written counterpoint. The fact remains, however, that the Eliot of 1935 could not possibly have foreseen the splendours and terrors of 1942 that were to make "Little Gidding" the crown of the whole work. The contingencies of a dreadful moment of world-history, you will say, filled the blank in for him. But to call it a blank is to prejudge the whole question. If "Little Gidding" must in some sense be present, in 1935, at the birth of "Burnt Norton" for the latter to be really a quartet, is it sufficient to say that it was present as a certain number of modifications of the abstract notions of succession, the moment, the meantime, and eternity? Did we not say that for one poem to be actually *a quartet* the other three must sound simultaneously in it, in the completest possible manner? And is the full meaning of "Little Gidding" separable from those contingent events through which it is conveyed? I think not. Then what had not happened yet precipitated and compelled an event which it followed years later? Perhaps: though not of course in the technically absurd sense of saying that "Little Gidding" was *written* before it was written. At least let me suggest, in the spirit of the *Four Quartets*, that a pattern laid down in humility in a "moment in and out of time" in 1935, kept waiting in stillness and patience until 1942, could turn out actually to have *been always*, before the beginning and after the end of the writing. Hazardous assertions, certainly; and to any such suggestion I would expect the author to reply "For us there is only the trying; the rest is not our business." Yet the doctrine of time's redemption which the *Four Quartets* expound in incomparable poetry, may, for all that, be confirmed in the very tissue of its verses.

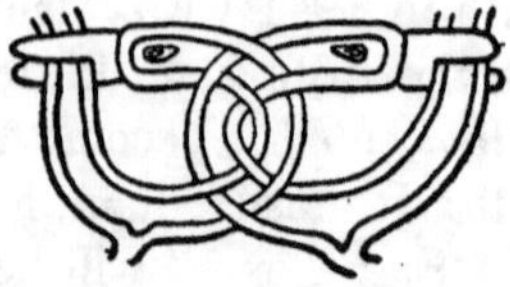

THE GROUP OF SEVEN: A RETROSPECT

AS it is now twenty years[1] since Lawren Harris, Arthur Lismer, J. E. H. MacDonald, J. W. Beatty, and others first startled Toronto with a show of pictures which seemed to defy all tradition and break with the whole past, it seems worth while to attempt an impartial stock-taking, to assess the movement and its probable influence, and to try to formulate in abstract language its central aesthetic achievement.

Externally, that is in terms of public opinion, the movement has run through the curve of vicissitudes which characterizes all important innovations: initial vituperation, of a violence and crudity which would be incredible, were it not for the evidence of the old newspaper files; contemptuous hostility; good-natured indifference; increasing enthusiasm; patriotic pride; until recently (sure sign of success) the rumour arises that the New Movement has fulfilled its promise and become a thing of the past, that we know just what to expect from its members and get it.

Negatively, the movement has achieved the extermination of the tradition which dominated the opening of the century, so that it is impossible for a young painter starting today (or even for an intelligent amateur) to reckon without "the group"; even those who disagree with the mood or technique of the new school are bound to start with them, in order to give their disagreement point, to find something of their own.

More positively, the achievement of these twenty years has been to provide Canadian painting with a tradition which is believed to be its

[1]This essay was first published in 1933.

own—that is with self-confidence, the conviction of being indigenous to itself. And in consequence the educational effect of the group, direct or indirect, has been of great importance for the future. The influence of all its leading members is evident even in such an independent group as the "Art Students' League" of younger artists, but of them all it is Lismer who deserves most of posterity for the patient devotion with which he has given himself to the task of preparing the future through all available channels of advice, guidance, public lecture, or exhibition. At present his interesting methods of instruction are drawing most significant results from a group of six hundred school children who work at the Toronto Art Gallery on Saturday mornings.

When we turn from the external symptoms of achievement to what is after all the important thing, the inner nature of what has been achieved, the spiritual fact, attitude, revelation, or whatever it is called, which has been the inner strength of the school, we find little agreement, indeed very little to go on. The artists themselves, probably rightly, have largely refrained from explaining what they were doing, being too busy doing it. At most, in the heat of controversy one finds politico-geographical terms such as "Canadian Art," "Canadianism," "The Canadian North," or Lawren Harris's "The North" bandied back and forth, denied, or asserted to characterize the new movement in its essence. In the heat of controversy the use of terms intelligible to the public precisely because they are not art terms served a useful purpose in drawing attention to the fact that Canada now harboured eminent painters of her own doing excitingly original work; but the fact remains that the language of politics or geography is as unsuited as that of arithmetic to formulate the essence of an art. Terms like Egyptian, Greek, Italian, Canadian when used in art are devices for classifying facts, and nothing more; they do not explain or account for the inspiration of a single great work. Thus, in a word, the great Greek sculptors did not produce immortal works merely because they were Greeks, certainly not because they were trying to be Greek, but because they had something to say. And what they had to say allows of abstract formulation only in the language of aesthetics.

Actually, like most well-meant propaganda in a good cause, this talk of Canadianism has created myths which stand in the way of a proper appreciation of the movement. Take the case of that great, and in some ways solitary genius, Tom Thomson. The public has eagerly seized him and built up a myth about him. He has become a national, even a political, symbol, even a symbol of our recent emergence from political tutelage. For here, against a general background of effete academies, especially the Royal Academy, arises a true earth-born artist, untouched by the past, untutored and unspoiled, who depicts Canada in an idiom which is genuinely Canadian, who brings the fire down from heaven in a new land and founds a flourishing native school. It is a curious revenge of facts upon this quasi-political legend that its originators ingenuously take the universal success of the Canadian pictures at Wembley as the climax of their little drama.

Certainly Thomson is amazing, and there is nearly enough truth in the above account to let it pass, but not quite enough. If you examine his early work when first as a member of the commercial art firm of Grip, Ltd. he tried his hand at painting the woods, you feel indeed that Thomson is there, but enveloped as it were in a cocoon; moreover, in these large, flat, decorative, rather poster-like, rather flamboyant canvases there is nothing to lead you to expect the cocoon to break. Compare this with the work of his brief maturity, before his lamentably early death in 1917; everything in these intensely felt, luminous, admirably organized, admirably restrained and economical pictures speaks of what he has learned; in the interval he had come in contact with MacDonald, Harris, Lismer, A. Y. Jackson, and through them with the whole of contemporary painting and with the past. For all these men had studied in Europe, all of them show influences of the vital traditions now at work in the world of art. Jackson's delicate and tender colouring, for example, is an individual expression of the influence at work in Morrice, and by him derived from the French. One is often reminded, when confronted with the luminosity of Harris's paintings, and the finish of his forms, of similar qualities in, say, Ingres. And who can observe the deliberately rhythmized hills and clouds of Lismer, or Jackson, without recalling Van Gogh and others whom he influenced, or who influenced him? Here, as everywhere else, scrutiny reveals that true originality is never a break with tradition for the break's sake, but a transformation of the traditional, arising not from contemptuous ignorance but from sympathetic acquaintance with the whole past achievement of the race. Behind the Thomson legend we find a straightforward story of a man of genius springing into virile maturity through contact with the great traditions of Western painting, and, along with his companions, forging them to a new expressiveness; a scholar, rather than a mythical fire-bringer, not so much a founder as a "member in full standing," one who has much to take from as well as to give to his group. I avoid the term, except in my title, "Group of Seven," remembering Wordsworth's difficult wrestling with that number; but from the first the phenomenon has been a group phenomenon, maintaining over twenty years an informal corporate identity. It is precisely in such a grouping that individual achievement is likely to be most incalculable, that the individual is most likely to do better than he knows, since he works along unforeseen lines towards a goal which is not clearly defined in advance, but arises out of the common effort itself. In this sort of group you find marked individual differences in style, temper, and technique, along with that elusive thing, "a marked family resemblance."[2]

The "Canadian" or "Northernist" theory, then, forces its supporters to exaggerate the originality of our artists beyond what is plausible. Whatever point the theory possesses can be retained without transferring the antithesis between Canadian and British from politics, where it originated, to art, where it has little or no meaning; much clearness is gained by substituting the word "provincial" for the word "colonial" in these discussions. For the real antithesis is that of the metropolitan and the provincial, of the life lived at the artistic centre of interest and growth, and the life slept out on the periphery in passive acceptance of time-worn conventions; and England used to be as provincial as Canada. The transformation brought about there by Nash, Fry, Gill, Kennington, Nevinson, and others is, like our own movement, an abandonment of provincialism under metropolitan influences. Both are significant incidents in the rebirth of the art of painting in the West. Essentially, an art style is a universal spiritual fact, a mode of man's feeling toward his world, and as such is the property of no race or people, but of mankind, originating from and returning to rest in the collective effort of humanity, in the international sense. It follows that any definition, however tentative, of the essential contribution of this school of painting must be in properly aesthetic language.

We have to start with man's feeling toward his world, and the general principle that innovations in art are to be understood in terms of new technical conventions with their correlative new modes of sensitivity. It is unnecessary at this date to labour the point that imitation of nature, fidelity of copying, is not the painter's real aim. The old art history, conceived in terms of this prejudice, inevitably distorted the aesthetic facts, because it assumed that men had always wanted to paint like the nineteenth-century painters, but that they only gradually acquired the necessary skill. The new history denies this single constant direction of will, and assumes instead a constancy of ability, or what is roughly true, that at any stage men are able to do what they want to

[2]The Group of Seven is now one of twenty-eight. Owing to the recent organized activity of reactionary forces, it has been deemed advisable to dissolve the Group (but can you formally dissolve what has never been formally organized?) and merge it in this larger unit. This time the organization is explicit and official, which, superficially, is to be regretted; but the effect of this move is not likely to be any deadening conformity to a preconceived formula, but rather the reverse; the movement has proved more than once that it has the secret of growth. H. R. M.

do. It admits many divergent directions of the "form-will," none of which can be given absolute aesthetic superiority over the rest. Thus it recognizes the value of the abstract art of primitives and Negroes and reveals behind it their shyness, even dread, of the world of living nature with its menacing, protean lability. Or it shows behind the organically flowing line of Greek art a different mode of sensibility, a fusion of man and the world in which nature is felt to be essentially friendly, a thing to be accepted in every fugitive sinuosity of contour. Or in Gothic art abstraction, geometric formalism, reappears with a new meaning, as a sort of penance, a mortification of stone by which the world of nature may be caught up in the great drama of redemption, swept upward, elevated and transformed into super-nature. Interpreted in this way, each epoch of human vision is seen to have its own unique value, and to require measurement by its own measures; further, the vicissitudes of vision, and the fact that no age is content to see with the eyes of the past, can be understood once we realize that the whole emotional and intellectual life of a period determines what type of line or form the artist shall choose.

To attempt to situate the Canadian school in this series of vicissitudes is really to discuss a much broader movement, namely, the spearhead of advance in contemporary world art. And yet since aesthetic discussion is condemned to sweeping transitions from the extremely general to the extremely particular, we may even formulate our problem as follows: What is the specific feeling common to Thomson's "West Wind," Harris's "Above Lake Superior," Lismer's "Evening Silhouette," Jackson's "Winter, Georgian Bay," MacDonald's "Solemn Land," and Carmichael's "From the Heights"? Each has its individual qualities, ranging from the gentle lyricism of Jackson to the almost religious austerity of Harris, yet underlying is the "family resemblance"—a common mode of feeling toward nature which should permit of at least tentative formulation.

Of the three most general attitudes toward nature, hostility, indifference, and acceptance, it is obviously the last which marks these landscapes. But not simply by virtue of their being landscapes; the depiction of a certain type of subject-matter guarantees nothing, one way or the other, about the artist's point of view, and many a modern landscape evidences an indifference to nature as complete as that of the industrialist, who can only see the world as something to exploit.

Yet these painters, and the wider school to which they belong, do not achieve a synthesis or immediate identification of the human and the natural: they are dualists, in the sense in which the Greeks, with their direct insight into, and identification of themselves with, the unstable and flowing forms of nature, were *not* dualists; lines, forms, and masses here are architectural, stable, formalized; abstract, rather than organic.

Partly under the influence of what Winckelmann and others conceived to be the Greek spirit, partly inspired by Rousseau's sentimental return to nature, and partly by inheritance of the Renaissance tradition of naturalism, nineteenth-century painting had attempted a re-identification of man and nature. But alas, the Greek miracle was no longer possible. The attempted union proved largely sterile. It is possible to account for this sterility in terms of the influences just adduced: the romantic misinterpretation of the Greeks, the romantic flight into the past (e.g. Pre-Raphaelitism), the romantic sentimentalism of Nature-worship. But it seems to go nearer the heart of the matter if we say that Romanticism conceives the union of man and nature in terms of the obscure promptings of animal vitality, at the expense of what is distinctively human, that is, intelligence and reason. Romanticism takes this union as fundamentally biological, and trusts it to work itself out through oracular utterance inspired by that instinctive, vital, even vegetal make-up which man shares in common with the rest of creation. The consequence is that order, the specifically human contribution of intelligence, is neglected, or disdained; and since order is the source and bearer of all values, it is no wonder that Romantic "nature" strikes us today as thin and poor.

For the most remarkable characteristic of the present age is its renewed interest in order, and what is still more significant, its sense of alternatives, its faith in the fertility of order. The nineteenth century took order in most of its forms at second hand, either accepting it, like Euclid's geometry, as a dull business on which the last word had been said, or romantically and ineffectually revolting against it. But the last word had not been said, even by Euclid; and—following the lead of the metageometers—musicians and painters, sculptors and writers initiated a series of revolutions in art which combine to make the present one of the most stirring and creative periods in world history. In each art in turn it was discovered that the reigning postulates of order and laws of form constituted only one of the total set of possible conventions, each of which has just as much right to be developed, and each of which contains radically new possibilities of beauty. This was not a revolt against order, but a widening of the idea of order itself.

Given this revived faith in abstract order, and this vigorous sense of its possibilities, what will the contemporary painter's feeling toward nature be? Certainly no "Back-to-Nature" sentimentalism. Our artists are not turning to vegetables and rocks in search of wisdom. Nor are they seeking to avoid the problems of a scientific civilization (which are also problems of ordering) or trying to escape from dreariness to an imaginary world of facile compensations. Nowhere is the idea of art as a romantic dream more ludicrously inapplicable. What they are doing is to show us a world of nature which would be really fit to live with, not to exploit one which exists already about us, if we have eyes to see. They show us a nature which is not a romantic dream, or an inhuman force, or a superhuman divinity, or a subhuman mechanism, but one which is the precise counterpart, so to speak, of man's ordered and ordering mind. In their decorative stylization of forms and abstraction of line you look in vain for the Gothic "form-will" which moulds and compresses nature into super-natural vitality. Abstraction here, it is true, is still used to heighten or enhance nature, rather than to turn away from it; but it is enhanced only up to the level where it becomes human, namely, something with which we can recognize our essential kinship.

Nature here becomes something which we can approach with frank and loyal openness; no more cant ("Isn't Nature grand!"), no swooning, none of the exaggerated pretentiousness which is simply the obverse of the industrialist's complete contempt; instead, a straightforward male reliance and reliability, a companionable attitude of trust with its answering trustworthiness—this is the specific way in which the world order is felt by our artists. In this *order as felt*, that is, in the profound agitations of the intelligence and of the whole man and their pacification through an ordered pattern of forms, the contemporary man is able to experience something which, in its vigour and robustness, he finds precisely apposite to his needs.

Of technique in general only artists can discourse fruitfully. Yet of the technique correlative to this new mode of feeling toward nature it is possible to say something by appealing to the reader's own experience as an artist. Imagine, then, your hand holding a pencil, and somewhat detached from *you*—let us say you are absorbed in telephone conversation. If your mind is at rest, if you are pleased, if the tone of the organism is resilient, the chances are that the tip of the pencil will flow in easy curves, spirals and the like. But if the conversation upsets you, or moves you deeply, the character of the tracing will change; straight abrupt lines, brusque angles and changes of direction, and a relatively complicated geometrical maze will be likely to result. Here we have the two complementary technical poles, abstraction and empathy, in their simplest and barest expression. Here we have the organically flowing line and the geometrical, fixed line traced to their sources.

Now imagine that, instead of being traced at random, these lines are part of a conscious and deliberate work of art; put the intelligence and the whole man behind the hand, put the intelligence *into* the hand and its movements. The first, which was a Romantic line, an uncriticized improvisation at the behest of instinct, or of sheer organic vitality, now becomes the Greek line, still vital, flowing, organic—as in the Parthenon, where not a single line is straight—but yet penetrated with intelligible and intelligent architectural order. And the second, which was the primitive line, designed less to convey natural beauty than to express depth of feeling, implying, that is, conflict and dualism, becomes, when similarly suffused with intellect, the line characteristic of contemporary art at its best. Instead of turning away from nature, like the primitive line, it turns toward nature, attempting even to capture the changing loveliness, which attaches so naturally to organic forms, within its rigid network. But it always retains something of the underlying dualism; it is a line which originates from within, and goes outward to seek an object which it may raise to its own level of exalted feeling. It is a disturbed and disturbing line but, when controlled by intelligence and subordinated to a concern with order, capable of attaining a calm mastery over its own agitation that makes it classical, in a new sense of that much-tried word.[8]

Artists have always been among the really genuine innovators, to whom mankind owes the respect it pays. For what starts as a new emotional complexion, a novel mode of feeling, inevitably makes its way into moral, political, social, and even—though this is not often recognized—into intellectual life. The formula attempted here must then necessarily be defective, since it deals with a process which is still in happening, as if it were something completed and done. At the same time it is advanced with some confidence in the conviction that it can be readily modified to take account of the wide repercussions upon all phases of our national life which this art movement is certain to have in the next fifty or a hundred years. Further, at a time like the present, when people are beginning to look about them for something more solid than material goods, it is well to recognize who our true benefactors are, and to reflect upon what they have done for us.

[8]What appears here to be a sort of mythology of lines is simply metaphor, or concentrated statement. The word "line," namely, is a convenient abstraction representing also masses and volumes and their arrangement, illumination, colours and their interplay, in fact the whole formal pattern of the work of art. H. R. M.

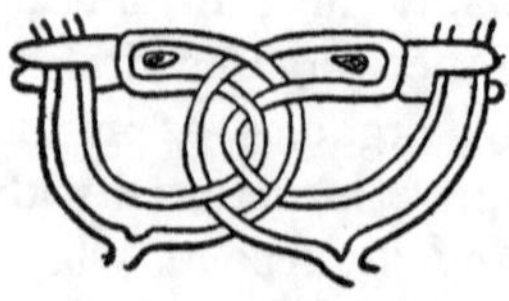

CONTEMPORARY AESTHETIC THEORY

THE scandalous confusion of contemporary aesthetic theory is not without its honourable side: it rises largely from the stubborn attempt to do justice to all the facts. A carpet, a joke, a triumphal arch, a procession, a gown, a garden, a psalm, an aeroplane, a fairy-tale, as well as a statue, painting, poem, or symphony, are proper objects for aesthetic reflection. How then can any theory be stretched to include them all without splitting, or, alternatively, becoming harmlessly inane?

Add that the vicissitudes of taste make any attempt to order this vast material precarious. There is only too attractive a variety of ways in which the historical material may be dealt with. Add also the variety of points of view, for the aesthetic of a creative artist is likely to differ essentially from that of a critic, or a spectator, or a philosopher with a general theory of value.

Finally there is the confusion arising from recurrent infidelity to the principle of the autonomy of art, which has been the cornerstone of aesthetic theory since Kant with a firm hand laid its foundations in the eighteenth century. From admitting that ideas are essential to a poem, usefulness to a building, representation to a painting, it is but a step to denying the existence of any specific and unique type of value in art, and making it an appendix to morals, the handmaid of truth, the servant of practice, or even *meretrix ecclesiae*. Accordingly, that step has been taken.

It is thus easy to see how eclecticism, that is, confused and incoherent thinking, is the rule in the subject. Hermann Nohl—to take an example of the avowed eclecticism which must be preferred to the unconscious variety—admits four coequal first principles of aesthetics: Expression, to cover arts like music which cannot be forced into the mould of representation; the Will to Reality, for those arts like painting which are representational and so cannot be made to fit the formula of mere rhythmic pattern; Beauty, to cover those arts of pure design which do not contain any hint of the revelation of unseen presences; and finally Symbolic Significance, for those arts like architecture, which do. The theory based on this interesting method of residues contains much that is valuable; yet it is very insecurely grounded. If the essential worth of art can consist here in the satisfaction of theoretical curiosity, there in that of religious needs, and so on, what good reason would there be for excluding other claimants with titles no more and no less well founded, such as pleasure, practical utility, eroticism, moral value, patriotic or social expediency?

It is not my purpose to reproduce—or aggravate—this chaos by attempting a complete catalogue of names or an exhaustive review of theories,[1] but rather to deal with the chief alternative types of theory, at the risk of some injustice, since few theories accurately conform to type. The clue to the maze will be the dialectic process whereby, if a theory is so wide as to include obviously non-aesthetic material, or so narrow as to be confined to a restricted group of arts, the opposite theory will be called up by the outraged facts to do vengeance for them.

We may start with a low-grade theory, that which unhesitatingly asserts that aesthetic value is just pleasure. Fechner, the hard-headed parent of laboratory aesthetics, who defines it as a branch of alghedonics, the psychological study of pleasure and unpleasure, is here in agreement with the most dilettante aesthete of the Wilde period or our own. A list including Groos, Guyau, Basch, Allen, Bell, Santayana, and Marshall, would contain both hard-headed and soft-headed specimens. The well-worn arguments against hedonism, which are as valid for aesthetics as they are for ethics or logic, need not be repeated. It is enough to note that the theory is too wide. Either pleasures are frankly admitted to be on a single level and to differ only quantitatively, and then with Guyau we shall have to include gastronomical, sexual, and indeed all other pleasures in our subject, or else recourse must be had to the old sophism of "higher" pleasures where a surreptitious appeal to standards other than pleasure is involved. H. R. Marshall, for in-

[1]In a Bibliography, appended to the article, are supplied the titles of some of the principal works in which these theories are advanced or summarized.

stance, distinguishes aesthetic from other pleasures as being *relevant*, i.e., projected into the object, not thought of as inhering in the subject, and as *common*, i.e., capable of being shared. Clearly it is only by supposing something peculiar in the objects of aesthetic experience that such distinctions, which are not contained in pleasure as such, can be established.

There can, in fact, be no reason to regard pleasure and delight in aesthetic experience as anything more than they are when any other human value is realized, viz., a concomitant or resultant of value, not its essence: a reflected glow, not the source of light.

In another way the theory is too narrow, since works of art with an ugly or tragic content do not please in any *prima facie* sense. Thus arise, dialectically, anti-dilettante theories (Tolstoy, Laurila) which assert that art is dead earnest, an affair of the utmost importance for humanity, and which tend to the opposite extreme of identifying art with morality.

The play theory of Groos, von Stein, Menzer, and others is a disguised form of the pleasure theory. Play, it asserts, is the art of children, and art the play of adults. Bentham's remark, then, can be improved on: not only is poetry no better than pushpin, it is pushpin. There is certainly a core of truth in the analogy between art and play, and Kant and Schiller who introduced it in modern times meant to say that art is completely disinterested with respect to useful ends. But it is only an analogy, and taken seriously breaks down in both its terms. For the child's play, pursued as if it were an end in itself, is largely a means to biological ends, the pre-exercise of functions that are to have serious importance. And, as Delacroix has acutely observed, adult art, which really is an end in itself, shows no trace of the indifference to material that characterizes play. In the realm of make-believe any object can stand for any other. The artist's passionate concern with every refractory knot or yielding grain of his material puts him in a different category from the player.

Even the sound element in this theory, its recognition that art and use lie along different dimensions of order and value, proceeds to arouse its dialectical antagonist in the "work" theory. Thus the "functionalism," professed by engineers or architects like Le Corbusier, directly equates beauty with fitness to perform a given function, i.e., with utility of the sort typified by the arrangement of parts in a machine. "A house," says Le Corbusier, "is a machine for habitation." This theory is probably a by-product of contemporary practice rather than its explanation. New forms appear in house-furnishing or architecture under pressure of a new mode of feeling; since a certain stark simplicity characterizes these forms, the theory of unadorned usefulness seems plausible. But function is relative to the total complex of styles and manners in any period, and, as a concern of cabinet-maker or architect, may fairly be taken as a constant, so that some other principle is required to explain fundamental differences in style. How functional, for instance, would one of our low, deep, thick-cushioned chairs be in an age of courtly etiquette and hoop-skirts?

Further, being tied down to the building arts, functionalism is too narrow. It is true there are profound affinities between, say, contemporary music and architecture, such as austerity and the avoidance of adventitious ornament; but to call this functionalist music, and to explain that each part is strictly constructed with a view to its function in the whole, is to be paid in words; it is to confuse the mathematical, formal sense of the word function with its biological meaning. And it should be clear that music as such—that is, exclusive of the National Anthem, the Red Flag, and the like—is and must be useless in any direct sense of the word. It is not good for anything, because it is good in itself.

The dialectical couple "useful-useless," which appears in one form as "work-play," may also appear as "real-unreal." Thus we find variants of the play or pleasure theory in which illusion, appearance, dream, or escape are supposed to constitute the value of the work of art. There are those like Vischer and K. Lange who hold that an immediate pleasure is yielded by a deliberate and conscious self-deception, issuing in a rapid oscillation between the illusion of reality and a sense of unreality. It is not at all clear why this situation should be pleasing rather than irritating, comic, perplexing, or downright agonizing. But having already rejected the pleasure principle, we need do no more than detach the kernel of truth in the illusion theory, which is that the work of art is isolated, islanded in stage or picture frame or their equivalent, in order to mark it off sharply from the surrounding physical reality. Physical objects necessarily refer beyond and outside themselves; the frame or pedestal is the artist's way of announcing that his work is not to be taken as a physical object, that it is self-contained. If to be real means to be ordered like a natural object in spatial, temporal, and causal relations to all other objects, then the work of art is certainly unreal.

In a second form the illusion theory finds pleasure-value arising indirectly through escape to a realm of facile compensation for the stern rebuffs of reality. Romantics everywhere, and to some extent the psychoanalysts, are chargeable with this view, though in justice to Freud it should be said he is expressly sceptical about it. For Professor De Witt Parker "a beautiful house is a dream of a house." The jargon of wish-fulfilment seems to me to throw less light and more genuine obscurity on art than any other. Art on this theory is simply self-magnification, and the cowardly retreat of a man who is too weak to face life: it realizes no genuine human value whatever. What can be admitted is that this day-dream theory correctly explains much bad art. If it must be a question of escape, surely true art enables us to escape from the intolerable, sterile day-dreaming of the romantic imagination back to the world of men.

In other words, illusion theories inevitably call up "objective" theories, which in turn (Alexander, Kallischer, Haeberlin) tend to the opposed extreme of endowing the work of art with the same order of reality that we attribute to physical objects, a view which is equally unacceptable. Here Kant's discovery of a special sense of the term subjectivity in art may be used to get out of the dilemma.

Kant started with the paradox that the aesthetic judgment while being subjective in the old sense, i.e., personal and private, yet claims universality. When I say that the *St. Matthew Passion* is better music than *William Tell*, the judgment expresses the way the objects affect me. But it is a true judgment to which everyone ought to agree, whether they do or not. Yet how can a judgment be both private and necessary, both true and incapable of proof? In answer, Kant was led to explore the experience of beauty and find in it a new kind of communication in which a certain sort of knowledge is passed from one person to another without employing the usual means of communication, namely concepts, at all. Sounds, for instance, as dealt with by science are translated into conceptual terms; the objective nature of sound expressed in numbers and measures can be learned from any text-book, even by a man born deaf. But the musician communicates in a different way: he can convey what a sound does to him, what he privately feels about it, by arranging it with other sounds in a pattern. What becomes objective, communicable, and public here is not the nature of sound, but the subjective experience itself. In other words, the term subjective here has lost its derogatory sense, and signifies what reveals the true nature of a subject or person; it no longer means unreal or lacking in objectivity, but refers us to an order of objectivity radically different from that of the physical object, namely the reality of other minds, and of our own, and of their states. When Kant stoutly maintained that there are no scientific geniuses, he meant no disparagement but simply that the great scientist is a man who succeeds in eliminating every trace of himself and his private states from his work; whereas the artistic genius makes the subjective itself objective, makes himself accessible to all, and for all time.

This would appear to be an important turning point not only in aesthetics, but in modern thought generally. After Descartes, and in spite of his dualism, confusion of the order of subjects with the order of physical objectivity was common; Descartes, in fact, did not work out the consequences of his dualism with sufficient rigour. In the interests of the new physics he was concerned to eliminate all anthropomorphism, all talk of purpose and ends, from the study of matter. He failed to bring out with sufficient distinctness the other side of his assertion; if it is a mistake to treat things as persons, it must be a mistake to treat persons as if they were things; or, if there is one sphere where anthropomorphism needs no apology, it is the study of man. The result of the one-sided direction imposed by Descartes on modern thought is that we still know less about minds and selves than medieval thinkers knew about matter. The methods of physics and mechanics confine us to the surface-play of personality and make its depths almost entirely inaccessible.

The *Einfühlung* or empathy theory of Lipps is a border-line case between objectivism and subjectivism, and may be regarded as something like a parody of the Kantian position outlined. Lipps calls aesthetic enjoyment "objectified self-enjoyment." The perception of a building, for example, sets up certain minute motor responses, it begins by changing the state of the body; but the next step is for us to change the object by endowing it with, projecting into it, the inner life, the organic rhythm whose actual locus is within us. It is what happens in our bodies which we read into the building when we call it light and airy or heavy and imposing, and so on accordingly with the other arts. Of special importance is the fact that for Lipps it is not pleasure or unpleasure, i.e., the feeling-tone, which matters in this act of empathetic insight, but the heightened inner life and self-activity. When an object enriches, extends, and strengthens my sense of life, it is aesthetically valuable.

But *Einfühlung* is expressly asserted to be a much wider phenomenon—indeed the general basis of our knowledge of other minds and their states—of which accordingly, aesthetic experience is a special case. In the final issue, then, it is the vitality of the architect which stimulates my sense of life. And yet in spite of all this Lipps's theory falls across the border into illusionism. "Feeling oneself into the object" means not that we feel the object as actually a revelation of someone else's conscious state, but that we feel *ourselves, as if* we were in the object. And again he says: "The other person is made by me out of myself." But it is clear that if the other centre of consciousness is simply a projection of my own, there is no real contact with it, no guarantee that it is anything more than a phantom. The life of others and (what is directly to our purpose) the life of a work of art remain a piece of psychological illusionism, the product of an "empathetic fallacy."

Illusionism and objectivism are both in part true and in part false. As regards the first, we have seen that art, judged from the point of view of the scientific order of objects, declares itself unreal by retreating within a frame. For the scientist, the historian, the police-magistrate, the events depicted in *Hamlet* simply do not occur; but who ever supposed them to be real in this sense? And by the same token, the proceedings of the scientific or demonstrative intellect are apt to appear absurdly inadequate, if not unreal, from within the other order, that of subjects or selves in their interrelation—for example, if we try to prove what we may know beyond conjecture, that a certain individual is frightened or in love or bored. Again, to the eye of a dramatist an event like a collective panic in real life will appear as unsubstantial as a nightmare, in spite of its physical and material objectivity; for he will sense the absence of anything but disorder, a chaos of constricted muscles and pounding hearts, an agitation without name or human semblance. From within the order of subjects it may be rightly claimed that it is the world of *Hamlet* which is real, that of science which is unreal.

Intellectualist and objectivist theories in turn are right in asserting that art reveals reality, but wrong in assimilating this reality to that of the physical object. Thus Witasek compares the aesthetic judgment with the judgment of perception and finds the sole difference in the fact that the former is concerned with an ideal object. Fiedler defines art as intuitive thought, the development of representations, in the same way that logical thought is the development of concepts. If you ask what this intuitive thought is about, he replies, "the real essence of things." Delacroix similarly says that in art man, liberated from practical aims, finds himself face to face with things as they really are. Croce of course regards artistic intuition as a theoretical activity, though taking place prior to the distinction of real and unreal.

Another group of objectivists, Hildebrand, Cornelius, and Wölfflin, are so influenced by scientific naturalism that they define painting as exposition for the eye. A cube, for instance, seen head on appears as a square. Through perspective and other devices painting aims at exhibiting objects in such a way that the beholder will have the completest possible representation of their true form: it renders thoroughly visible what is only partially so in random everyday perception. Against this pseudo-scientific objectivism is the fact that what from the point of view of physiological optics would be distortion may be, and often is, great painting. The laws of art simply are not the laws of nature, and spatial form in painting has a different basis from the theoretical elaboration of space-relations which underlies our knowledge of objects.

There remain anti-intellectualist objectivists such as Bergson, who define art in vague terms such as the revelation of human personality, intuition of life or of individual character. The knowledge which art conveys is in this definition properly restricted to the order of subjects. Further, in emphasizing its non-intellectual or intuitive character, they are asserting that this knowledge of the states of others is direct, not mediated.

But granting this, they are open to the sweeping objection, which is the final objection to the miscellaneous theories included under this topic, that they all commit the error of confusing aesthetic value with truth value. Knowledge is power, and art (as Plato knew) is also power, but that can be no reason for subordinating either of them to practical purposes; in fact they rapidly lose their specific values if you do. In exactly the same way, though art does yield basic knowledge of the order of subjects or selves, it is not as knowledge or truth, but in some other specifically aesthetic way, not yet determined, that it is actually valued. I should say it is valuable as the actual experience of some human emotion. The only direct communication between subjects is the communication of feeling; and though this has weighty consequences for psychology or philosophy, it is not as having these consequences—i.e., not as knowledge—but directly as emotion felt that art is valued.

We thus reach the theory that the essence of art is the expression and communication of emotions. In modern form it originates with Kant, though it could be traced to Aristotle, especially in his theory of music, or to remarks of Plato in the *Laws, Symposium*, and *Timaeus*. Tolstoy, Volkelt, Hermann Cohen, Baensch, Odebrecht, Jonas Cohen, Ducasse, Bosanquet, Carritt, provide variants on this theme.

Croce fits into it only in the second instance; for his identification of expression with intuition, like other celebrated identifications, that of philosophy with history, or of aesthetics with general linguistics, is both arbitrary and indefensible. Intuition, we saw, was a preliminary form of knowledge; but if so, we must effect a disjunction between it and expression in the emotional sense, which is clearly not primarily theoretic at all. If in spite of this Croce, outside the covers of his *Estetica*, emphasizes the lyrical character of all art, and defines it as a feeling enclosed in the circle of a representation, this is simply the dialectical revenge by which the true sense of the term "expression" forces its way through a hard crust of resisting theory.

Another variant which we should reject is the "significant form" of Fry, Bell, and Read. When absolutely compelled to, but not otherwise, they explain that a significant form is one that arouses aesthetic emotion. It is significant, then, emotionally, and so far so good; but it is significant of and for only one unique *ad hoc* emotion which, like Witasek's *ästhetische Gefühl* or Sully's aesthetic sentiment, has nothing in common with feelings such as pity, fear, or love, emotions of real life. And if so, this phantom aesthetic emotion is impossible to distinguish from the dilettante's rapture—i.e., it is simply a synonym for pleasure.

At the same time formalism is an essential component of the emotion theory—if the whole range of human emotions be taken as the material to be formed. Pattern and rhythm are the categories or principles of order generating emotional value and emotional objectivity, just as in another dimension of order, space, time, and causation generate theoretic objectivity and value for knowledge. To establish this point we must examine a capital distinction made by Alain, Baensch, and others (and traceable in classical aesthetics to thinkers like Hegel and Aristotle), the distinction between what we may call "commotion" and emotion: between the crude physiological disturbance which is not art, though it is the indispensable material for art, and emotion as it exists when this agitation has been composed through being subjected to order in a pattern.

The chief objection to the emotion theory is that it is too wide. "The spontaneous involuntary expression of fear, anger or delight," says the Earl of Listowel, "is surely in itself neither beautiful nor artistic." And Moritz Geiger: "To allow feelings to stream forth in words, sounds and gestures, is not art, nor even a necessary feature of the artist's activity. What is necessary is rather the forming of material to an artistic pattern, of stone into a statue, of sounds to a melody, of bodily motions into a dance."

As applied to commotion all this is perfectly true. It is not art; it possesses no human value; it is not even expressive, as you see from the failure of psychology to go beyond the coarse discriminations of common sense in its attempt to classify emotions on a physiological basis, or from the fact that no face is less expressive than that of a man who has lost control of his features, or from the fact that nothing resembles the paroxysm of one passion more than the paroxysm of another. Commotion is a form of physiological bondage which weighs heavily on man's spirit, and rightly; and it is generally in vain that he seeks deliverance through taking thought, or through energetic willing. Thus we are in a position to see how emotion as a liberation from such bondage would contain its own worth. Such liberation occurs where the disintegrated body is restored to order through the agency of a formalized pattern of bodily motion, or dance—and all the arts may be traced to this source—whether it be the muscles of the arm, of the throat and chest, or of the whole body which execute the dance. It is through pattern that commotion becomes emotion, the primitive cry a song; agitation becomes composure through the agency of composition. If, as Geiger would have us, we hold the two terms, form and feeling, apart, nothing remains but composition—the dull academically correct song with no cry in it.

Thus there emerge two complementary truths which seem to throw a flood of light on our subject: Nothing which does not move us can be a work of art; Nothing which merely moves us can be a work of art. Pattern without commotion is arid; commotion without pattern is turgid. Fused, they reveal some form of human emotion, heighten, enlarge, extend, or clarify the possibilities of feeling.

The theory in question admits terms like initiation, understanding, discovery, and learning, so long as it is expressly recognized that intellectual initiation, understanding, etc., enter into the matter only in auxiliary and secondary respects. The human being is not born emotionally ready equipped, but has to learn to feel humanly, just as much as to think rationally or to act morally; and learning to feel is not the same as learning to think, though it is true that these functions are not exercised separately, and that thinking may have profound bearings upon feeling. Thus after a child attains the age of reason he will need different poetry and music than before. So too with the race: it may be the progress of the intellect which makes it impossible to feel as our own the emotions of an earlier age; but the fact remains that what is acquired in such a change is not an intellectual truth, not a thought-value, but a feeling-value, and it will be embodied not in philosophy or science, but in art.

This has the advantage of removing a paradox: that we rightly revere the great art of the past as unmatched, and that we rightly match ourselves with it. A man who, as Comte said, learns for the first time the true nature of grief by reading a poem two thousand years old, may be impelled to write a poem of his own because in no two ages does the same passion or emotion appear in identical form. We can learn what men felt in the past from their art; we can even feel it, but not as our own. Emotion strains forward towards the future as surely as knowledge or action does.

It may be of interest, in conclusion, to interpret a familiar document, the *Symposium* of Plato, in this sense. It is true that only one emotion, that of love, is envisaged here; but its importance and range are such that several thinkers, such as H. Cohen and Gentile, are prepared to regard it as the primary concern of aesthetic experience. Lucka, for another, says that any work of art is love become visible.

The Platonic Eros is the offspring of a divine father, Expediency, and a human mother, Poverty; he is thus perpetually in straits, indigent, and at the same time inexhaustibly resourceful and full of ruses. This means, first, that we should avoid confusing love, as a creative or demonic function, with the object loved. The function has none of the qualities of the object. Love is not lovely, but terrible—a terrible burden of fecundity, physical or spiritual. In itself it is indigence, privation, the absence of those values, such as beauty, which are found in the loved object. As we said of commotion, it is a positive dis-value, a form of bondage; tending blindly to overflow into expression, yet at the same time constituting the greatest single obstacle to expression.

Further, the indirectness and ingenuity displayed in artistic creation correspond well enough to the fertility of expedient through which the demon achieves his object, generation into beauty. Liberation from commotion comes through a doubly indirect process; not by acting on the commotion itself, but by shaping some physical object, which in turn, as we saw, means subjecting the disturbed body to a rhythmic order of motions or dance. Only through this expedient can agitation resolve itself into composure; only by this indirect process can minds be brought into direct communication; only through this ruse is actualized the saving grace of pattern, of which Plato wrote elsewhere, "The Muses have given us harmony as an ally of our soul in its efforts to reduce those disordered movements within us to order and unison."

The *Symposium* culminates in the picture of a progressive initiation in love, which necessarily follows from these dynamic premises. It seems to be an emotional development parallel to the growth of knowledge and science, but not to be confused with the latter. It is an increasing liberation from the bondage of commotion, which nevertheless remains a constant, the same primitive urge to creation. It is a progressive advance towards ever new and unsuspected depths of love. I may be mistaken, but I will suggest that if you were to pass from, say, Greek sculpture to the poetry of Dante and Petrarch, and then to the music of Bach, you would be exhibiting stages in just such a progressive initiation as Plato here has in mind.

Bibliography

ALAIN, *Système des beaux-arts* (1926).
——— *Vingt leçons sur les beaux-arts* (1931).
S. ALEXANDER, *Beauty and Other Forms of Value* (1933).
O. BAENSCH, "Kunst und Gefühl," *Logos*, XIII (1923).
V. BASCH, *La poétique de Schiller* (1911).
C. BELL, *Art* (1914).
H. BERGSON, *Laughter* (1911).
B. BOSANQUET, *Three Lectures on Aesthetic* (1915).
E. F. CARRITT, *The Theory of Beauty* (1914).
——— *What is Beauty?* (1932).
E. CASSIRER, *Kants Leben und Lehre* (1921), chap. VI.
H. COHEN, *Aesthetik des reinen Gefühls*, 2 vols. (1912).
B. CROCE, *Essence of Aesthetic* (1921).
H. DELACROIX, *Psychologie de l'art* (1927).
C. J. DUCASSE, *The Philosophy of Art* (1929).
R. FRY, *Vision and Design* (1920).
——— *Transformations* (1926).
M. GEIGER, *Zugänge zur Aesthetik* (1928).
G. GENTILE, *The Philosophy of Art* (1932).
K. GROOS, *Der Aestetische Genius* (1902).
J.-M. GUYAU, *Les problèmes de l'esthétique contemporaine* (1891).
T. LIPPS, *Aestetik*, 2 vols. (1903-6).
Lord LISTOWEL, *A Critical History of Modern Aesthetics* (1933).
H. R. MARSHALL, *The Beautiful* (1924).
H. NOHL, "Die Mehrseitige Funktion der Kunst," *Deutsche Vierteljahrschrift f. Lit.-u.-Geistesgeschichte* (1927).
R. ODEBRECHT, *Aestetik der Gegenwart* (1935).
DE WITT PARKER, *The Analysis of Art* (1926).
H. READ, *The Meaning of Art* (1931).
W. T. STACE, *The Meaning of Beauty* (1929).
S. WITASEK, *Grundzüge der allgemeinen Aesthetik* (1904).
H. WÖLFFLIN, *Principles of Art History* (1932).
W. WORRINGER, *Abstraktion und Einfühlung* (1907).

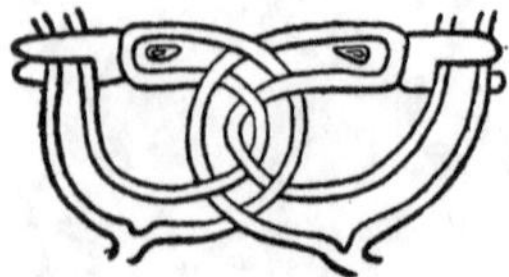

THE IDEA OF MAN

THE Delphic admonition "Know thyself" may still claim to be the clearest statement of the aim of philosophy; also, properly understood, of its distinctive subject-matter. No one has ever turned to philosophy without desiring, blindly or explicitly, to answer some form of the question, "Exactly who am I?" or, "Can my existence be given any sense?" And every philosophy is the ordering (subordination and superordination) among themselves of the various, multiple, partial answers a man gets to this question, whereby some sort of single and total answer is fashioned.

The first major point raised by this formulation concerns the relations of philosophy and science. The philosopher's concern with the physical universe is not, or should not be, strictly scientific, because it does not terminate upon the universe; the riddle of the sphinx is not for the philosopher the inner nature and structure of matter, the limits, if any, of the universe in space, or any puzzle of that order. Even in the deceptively childish conundrum current in antiquity, it will be remembered, the answer to the riddle no one could solve was, Man.

The fact is that there are two main sets of answers to the question "Who am I?" the first of which primarily concerns a man as a physical object, a body, while the second primarily concerns him as a conscious person. The issue raised is that of the distribution or redistribution of weight between these two sets of answers, between the natural sciences and what, for distinctness' sake, might be called the anthropomorphic disciplines: history, economics, law, political and social theory. One merit of the simple Delphic definition of philosophy is that it involves from the outset a shift in the usual distribution of weights and emphases between these two, putting us on guard against the excessive temporary prestige enjoyed by the natural sciences in our age; considerations derived from economic or social theory, from morals, aesthetics, or history, are as likely, perhaps more likely, to be relevant to this question than those derived from mechanics, chemistry, astronomy, physics, and the rest.

In an age like this such an assertion has to be defended. So let us look at the first set of answers. Mathematically regarded, a man will be assigned certain linear, plane, and stereometric coefficients, a number which we call his age, etc. Mechanical science determines his weight, specific gravity, and the like; chemistry and physiology such things as his metabolism, endocrine equilibrium, idiosyncrasies and allergic sensitiveness to certain substances; the biologist will specify, for instance, certain unit characteristics inherited according to Mendelian law. The psychologist as natural scientist, i.e. the experimental psychologist, will supply a psychograph, an I.Q., individual reaction-times. This list of answers, a very incomplete sample of what the individual would obtain if he were thoroughly gone over by a board of experts, will yet serve to indicate the common tendency and defect which, philosophically speaking, all answers from the natural sciences exhibit.

The tendency is inherent in the method of these sciences, that of registering coincidences between ruler and ruled, i.e. between some part of a graduated scale and the object measured. The assumption behind this method, in turn, is that the observer can largely, if not entirely, stand outside the observation, that he as a person is not implicated in it. We cannot here discuss the technical question of the allowance made for the subjective factor in the reading of scales; this "margin of error" itself is dealt with in a rigorously impersonal way. Nor is this the place to discuss the admitted breakdown of the assumption where events at the subatomic level are concerned. By and large it remains true that the elimination of the observer as a person is the condition of the natural sciences.

The defect common to this first set of answers is not inaccuracy. On the contrary, these numbers and pointer-readings do really and truly attach to me; even, if carried out in sufficient profusion, detail, and precision, they serve to specify me uniquely; they may also serve to indicate, within those limits which a prudent scepticism sets on taking the advice of experts, what things I should and should not attempt to do. Thus the defect is not irrelevance either, though, in the strict theory of scientific positivism by which "all is coincidence," it may sound like irrelevance for a scientist to say "these are the measurements, there is no explanation, no sense in asking why they should be just these and not other measurements." But then it is doubtful whether such positivism is more than a pose, useful for certain limited purposes. Certainly the history of science shows these sets of measurements as developing against a provisional background of physical, chemical, or biological theory which is always understood to be explanatory and thus relevant to the properly metaphysical question, what total idea I am to form of man and of myself as man. For each of these theoretical constructions throws light, in varying degree, on what it means to be in space and in time, to be a piece of matter, to be alive; and I am all these things.

No, the defect is not irrelevance, so much as minimal relevance. This may be illustrated in a kind of parable. If I say, "I want to know who I am," and someone, taking out a measuring tape, replies, "Just a minute and we'll see," it is the answer and not necessarily the question which is absurd. For all its numerical accuracy, the answer obtained would be relevant in only one situation, and that the "minimal" one, when I am suffering from amnesia and my metrical record is kept at headquarters. Accordingly, that construction, the one with the least human content, is forced upon my question. It is a case of an accurate answer being no answer at all. Presumably the giver retorts that my question is no question at all, but as I am indisputably aware that I am in full possession of my faculties, I am entitled to unload the burden of proof upon him.

When philosophy is variously asserted to begin with the sense of wonder, or of anguish, this is a way of pointing to its demand for a completely relevant answer. It is a way of saying that the question, "Can my existence be given any sense?" is not to be answered by the fiction that I can stand outside myself as an impartial second or third party, when in fact all my actions, emotions, and thoughts are implicated in the question itself and the attempt to answer it. More than this: it is the recognition that no other self can be properly dealt with in terms of this fiction either. Where what we are concerned with is "anthropos" himself, the scientific aversion to anthropomorphism is, to say the least of it, misplaced; what other shape than his own could be more appropriate to man? Declare purpose, feeling, striving, conviction, faith, and the like to be irrelevant and misleading factors which, in accordance with the assumption of the natural sciences, can and should be disregarded in the observer and denied of the object observed, and you make nonsense of even our most ordinary awareness of one another. The human order is one in which objective judgment is possible, but on condition that everything that makes it human should not be removed to begin with; the judgment is objective in regard to subjects, not to space and time, or electrons, or chemical compounds, or living cells and tissues. In this order the "scientific elimination of everything personal" leads not simply to reduced relevance, but to the disappearance of what you set out to observe. In law, economics, history, ethics, sociology, there are, as E. H. Carr has reminded us, "no facts existing independently of what anyone thinks of them." Who makes a statement in any of these fields, why he makes it, what he believes—all these must in some degree be appreciated if the statement is to make sense. What the judge thinks about the facts in a case at law is itself one of the facts in that case. The judgment passed by the economic expert on tariffs or the control of foreign exchange, if it helps determine national policy, is not a mere "opinion" but itself an important economic fact. And in each of the cases of this sort, which could be indefinitely multiplied, the strictly relevant question "Who is this man, anyway?" demands some sort of answer if we are to understand the facts in the case; which is to say that the attempt to eliminate the personal, both in the observer and in the person observed, is ultimately self-defeating.

To compare the answers the philosopher obtains from the natural sciences with those given in the "anthropomorphic disciplines" should make clear the superior relevance of the latter to the question, What idea am I to form of man, and of myself as man? The answers are, that I am an historical figure in so far as records of my acts survive, and even if they do not, an anonymous historical figure in so far as these acts will affect the life of those yet unborn; that I am a legal person, possessing a complex of rights and responsibilities enforcible in police-court or elsewhere; that I am a political subject, determined in my action by (and, in perhaps imperceptible ways, helping to determine) the organized network of power-relationships which marks my nation off from others; that I am a moral subject with duties toward myself and others, which are unique and therefore ineffable as far as legal codes are concerned; that I am an aesthetic subject—appreciator, critic, artist in my measure (i.e., that I am familiar with a certain range of human emotions, have myself a certain temperament, and am able in some degree to convey experience of this sort to others through a personally expressive fashioning of speech, gesture, intonation, through dramatic skill in the choice and arrangement of objects, acts, ideas, etc.); that I am economically subject to a productive and distributive network of relations between people and economic goods which I, both as a worker and as a consumer, affect in some measure; that I am a social being, a vague term often used to lump together all human relatedness whatsoever, but perhaps more narrowly specifiable as membership in all those subordinate groupings (from the family to the chess club) which cannot be regarded as primarily political or economic in their purpose; that I am a religious being, a statement which may be taken first, subjectively, to mean that as a man I am compelled to live by some myth as to the destiny of myself and my fellows which will be either one of the collectively elaborated myths which I find to hand (Atheism, Communism, Nazism, Islam, Buddhism, Christianity, etc.) or else a myth of private fabrication or some mixture of the two, or second, phenomenologically, that the world of human experience is necessarily articulated for every man, in one way or another, under the fundamental religious categories of the holy (the extraordinarily attractive and repulsive) and the profane or commonplace.

These answers, each of them momentously relevant, and together constituting the central human fact, show why philosophy cannot afford to "sell out" to the natural sciences—though, of course, it should not ignore them or treat them with contempt. But in our times the prestige of these sciences has kept philosophy in a sort of muscle-bound catalepsy before such questions as whether there is an external world or what the relation is between objects and *sensa*—questions which belong to the same sphere, and are therefore respectable, but which can largely be ignored in the taking of measurements, so that no natural science is seriously concerned with them. The relief which the recognition of the philosophical primacy of these central human facts brings with it, is no doubt the same (for in principle it is indifferent to the stage reached by natural science) as that reported of Socrates, when he turned from his earlier "hope in vortices, relative velocities, sockets, joints and the tension of sinews" to the conviction that the sense of life is to be sought in "Mind." Shaftesbury, among others, lays the emphasis adroitly in the right place when, discussing the current scientific dispute about the "simple ideas" of body and extension—today it might be the dispute whether matter is simply peculiarities in space-time or something more—he says: "The mathematicians are divided, and mechanics proceeds as well on one hypothesis as the other. My mind is concerned on neither side. . . . Philosopher, let me hear concerning what is of some moment to me: concerning life, what the right notion is, and what I am to stand to upon occasion; that I may not, when life seems retiring, cry vanity, and at the same time complain that life is short and passing. This is of some moment to me, this is worth my while. If I can come to nothing certain here, what is all the rest to me?"

Philosophy may then be viewed as an attempt to reach some comprehensive notion of man which, though recognizing the restricted relevance of the natural sciences, yet assigns the central and primary role to the "anthropomorphic" or humanistic disciplines. Innumerable considerations, inhibited by the current academic view of what philosophy ought to be, at once throng to the surface. Here we have room to deal summarily with only two points.

First of all, when we speak of objectivity in regard to the personal, to the order of subjects, a reference to some distinctive type of necessity is always implied. There are as many such specific types of necessity as there are disciplines in our second list. Indeed the very term "subject" in the sense of conscious self or person might be said to imply *subjection* to these various distinct but interlocking types of necessity, each embodied in some human institution, order, or network. Thus, for example, the legal obligation of completing work as contracted is one thing, and specifically different from the aesthetic compulsion whereby a rhythm or pattern must be completed in one way rather than another; and again from the moral duty of finishing a task in such a way as to be satisfied that one's best effort has been put into it; this from the economic necessity of terminating an enterprise with a credit balance; and all of them from the religious necessity of preparing in some way for the termination of life. In all these respects a reference to an objective, interpersonal network is required to define the subject himself.

This is to say that what I am is what others take me to be. But such a two-edged statement is easily misunderstood. It is true that we are none of us too sure what we are, that every man is blind about himself, unable to judge and estimate himself, that others, if he can get them to tell him, are in a better position to say what he is really like than he is himself. Superficially this might be held to justify me in sacrificing everything to create and nourish a favourable public self. The very derivation of the word "person" from the actor's mask, or the voice sounding through it, seems to give weight to such histrionic practice, suggesting the equivalence of "person" and "impersonation." But more profoundly, the statement "I am what others take me to be" may mean that the reputed or public self is not a disguise but an unmistakable revelation of private personality. It is through the assumed role that the actor's real quality, his ability or the reverse, is made publicly manifest. Nothing shapes the person more decisively than the attitudes he adopts and the roles he takes up in the various networks. When what began as a role ends in earnest, when the life grows into the attitude, personally characteristic and expressive being is achieved. Or again, if it is extremely trivial of me to seek others out with the intention of impressing them, nothing could well be more momentous than genuinely to hand myself over to another for consultation or advice, or in trust, or in any other way.

The same dialectic between the individual and the network arises in respect of freedom. Superficially freedom is revolt against necessity, insubordinate assertion of the self against the sovereignty of such aesthetic, legal, economic, religious, political, moral networks of relatedness as we have pointed to. But the assumption that the self means or is anything apart and in divorce from these necessities is one we have just seen grounds to question. The popular notion is a survival of the very primitive idea of "a little man inside the chest" (or the belly) whom the anatomist's scalpel ought to reveal, though we all know by now that it doesn't. Hume's destructive analysis of the idea of self is valuable as calling for a revision of that idea, a revision which he did not himself make. The error is to insist that if the self is real it must be in principle an observable entity, a datum. But everywhere we find that to give meaning to the self is possible only in reference to the various networks; that the self is not something given, a datum, but a problem or, better, a task—something which does not exist except as a task exists before it is completed—a task to be realized socially, in terms of common action and then only over a stretch of time. To confine the self to the present and look for it purely "within" is to transform the *me* into an *it* and thereby make sure that I shall be found missing. Everything thus points to a corresponding revision of the notion of freedom. True, and not illusory, freedom does not reject but accepts "subjection" in the senses outlined above. Just as it is through the various specific human networks that the quality of the person takes shape, so it is only through submission to the necessities governing each that free—and that is effective, and effectively personal—action is possible.

However inadequately, the general outline which philosophy would take in accordance with the Delphic formulation of its object has been sketched. The idea of man would be the networks of historical, economic, aesthetic, religious, ethical, legal, political, and social determination, not forgetting, in due subordination, those provided by the natural sciences: or rather perhaps it would be the network of these networks. I myself as man would be knowable as an answering complex, to be specified in terms of the "places" I occupy in these various series and networks, over a duration of time.

It remains to say something about interrelations. An argument about philosophy, such as this, which does not pretend to be an exposition of specific metaphysical content, must be satisfied to state that there are manifold tensions and conflicts between the various constitutive aspects and activities of man, which it is the object of philosophy to resolve; this is another way of stating the characteristic philosophical demand for completeness, total relevance, a comprehensive answer to its question. But there is only too attractive a variety of ways of evading this demand. Accordingly we find in the present, when philosophy has so largely failed to perform its proper task or to concentrate upon its proper object, a proliferation of pseudo-philosophies. Their common feature is a method of reduction whereby one human function is taken as substantive, constituting the "real" man, and the others are reduced to the status of adjectives, appearances, or disguises thereof. With Marx the "real" man is the worker; the real as opposed to the illusory or reputed self is the actual place a man occupies in the process of production—a view whose affinity with the capitalist reduction of persons to "hands" in industry should be noted, and is not an accident. Everything else, such as law, politics, morals, is an "ideological superstructure," a transposition into other and less proper terms of these basic economic realities. It is true that the Marxist protests that he does not deny all autonomy, all effective reality to these other things, but these protests are revealed as perfunctory, to say the least, by the basic tenet of Marxist orthodoxy that economic forces will blast their way through to their effects whatever the "superstructure" may be. With Freud, the "real" man is the sexual function, psychologically rather than biologically conceived—as libido, mechanism of repression, complex, transference, sublimation. Freud's excursions into art, mythology, or social theory (again, in spite of his followers' protests that it is not Freud but we who oversimplify) reveal the unmistakable *parti pris* of regarding everything else as a disguise for this pervasive sexuality. With the social relativism of various schools of anthropology since Durkheim, the "real" man is the tribe: the substantive terms are terms like society, collective representation, "folkways." Thinkers who do not recoil from the conclusion that even astronomy reveals more about folkways than it does about the heavens will be inclined to agree with M. Halbwachs that separate individuality is itself a tribal representation, authorized momentarily by the collective mind at a given stage of development. Why anyone should pay any attention to such views, which are, taken at the face value set by themselves, simply products and illustrations of the folkways of contemporary France or America, something thrown up now to be washed away later, is indeed another question. With the aestheticism which began with the Romantics, and still flourishes in some quarters, the "real" man is the artist: law, economics, morals, etc., must either be auxiliary to the prime object of converting life into a poem, a beautiful symphony, or they are obstacles to be destroyed. With a man like Hobbes who views everything *sub specie legis*—it is true Hobbes is long dead, but logical positivism is with us—all things else are sacrificed to the category of legal convention. And so on, though not indefinitely: there are only just so many startling "discoveries" about man to be made by this reductive procedure.

The point of calling them pseudo-philosophies is not to deny that each serves to throw light, if a somewhat fitful and treacherous light, on the subject of man. It is important to recognize that man *is* worker, or artist, or legal subject, and is such by his very essence. The point is rather to assert that any philosophy deserving the name must exhibit balance and sense of proportion enough to recognize that man is also essentially and necessarily all these things at once, and to do full justice to each constitutive activity and aspect of human nature, denying none. The philosopher will seek to resolve the tensions between one and another, but not by the easy and spectacular method of short-circuiting which we have just examined. On the contrary, to pursue the electrical metaphor, he will patiently preserve each separate current, leading them all into a common switchboard where the systematic ordering of forces in tension permits him to obtain effects which are at once elaborate, harmonious, and precise.

Thus, to conclude, the readiest sign of philosophical defect is that a theory sets out to explain away any one of the authentic constituents of human personality. On this score alone, philosophy should pay far more serious attention to religion than it does, for *prima facie* there is as much evidence that man is by nature a religious being as that he is by nature an artist or a worker. And in fact there is no more astonishing illustration of the havoc and intellectual chaos wrought by the proliferation of pseudo-philosophies than the situation with which the common man is now confronted in this field. He supposes himself to believe, along with multitudes of other men both primitive and civilized, in the actual existence of a Being, personal or superpersonal (but not subpersonal as a law or principle would be), who created and sustains all things. On every hand he finds it explained to him that he does not and cannot believe this; what he thinks he believes is really just the Oedipus complex, the continuous germ-plasm, or the life-force of the species; the economic process in so far as we fail to take hold of and control it, i.e., in so far as it seems mysterious and uncontrollable; the tribal sense of community, or "the sum of the social consciousness," and a variety of other things so bewilderingly various, so clearly incompatible with one another, as to be ludicrous. I imagine that the plain man who tried to survey this field would, however, be less amused than alarmed and repelled by what he found, and perhaps rightly so.

However, further discussion of such an issue would take us beyond the limits set in this paper. The concluding point of these reflections is that it is unphilosophical to restrict authentic human experience to any one of its ranges. To narrow it down, with the natural sciences, to the experience of external sense; with aestheticism, to the experience of aesthetic form; to confine it to moral experience or economic experience, or religious experience, or social experience or any other single distinctive type of conscious happening, is in the end to lower, impoverish, mutilate, and dehumanize the notion of man. Philosophy holds tenaciously to the variety of this experience in the whole wealth of its specific forms, and proceeds on the assumption that the most likely way of achieving a comprehensive and completely relevant answer to its question is to put upon this experience the highest, and not the lowest possible construction.

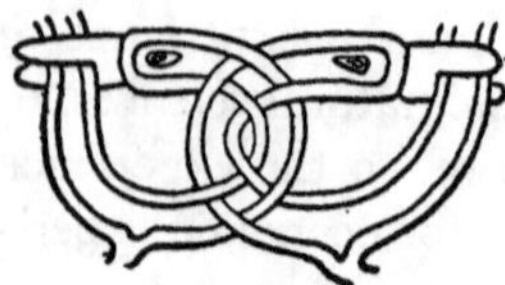

FIRST & SECOND SELF

IN Burckhardt's epoch-making book there is a remark to the effect that prior to the Renaissance "man's awareness both of himself and nature lay dreaming or half-awake beneath a veil. Man was conscious of himself only as a member of a race, people, party, family or corporation. . . . With the Renaissance man became a spiritual individual and recognized himself as such."

A single sentence from the *Phaedo*, or from the New Testament, might be considered sufficient to ruin and dislodge this startling generalization. When his friends ask the dying Socrates if he has any commands for them, he replies: "What I always say, nothing new; by taking care of yourselves you will oblige me and mine, whatever you do; but if you should neglect yourselves, even though you were to promise me much now, and earnestly, you will do no more good at all." Or, more succinctly still, there is the publican in the Christian parable: "God be merciful to me, a sinner."

The Greeks were evidently capable of taking seriously the admonition of the Delphic oracle, "Know thyself." And Christians thought of themselves as persons for whose saving God had been content to die on the cross—that is, in a fashion basically hostile to the sway of a collective consciousness of race, tribe, party and the rest. Yet for all that, it may be that Burckhardt's view points toward a truth; for it does not follow that the self-awareness of the "spiritual individual," as experienced by Greek or Christian, is identical with that of the Renaissance man. To put it bluntly, the self they were aware of may not have been the same self. It is tempting to suggest that they differed in fact as widely as "I" from "me."

The subject-self, indicated by the word "I," is like the organ of vision, which has to be invisible to itself just because it does the seeing; whereas the "me," the object-self, is like the reflection of the eye seen on a mirror surface. No doubt, if words like "object," "objective" properly apply to this reflection, it is because it *is* the eye (or the self) in reflection, a reliable image, for certain purposes, of the thing reflected. The colour of your eyes, which you cannot see, is actually that perceived in their reflected image, for example. It is only where the reflected image (or the "me") is supposed to be the full equivalent of the organ of vision (or the "I") that this objective attitude reveals its limitations by precipitating us into error: when, for instance, the eye seen on the mirror surface is mistaken for a living eye, returning our glance, for the eye in the mirror is, in fact, inactive and unseeing, a blind eye.

Let us term these two, "I" and "me," the first and second self, following the lead of George Macdonald when he remarked: "When people seek advice it is too often in the hope of finding the advisor side with their second familiar self instead of their awful first self of which they know so little." It will be maintained here that the specific "discovery" of the Renaissance, bequeathed by it to modern psychology, is that of the second or object self, rather than the discovery of the "spiritual individual as such." The legacy is one that only the so-called "depth-psychology" of our day has shown any reluctance to accept.

If we examine more closely the two illustrations previously brought under tribute, the force of these observations will be increased. No doubt one of Socrates' (or Plato's) chief discoveries was that of the "spiritual individual," the responsible self whose free decision, and not blind fate, determines its destiny here and hereafter: the imperishable pages of the myth of Er the Armenian, at the end of the *Republic*, demonstrate the fact. Socrates, the very prototype of the free, conscious, and responsible self, turns out to possess a demon—or, to translate *to daimonion* more adequately, some holy thing—within him, to which he turns in emergencies for consultation that bears all the appearances of being oracular. Superficially, then, he seems just like the tribal primitive, who is so embedded in the common life, awareness, and talk of his fellows that he is impelled to regard any intimations of individual selfhood with awe and mistrust and to treat this self as something alien to himself, which he must placate, and approach only with special precautions. *To daimonion*, however much it may look like this, must yet be something else, for Socrates is precisely the one who has made the most decisive break with the reassuring warmth of the collective of tribal consciousness, assuming the arduous task of constant individual wakefulness and alertness, in the conviction that the unexamined, i.e. unconscious, life is not worth living. Awe there is, toward something that transcends the self, and upon which the self is most intimately dependent; it is, however, a much profounder and more clairvoyant awe than that of the primitive—say, of Lawrence's Arab tribesmen in respect of the self-containment of the British troops attached to them toward the end of the war, of whom they wonderingly remarked that each seemed to be a tribe all to himself. It is an awe not prior but subsequent to the discovery of the object-self, and perfectly appropriate to the sources of the "awful first self of which [we] know so little."

Again, the medieval mystic (who, surely, of all men ought not to be charged with ignoring the "spiritual individual") shows very little concern with the familiar "me," or second self, though he is quite aware of its existence. The fourteenth-century author of the *Book of Privy Counselling*, to take a typical example, requires his reader to discipline himself in turning away from the second toward the first self, in order to be open to the promptings of the divine Source of all being: "I hold him brutish and untaught that cannot think and feel that he himself is; not what he himself is, but that he himself is. I am, and I see and feel that I am: and not only that I am but that I am so and so and so and so . . . thus mayest thou see that the beginning and end of thy attention is most substantially set in the naked sight and the blind feeling of thine own being." For all the emphasis of "brutish" and "untaught," the author makes no attempt to overcome the difficulty of catching a glimpse of that which catches glimpses. In common with the mystical tradition of the West, he simply affirms that it can be done and that the means to it is negative, a deliberate and systematic turning of attention away from the self that is "so and so and so and so," i.e. from the object-self. In this direction we immediately encounter *to daimonion*, a holy thing other than the self, in its Christian form: "He is thy being, and in him thou art what thou art . . . evermore saving this difference between him and thee, that he is thy being and thou not his." This is the lesson of our Lord when he says "Whoso will love me, let him forsake himself; as who saith: 'Let him strip himself of himself, if he will be verily clothed in me, that am the flowing garment of love and of lasting that never shall have end.' " It is as if the central assertion of the gospel were to be read, "He who seeks to save his second self shall lose his first; but he who loses the second for my sake, shall save the first."

Follow the diametrical reverse of this counsel, and you obtain something like the Renaissance form of self-consciousness, as represented by the major figures of Montaigne and Descartes. Montaigne sets out in the *Essais* most deliberately to depict "not man, but an individual," himself; and himself in process, the fluctuation of his feelings, circumstances, convictions in their passage. "I do not paint being," he says, "I paint passage; not that from one age to another—as the people say from seven years to seven years—but from day to day, minute to minute. If my mind could take foot and take form, I should not essay myself, I should resolve myself. It is always in apprenticeship and in trial." "I wish to represent the progress of my humours, and that each should be seen in its growth. I wish I had begun sooner, and would take pleasure in recognizing the succession of my changes."

The resulting portrait is that familiar "delightfully modern" piece of naturalism in full detail, which marks an epoch. Montaigne is the first human being to record of himself all such facts as that he likes a blanket to cover his feet, that he prefers to sit with his feet higher than his head, that he eats so gluttonously that he frequently bites his tongue, and even his fingers; the first to dwell lovingly and fully on what ancient and medieval alike would have rejected as trivial, unessential, transitory—namely, every twist and turn of the second self in its shimmering course through the ocean of events.

It is true that somewhat to his astonishment Montaigne discovers that no description is as difficult as that of oneself: that "'I' evades myself always, and hides myself from myself"; in fact, in at least one passage, we may detect a definite haunted recognition of the first self when he writes that he has constantly in mind and soul a certain dim image of himself "which presents me, as in a dream, with a better form than that I have employed; but I am unable to seize and exploit it." The alchemical (or chemical) alternative between "resolution" and "assay" (the term to which Montaigne gave a permanent new meaning by attaching it to his book) is a real alternative. Such a search for the first self as is engaged in by the author of the *Book of Privy Counselling* requires final decision, commitment, engagement: it is interested in obtaining a precipitate, a resolution, and after a certain point sternly prohibits any further assaying or sampling or tampering with the ingredients. It is because Montaigne cannot resist the fascination of watching the change and helping it along that the phantom image of a first self and of a possible resolution evades his grasp. Certainly few books have ever been given a more significant and revealing title than his.

With Descartes the question is transferred from a literary to a momentous metaphysical context. The whole future is at stake: he has in mind nothing less than the entire demolition of the planless slums and tortuous, haphazardly traced streets of the city of knowledge, to be followed by a rebuilding on the rational geometrical town-plan of a single architect of genius, Descartes himself. He sets out to reject and rid himself of "everything which has hitherto passed for knowledge," to doubt till doubt gives out, breaks down, cancels itself, and is replaced by absolute certainty.

This certainty eventuates precisely in regard to his own existence as a conscious being. "Je pense, donc je suis": such is the initial pronouncement of the Cartesian reconstruction, which, while everything else is still in doubt, cannot possibly be doubted. Jung makes the penetrating observation that the self that formulates this proposition—"I think, or am conscious, therefore I exist"—cannot be the self to which the proposition refers, for there is an implied and suppressed certainty prior to that with which we are presented. Let us then try to complete the statement: "I am, therefore I think, therefore I am"; if that is not a circular statement, it is because it is the first self, the subject or agent self, that is intended by the prefixed phrase; while the second "I am" refers to its familiar observable and observed reflection, the Cartesian "thinking thing" or object-self.

"Je pense, donc je suis," under the inoffensive mask of a truism, is quite as momentous a statement as Descartes claims; its influence persists through each step of his metaphysics, colouring each traditional theme—the existence of God, the theory of substance, the nature of matter, even the assertion of the freedom of will and the activity of intellect and imagination—with novel and peculiarly subdued hues. The *Méditations* show Descartes at work noiselessly transforming the correlative concepts of man and nature to accord with his conviction that the ego or me, the object-self, is the only self there is any sense in talking about. He is the first begetter of "psychology without the psyche," and of its physical correlate, nature as a system of thoroughgoing mechanistic determinism, and thereby the first begetter of the modern age.

Let us try to put the point once more in different terms. Others in plenty had sought knowledge in an act of introversion. "Do not go abroad," they had warned; or "Enter into thyself, there thou wilt find what thou seekest in vain without." But until Descartes none had limited the inner field to the "clear and distinct" ideas of "Universal Mathematics," i.e. a generalized science of "order and measurement" as such. Through this act of mathematical introversion, what Descartes finds within himself is precisely the outside, the objective *order*, to which the infinite particularities of the physical universe can be subdued and thus known. "Second self" and "world machine," I repeat, are not accidentally connected in this doctrine but mutually imply and condition each other.

Incomplete as these historical references are, they call for some measure of elucidation of the problem itself. Why and how is the "productive will," the source of energy of our being, so largely hidden from itself?

Here, since we cease to court the severe muse of history, we may employ a lighter, more familiar tone, and begin with a myth, the profound Greek myth of origins. According to this the brother Titans Prometheus and Epimetheus (forethought and afterthought) were charged with the making and equipment of man. Their gifts were good, so were their intentions, but yet the thing went wrong. This was mainly the fault of Epimetheus, who had not foresight enough to see that he was giving the gifts away too liberally to the beasts, before he reached man; no great swiftness or strength, no claws, no shell or wings were left by this time. But he did make and give him (as an afterthought) a woman, the first. She was Pandora (all gifts), a splendid creature with one flaw, the charming feminine weakness of curiosity; unable to resist opening the chest in which Epimetheus kept all unused ills, she let them loose; and there she stands, poor sweet Pandora, unable to catch them again, and weeping at what she has done. Superfluous evils have plagued man ever since.

The bargain was that Epimetheus would make man, and Prometheus check him over afterward. Whatever led them to exchange their functions that day, it must be at the root of the trouble, for a being planned by afterthought and revised by forethought is in a queer case. Anyway, Prometheus, seeing what a botch had been made, assaulted heaven, stole the sun's fire by lighting his torch at it, and so gave man the technological instrument by which he gained, and has since held and increased, his power. Sensitively enough, the Greeks had misgivings about this stolen gift; Prometheus, for the impiety, was chained to a rock, with eagles ceaselessly tearing at his liver—the organ whose dark, slippery, reflecting surface makes it the birthplace of dream-images and omens of the future. We, for whom it has been reserved to see the globe, on at least five occasions now, briefly and menacingly touched with the sun's torch will not make the mistake of taking Prometheus just for what the anthropologists call a culture-hero; he is himself an omen, and a symbol of a kind of bad conscience, of the sense of danger in knowledge.

Epimetheus' gift, which was to passion, was a good one; and so was Prometheus' gift to intelligence: yet awkwardly enough each adds to the tale of troubles and sorrows.

Since the parable draws our attention to time before and after, let us take a simplified look at that mysterious matter. Time is basically just flow or passage, and for the brutes seems to form a kind of pointland, such as a one-dimensional line would be; a point could have no means of looking forward or backward, its vision would be blocked by the ends of the line, i.e. the points on either side of it. With man, singularly privileged in respect of the power of reflection, time becomes more like a plane of flatland; he too is of course subject to the linear process of succession, but can, as it were, run out crosswise to it along another line and obtain a perspective on it: he takes certain bearings on passage in both directions, thus estimating the flow along which he is carried. Memory (or hindsight), and intelligence (or foresight) free him from the immediacy of the animal present and give him what might be called a second temporal dimension over and above succession—that of duration: not just passing, but lasting through passage.

He is freed by reflection from immediacy, to be sure, but is in consequent peril of losing any sense of the present by becoming absorbed in the backward or the forward look. Here we begin to see the full force of the myth of Epimetheus and Prometheus. Perhaps, man reflects, there is a third dimension to the queer thing, which, since he is a flat creature confined in flatland, he can never hope to perceive; "above" and "below" are strictly inconceivable to dwellers in flatland who, as someone has remarked, would just be enormously puzzled by the succession of round rings imprinted on their plane by any elephant happening to stumble across it. But, his suspicions aroused, man, we said, torments himself with the idea that there may be more; with great rigour, in the scientific theory of relativity (which is not our concern) he deepens the notion of simultaneity to cover events separated by millions of light-years—any event that takes place between the emission and return of a signal between two remote bodies being simultaneous with any other, in that frame of reference—and in philosophy and theology (which are our concern) he arrives at the notion of *eternity*, or of a restored present, for which the whole past and the whole future would be contemporaneous, thereby overcoming the antithesis of "backward" and "forward."

But (and this is the point of the myth) since he is in fact limited to succession and duration, to flatland, these intimations of eternity may simply lead man more powerfully backward or forward. Intellectually, the eternal seems to be within his grasp when he rises, in science, above the passing and particular to the knowledge of timeless laws; in terms of passion, his awareness of absence—that singular and disturbing privilege!—may turn into an effort to suppress time, and eternalize the past. In the first case he will be active, objective, extroverted, living ahead of himself—forward-going it is called—in a word, a scientist; in the second, passive, subjective, introverted, turned backward to the past, an artist.

We are talking of extremes here, and no doubt a sound distinction of science and art would have to add much to modify this contrast; yet extremes do exist, and must be reckoned with. The moral of the Greek myth still holds: though both art and science, both hindsight and foresight, are in principle good things, in fact, as a result perhaps of some division or inadequacy of will, each has been and is a fertile source of woe. Extremes too have the value of being exemplary or instructive. We can see that to be turned exclusively inward and backward in retrospection and introversion is a bad thing; it is to live in the moist darkness of unintelligent passion, like the bereaved and demented mother who daily expects the return of her dead child. Everyone should by the same token be capable of seeing, though in a "scientific" civilization like ours there is a prejudice against seeing it, that to be turned exclusively outward and forward, in extroversion and prospection, is a bad thing too; it is to live in the "dry light" of dispassionate intellect. Pathologically speaking, if the first involves loss of contact with the objective world, the second means loss of the sense of selfhood, and of other selves; each is an alienation, whether from outer or inner reality. It would be difficult to say which holds the more serious dangers.

No doubt there is a project, repeatedly favoured, to guard against these extremes by tempering Prometheus and Epimetheus with each other. The discipline of science will go far to correct a passionate nature, training in poetry and art to correct an inhuman intellectualism; yet like all compromise solutions this remains on the surface. If man's strange aspiration is not satisfied either in the "eternity," actually the unchanging character, of the laws of nature or in the false "eternity," sought by the artist who sets out like Proust, in search of Time Past, we should not expect any combination of the two movements to succeed.

Let us return to the diagnosis and to what may have been omitted from it. By reference to our temporal "flatland," we have specified two preoccupations (with knowing and with feeling) leading respectively ahead and backward and we have also made the conjecture or admitted the suspicion which may be expressed by saying that one side of the plane is lit and the other in darkness, for this is not to endow the flat creatures with a perspective out from their plane, but to present them with a puzzling difference on it; and the puzzle is reflected in an aspiration, which we have called the aspiration toward eternity. Next, we have said this aspiration can become misplaced, either immobilizing man in passionate brooding upon the past, or catapulting him ahead through his grasp of laws and of their technological applications, in frenzied motion and activity, till he lives in constant preoccupation with times that are not yet. In either case it is as if his present had dropped right out of the plane, or, if you prefer, as if all meaning had dropped out of the present. It is as Pascal says: he wanders about shamelessly in times that are not his at all, ignoring the only one that does belong to him. Thus robbed of his present, he is grieved at the brevity of life or appalled by its tedium, i.e. its endless length, or even—confirming the fact of a total dislocation of the present—makes both complaints concurrently.

Looking more closely, we may detect four things that make a present unbearable: impatience, anxiety, nostalgia, and remorse. Impatience and anxiety are for the future, one desiring and one fearing it (though by that very fear inducing precipitancy, the habit of jumping ahead of the *now*). Nostalgia and remorse play comparable roles for the past, one desiring it to be, the other not to be. By these four threads the lost present, subsisting no doubt somewhere in the darkness below the plane in our analogy, is connected with the past and present; along them the energies of man are distributed backward or forward or in both directions at once. His desire and will, that is to say, must be reckoned in, to complete the account so far given in terms of feeling and knowing.

The decisive term here is "will."[1] In it the various obscurities we have detected meet: the will is the "awful first self," the "dark under the time-plane" too, perhaps; certainly the cause of that loss of presence that sends the Epimethean Montaigne backward (in assay, not resolution) to perpetuate his past; and the Promethean Descartes im-

[1]The traditional threefold distinction of intellect, feeling, and will (cognition, emotion, conation) is impenitently employed in place of more sophisticated, and evasive, substitutes. I recently read a letter from an eminent psychologist in which he advised that these "overworked" terms be abandoned in favour of "intention-attitude—and direction-phenomenology."

Can it be that their horror of "faculty psychology" blinds people to the fact that faculties, or functions, were never taken to be mutually exclusive and non-communicating? Can it be, again, that eagerness to regard these as aspects of the total personality, the man as a whole, blinds them to the dis-integrity and lack of wholeness that marks our actual nature? H. R. M.

patiently forward to live in a scientific New Jerusalem of his own planning. The will is, also, I suspect, what psychoanalysts mean by the Unconscious—a term so negative as to be equivalent roughly to "the Question Mark," though in practice they endow this source of energy with representative and emotional ingredients inseparable from the will.

The term "will," moreover, expressly introduces us into the context of religious life and reflection, which is concerned with man's dividedness and its cure. Primitive myths dimly, the higher religions explicitly (though not with equal adequacy), trace the dividedness to the will, and present surrender to the divine will as the only means whereby man may be made whole—restored, that is, to his present without robbing him of either intelligence or passion. In the Christian scheme, for instance, the *libido sentiendi* (which produces a Montaigne) and the *libido sciendi* (which produces a Descartes) are alternative products of a more radical defect, a corruption of will itself: the *libido dominandi* or will to power, or tyrannical self-will. Here emerges the "familiar second self" of the Renaissance, the cherished mirror-image, for which presence and, with it, true energy (or activity) have lost their meaning; the residual unity of the resultant is no longer sufficient to permit us to say what it would be marvelous to be able to say, that it is the "whole man" who thinks and feels and wills. And if he cannot honestly say that he wills anything with his whole being, does that not simply show how far he is from having a whole being? Gradually, as art comes to be pursued for art's sake, not for life, science for science's sake not for life, even morality for morality's sake and not for life, the effects of the will to power grow more evident on an increasing scale.

If self-will is the disease, religion, we said, offers in some form the remedy of surrender. Morality it regards as no real remedy; for we are born having everything our own way, and regarding ourselves as the centre around which everything revolves, and this point of view, which we must get rid of, we cannot get rid of. Moral effort is a will to dominate the will to domination, and leaves man essentially where he was—in the dark beneath the plane. The purest of moralists (the Kantian, for instance, who always acts according to the law of duty) is one whom everything invites to form a very favourable opinion of himself, and there is no moral way out of this predicament. Surrender, in the religious sense of conversion, repentance, dedication of will may then seem impossibly difficult, even a sort of contradiction, if will is supposed to assert its own denial.

On the other hand, it might seem that nothing is more common or more absurdly easy, nothing more dangerous either, when *to daimonion* to which surrender is made happens to be some revival of primitive myth—as when the German people, suddenly discovering that they had a present, rushed to surrender their wills to Hitler. The temples of Venus, of Mercury the god of commerce, and of Mars the god of violence are crowded with devotees. Then there is that darkest religion of all, the one of which Macdonald says that the more devout a man is in it the fewer disciples he makes, namely, self-worship. But this is to swing back to where we began, with self-will and the conviction, so hard to overcome, that one is somehow terribly special. The fact is that these forms of "surrender" are more or less tainted with the will to domineer. The whole realm of myth lies in the dark, beneath the plane; religion begins only on the other side of it, in the light.

How much, finally, can be said about the first self and the dimension of eternity in terms of this illuminated side of the plane? Little, I imagine, that is more than a variant of what writings like the *Book of Privy Counselling* assert, unless we raise the question of the right by which those who profess to have had no experience in religion challenge the validity of such direct reports—and it is too late to deal with that now.

It seems, then, that the will to domination is tied up with a hypnotized vision of the second or mirror-self; as long as this occupies the focus of vision, every effort to let go simply reinforces the clutch of that will, just as in insomnia every effort to relax merely adds to the tension. The difficulty is that self-will cannot be yielded; the ease is that it is sufficient to ask for help, in a sustained way, and the giving-over takes place. It might not be an inaccurate summary of the evidence of those with most experience of what it is to say "Thy will be done" to suggest that a powerful attractive force from above the plane draws the present vertically up into it, from the darkness in which it lies absent and that it reintegrates therewith into the plane those threads of remorse, which becomes joy at the effacement of guilt; nostalgia for the past, which becomes gratitude for it; anxiety for the future, which becomes peace; and impatience, which is turned to hope or confidence.

This is what a "restored" present would be: not a return to the narrow immediacy of the animal moment, but an enlargement of the *now* to overcome the isolation consequent upon the "backward" or "forward" movement. If it brings awareness that there is no other time than now, that it is *always* now, no doubt this "always" is not quite eternity; only the sun that illumines the entire plane, if there is one, can take that view of the whole of succession and duration at once;

but this awareness is different enough from the rest of man's experience of time, enough like a participation in eternity, remarkable enough in its effects, to strengthen the flat creature's conjecture of a third dimension to time. Or, if you prefer, the fact that, collectively speaking, the plane of life is dotted with peculiar rings—the lives of those who do know that it is always now, and who live in the present—constitutes one of the main reasons for thinking that there is an elephant.

Only in such a present is will an unhampered source of knowledge and of feeling, passion suffused with intelligence and integrated with action, intellect both sensitive and practical; only such a whole man engaged in science, art, or moral action would be engaged in all three at once, to harmonious effect.

It might be enough to say that to live in the present is to live in love, but as people understand that word so differently, it would be better to end with an unpretentious pun: the present is a present, a gift.

INDEX

www.ingramcontent.com/pod-product-compliance
Lightning Source LLC
LaVergne TN
LVHW010448080826
844660LV00027B/1232